OXFORD READINGS IN PHILOSOPHY

A PRIORI KNOWLEDGE

Also published in this series

The Concept of Evidence, edited by Peter Achinstein
The Philosophy of Law, edited by Ronald M. Dworkin
Moral Concepts, edited by Joel Feinberg
Theories of Ethics, edited by Philippa Foot
The Philosophy of History, edited by Patrick Gardiner
The Philosophy of Mind, edited by Jonathan Glover
Knowledge and Belief, edited by A. Phillips Griffiths
Scientific Revolutions, edited by Ian Hacking
Philosophy and Economic Theory, edited by Frank Hahn and
Martin Hollis
Divine Commands and Morality, edited by Paul Helm
Hegel, edited by Michael Inwood
The Philosophy of Linguistics, edited by Jerrold J. Katz
Reference and Modality, edited by Leonard Linsky
The Philosophy of Religion, edited by Basil Mitchell
The Concept of God, edited by Thomas V. Morris
Aesthetics, edited by Harold Osborne
The Theory of Meaning, edited by G. H. R. Parkinson
The Philosophy of Education, edited by R. S. Peters
Political Philosophy, edited by Anthony Quinton
Practical Reasoning, edited by Joseph Raz
The Philosophy of Language, edited by J. R. Searle
Semantic Syntax, edited by Pieter A. M. Seuren
Applied Ethics, edited by Peter Singer
Philosophical Logic, edited by P. F. Strawson
Locke on Human Understanding, edited by I. C. Tipton
Theories of Rights, edited by Jeremy Waldron
Kant on Pure Reason, edited by Ralph C. S. Walker
Free Will, edited by Gary Watson
The Philosophy of Action, edited by Alan R. White
Leibniz: Metaphysics and Philosophy of Science, edited by
R. S. Woolhouse

Other volumes are in preparation

A Priori Knowledge

EDITED BY
PAUL K. MOSER

OXFORD UNIVERSITY PRESS

1987

Oxford University Press, Walton Street, Oxford OX2 6DP

Oxford New York Toronto Melbourne Auckland
Delhi Bombay Calcutta Madras Karachi
Petaling Jaya Singapore Hong Kong Tokyo
Nairobi Dar es Salaam Cape Town
Associated companies in Beirut Berlin Ibadan Nicosia

OXFORD is a trade mark of Oxford University Press

Published in the United States
by Oxford University Press, New York

British Library Cataloguing in Publication Data

A priori knowledge.—(Oxford readings in
philosophy)
1. knowledge, Theory of
I. Moser, Paul K.
121   BD161

ISBN 0–19–875084–6
ISBN 0–19–875083–8 Pbk

Library of Congress Cataloguing in Publication Data
A priori knowledge.
(Oxford readings in philosophy)
Bibliography: p.
Includes index.
Contents: Introduction/Paul K. Moser—A pragmatic
conception of the a priori/C. I. Lewis—The a priori/
A. J. Ayer—[etc.]
1. A priori. 2. Knowledge, Theory of. I. Moser,
Paul K., 1957–   . II. Series.
BD181.3.A2 1987   121'.3   87–1663

ISBN 0–19–875084–6
ISBN 0–19–875083–8 (pbk.)

Printed in Great Britain
at the University Printing House, Oxford
by David Stanford
Printer to the University

BD181
.3
.A2
1987

CONTENTS

Introduction   I

I. A Pragmatic Conception of the A Priori   15
   by C. I. Lewis

II. The A Priori   26
    by A. J. Ayer

III. Two Dogmas of Empiricism   42
     by W. V. Quine

IV. Wittgenstein and Logical Necessity   68
    by Barry Stroud

V. Analyticity and Apriority: Beyond
   Wittgenstein and Quine   85
   by Hilary Putnam

VI. The Truths of Reason   112
    by Roderick M. Chisholm

VII. A Priori Knowledge, Necessity, and
     Contingency   145
     by Saul A. Kripke

VIII. Kripke on the A Priori and the Necessary   161
      by Albert Casullo

IX. Analyticity, Necessity, and Apriority   170
    by R. G. Swinburne

X. Apriority and Necessity   190
   by Philip Kitcher

Notes on the Contributors   208

Bibliography   210

Index of Names   220

INTRODUCTION

I. SOME PRELIMINARY DISTINCTIONS

PHILOSOPHICAL questions about a priori knowledge revolve around
a trio of long-standing distinctions: the epistemological distinction
between a priori and a posteriori knowledge, the metaphysical
distinction between necessity and contingency, and the semantical
distinction between analytic and synthetic truth. Some of these
questions are: What are the necessary and sufficient conditions for
one's having a priori knowledge? Can we humans satisfy those
conditions? Must every proposition knowable a priori be analytically as well as necessarily true? Or, can there be a priori knowledge
of some synthetically true propositions or of some contingently true
propositions? A more recent issue, stemming from the epistemological writings of W. V. Quine, is whether the very notion of a priori
knowledge is philosophically misguided. Clearly, we cannot begin to
answer such questions without some prior conceptual clarification.

Let us begin with the distinction between a priori and a posteriori
knowledge. This distinction is epistemological inasmuch as it con-
trasts two kinds of *knowledge*. More specifically, this distinction
may be plausibly regarded as connoting two kinds of *epistemic
justification*, the sort of justification appropriate to knowledge.
Thus, an instance of knowledge is a priori if and only if its
justification condition is a priori in the sense that it does not depend
on evidence from sensory experience. Knowledge of mathematical
and logical truths, and even of the truth of one's own existence, has
been considered to be a priori in the present sense. In contrast, an
instance of knowledge is a posteriori if and only if its justification
condition is a posteriori in the sense that it depends on evidence
from sensory experience. Our assumed empirical knowledge of the
truths of natural science is widely regarded as a posteriori in that
sense.

The distinctive feature of *epistemic* justification is that it relates belief to truth in an appropriate way. A common assumption, accordingly, is that a belief is epistemically justified if and only if it is more likely to be true than its denial.[1] Philosophers disagree about just how much more likely than its denial a belief must be if it is to be justified; but there is virtual unanimity on the view that epistemic justification does not require certainty in any of three well-defined senses. The first relevant sense of 'certainty' is the truth-entailing infallibility sense according to which a belief is certain if and only if it (logically) cannot be mistaken. The second sense is the non-truth-entailing indubitability sense according to which a belief is certain if and only if it is not susceptible to any psychological doubt or any epistemic ground for doubt, however weak. And the third sense is the entailment sense according to which a belief is certain if and only if it is logically entailed by the evidence supporting it. This third sense is, of course, non-truth-entailing, since the relevant evidence may consist of false propositions; furthermore, it clearly precludes inductive or probabilistic justification of any sort. Yet the wide-spread assumption among contemporary epistemologists is that epistemic justification requires none of the aforementioned kinds of certainty. For what is ordinarily considered to be knowledge does not involve any of those kinds of certainty. Consider, for instance, our assumed knowledge of the truths of chemistry or biology. The denial of the assumption in question obviously leads to epistemological scepticism of a far-reaching sort.

We have, then, a concept of minimal a priori knowledge according to which an instance of knowledge of a proposition's truth is a priori if and only if its justification condition consists of evidence that (*a*) does not depend on sensory experience and that (*b*) makes the proposition in question more likely to be true than its denial. Given this concept, we can see that many of the features commonly

---

[1] Some philosophers have objected to this assumption on the ground that in lottery cases it allows for justified belief in each of the members of an inconsistent set of propositions; but let us bracket such cases for present purposes. Some relevant discussion of justification in lottery cases can be found in Henry E. Kyburg, *Epistemology and Inference* (Minneapolis: University of Minnesota Press, 1983), ch. 14 and 15, and Paul Moser, *Empirical Justification* (Boston: D. Reidel, 1985), ch. 1. Also, on the kind of probability relevant to epistemic justification, see Kyburg, op. cit. ch. 12.

attributed to a priori knowledge do not necessarily apply. For example, on this concept, a priori knowledge does not require epistemically irrevisable belief, self-evident belief, or innate concepts. Let us elaborate briefly on this point.

A justified belief is epistemically irrevisable, let us say, if and only if it would not be epistemically rational to give up that belief under any circumstances, including circumstances where the world is radically different. It is epistemically rational to hold such a belief *come what may*. Clearly, minimal a priori knowledge does not require epistemic irrevisability, since such knowledge is compatible with the fact that one's a priori justifying evidence might be altered (e.g. expanded) in such a way that what was justified a priori on the original evidence is no longer justified on the altered evidence. Thus, even if all our justified beliefs are epistemically revisable, we may still have minimal a priori knowledge.[2]

A belief is self-evident, in the literal sense, if and only if it is justified but does not derive its justification from anything other than itself. Clearly, minimal a priori knowledge does not require self-evident belief in this sense. Such knowledge might be *inferentially* justified a priori in the sense that its justification derives from the justification of other instances of a priori knowledge. For example, one might have a priori knowledge of a mathematical theorem that depends for its a priori justification on the justification of other theorems that are known a priori. However, a major question here is whether *all* instances of a priori knowledge are inferential in the sense specified. The view called *coherentism* regarding a priori knowledge states that all instances of such knowledge are inferential; and the view called *foundationalism* regarding a priori knowledge denies this, and states that any inferential a priori knowledge requires belief having *non*-inferential a priori justification, i.e. a priori justification that does not derive from the justification of any other belief. But of course such non-inferential justification does not require self-evidence in the literal sense; for such justification might be provided by something other than a belief (e.g. an intellectual intuition of some sort or a special state of understanding). Consequently, even if none of our justified

---

[2] For alternative approaches to the relation between a priori knowledge and epistemic revisability, see the subsequent selections III and V by Quine and Putnam.

beliefs is self-evident in the literal sense, we may still have minimal a priori knowledge.

The next issue is whether one's having minimal a priori knowledge requires one's having innate concepts, concepts that do not derive from sensory experience. (A common view, inspired by Plato, is that our concepts of abstract mathematical objects, such as triangles and chiliagons, are paradigm instances of innate concepts.) If we make the natural assumption that concepts are the constituents of propositions, we may recast the present issue as the question whether every proposition known a priori must consist of concepts that have not arisen from experience of sensory objects. It is doubtful that the concept of minimal a priori knowledge requires a 'yes' answer to the latter question. For that concept specifies conditions for the a priori *justification* of a belief; it does not specify conditions for the *causal origin* of the concepts constituting a belief, and so does not specify such causal conditions for the existence of a belief. (The operative assumption here is that we should not confuse the conditions for the justification of a belief with the conditions for the existence of a belief.) Of course it might be argued that whatever is justified a priori must consist of innate concepts; but in the absence of such an argument, we cannot plausibly hold that minimal a priori knowledge requires innate concepts.

Let us turn now to the question of how the epistemological concept of minimal a priori knowledge relates to the metaphysical distinction between necessary and contingent truth. A proposition is necessarily true if and only if it is not possibly false. (Many philosophers take the truths of logic and mathematics to be paradigm instances of necessary truths.) Leibniz tried to make the notion of necessary truth somewhat accessible by characterizing necessarily true propositions as propositions that are true *in all possible worlds*. Furthermore, according to Leibniz, contingently true propositions are true in the actual world, but not in all possible worlds. Less metaphorically, we might say simply that contingently true propositions are true propositions that are possibly false. The truths of the natural sciences are paradigm instances of such truths. Most philosophers hold that a proposition is a candidate for a priori knowledge only if it is necessarily true. The relevant assumption here, it seems, is that if a proposition is possibly false, it requires justification consisting of sensory experience. Saul Kripke, however, has argued that contingently true propositions can be known a priori.[3] Kripke gives the example of one's knowledge that stick S is one metre long at a fixed time, where S is a certain stick in Paris. (However, knowledge of the truth of one's own existence might also be considered in this connection.) More specifically, Kripke claims of a person that if he uses the stick S to fix the reference of the term 'one metre', then due to this special kind of definition, the person knows a priori that S is one metre long. Yet the truth that S is one metre long is evidently contingent; and, on this basis, Kripke concludes that we should countenance a priori knowledge of some contingent truths. Kripke's conclusion has generated a good deal of philosophical discussion, some of which is represented below in the selections by Kitcher and Casullo. Without engaging that discussion here, we should note that the relevant distinction between necessary and contingent truth is metaphysical, and not epistemological, inasmuch as it concerns only the metaphysical status of truths and does not directly concern ways of knowing. Furthermore, the aforementioned concept of minimal a priori knowledge is straightforwardly epistemological, and does not directly concern the metaphysical status of truths. Consequently, argument independent of that concept is needed to warrant the thesis that propositions known a priori must be necessarily true. A related moral here is that we should avoid any *conceptual* confusion of the epistemological category of the a priori and the metaphysical category of the necessary, even if the two categories are coextensive inasmuch as they happen to include the same propositions as members.

The third member of our trio of relevant distinctions is the semantic division between analytic and synthetic truths. Kant held that analytically true propositions 'express nothing in the predicate but what has been already actually thought in the concept of the subject, though not so distinctly or with the same (full) conscious-

---

[3] See Kripke, *Naming and Necessity* (Cambridge: Harvard University Press, 1980), pp. 54–7. The relevant discussion is reprinted below in selection VII. In that selection Kripke also argues against the view that every necessary truth can be known a priori.

ness'.[4] Two common examples of analytic truths are 'All bodies are extended' and 'A bachelor is an unmarried man'. Accordingly, we might hold that analytically true propositions are true just in virtue of the meanings of their constituent terms or concepts. In any case, such propositions cannot be denied without self-contradiction. A proposition is synthetically true, in contrast, if it is true but not analytically true, i.e. not true solely in virtue of the meanings of the terms it comprises. The so-called truths of experience are paradigm instances of synthetic truths; for example: 'Some professors are pedantic' and 'Some epistemologists are long-winded'. Clearly, the denial of such truths does not entail self-contradiction. Although philosophers such as W. V. Quine have challenged the conceptual viability of the analytic–synthetic distinction,[5] this distinction persists widely among contemporary philosophers.

One major issue of debate is whether any synthetic truths are necessarily true and known a priori. Kant held that some synthetic truths 'carry with them necessity, which cannot be obtained from experience'.[6] One of Kant's examples comes from mathematics: 'A straight line is the shortest path between two points.' Kant held that synthetic truths of that sort can be known a priori, i.e. solely by means of pure understanding and pure reason without any evidence from sensory experience. Indeed, a central Kantian view is that such synthetic a priori knowledge constitutes genuine *metaphysical* knowledge. But Kant's thesis of the synthetic a priori is still a topic of philosophical controversy; it receives contrasting treatments below in selections II, VI, and IX by Ayer, Chisholm and Swinburne. The key issue here may be put succinctly: How can a proposition be known (specifically, justified) a priori if it is true in virtue of considerations other than the meaning of its constituent terms? An answer might be sought in the apparent fact that some synthetic truths, such as 'Everything that is square has a shape', are characterized by a kind of necessity that does not entail analyticity.

---

[4] See Immanuel Kant, *Prolegomena to any Future Metaphysics*, ed. L. W. Beck (Indianapolis: Bobbs-Merrill, 1950), sect. 2a.

[5] See Quine, 'Two Dogmas of Empiricism', reprinted below as selection III. It should be noted that Quine's essay has also been regarded as questioning the very notion of a priori knowledge. Some critical discussion can be found in selection V by Putnam.

[6] See Kant, *Prolegomena*, sect. 2c.

This apparent fact may provide the beginning of an answer; but a full answer requires, of course, an explanation of how propositions characterized by such necessity can have a special *epistemological* status, the status of being knowable a priori. Notice, in this connection, that the aforementioned concept of minimal a priori knowledge does not obviously restrict the category of propositions knowable a priori to analytically true propositions. Independent argument is needed to set such a restriction or, alternatively, to reject such a restriction by including synthetic truths within the category of propositions knowable a priori. And this open-ended feature of the concept of minimal a priori knowledge is wholly appropriate, given the fact that the concept is epistemological and the analytic–synthetic distinction is not.

More generally, given the epistemological character of the concept of minimal a priori knowledge, we should recognize the elliptical character of the common talk of a priori *truth*. The modifier 'a priori' does not connote a kind of truth; rather, it connotes a kind of knowledge, or more specifically, a kind of epistemic justification.[7] And this point holds even if it is shown that all instances of a priori knowledge involve a special kind of truth, viz. analytic truth or, more generally, logically necessary truth. Let us understand, then, the common talk of a priori truth as elliptical for talk of truth that can be known a priori (by us humans).

A long-standing controversy among epistemologists stems from the issue of what constitutes the distinctive feature of truths that can be known a priori by us. The issue, in other words, is: What is the defining criterion for truths that can be known a priori by humans? The prominent positions on this issue may be designated and defined as follows:

(*a*) Psychologism: A true proposition can be known a priori by humans if and only if humans are so constituted psychologically that they are unable to think of that proposition as being false.[8]

(*b*) Pragmatism: A true proposition can be known a priori by humans if and only if it describes only a human intention to employ

---

[7] The present point accords with Kant's talk of a priori *modes of knowledge* in the *Critique of Pure Reason*, A2, B3, *et passim*.

[8] Edmund Husserl defended a version of psychologism in his *Philosophie der Arithmetik* of 1891, but later opposed the view in his *Logical Investigations* of 1900.

a certain scheme of classification for the ordering of human experience.[9]

(c) Linguisticism: A true proposition can be known a priori by humans if and only if the (conventional) rules of human language-use would be violated upon our denying that proposition.[10]

(d) Anthropological Conventionalism: A true proposition can be known a priori by humans if and only if human forms of life (i.e. human nature as determined by human biology and cultural history) preclude the intelligibility (for humans) of the denial of that proposition.[11]

(e) Understanding Intuitionism: A true proposition can be known a priori by humans if and only if a human's understanding that proposition is all the evidence needed for him to see that it is true.[12]

(f) Rationality-Based Apriorism: A true proposition can be known a priori by humans if and only if that proposition is certified by the nature of human rationality in the sense that it would be irrational for humans to deny it under any circumstance.[13]

(g) Necessity-Based Apriorism: A true proposition can be known a priori by humans if and only if that proposition is necessarily true in the sense that its negation is incoherent (i.e. entails a self-contradiction), and humans can know that proposition to be necessarily true.[14]

(h) Reliabilism: A true proposition can be known a priori by humans if and only if their believing that proposition can be

[9] This view is suggested by C. I. Lewis, 'A Pragmatic Conception of the A Priori', reprinted below as selection I.

[10] Linguisticism is represented in selection II by Ayer. See also Anthony Quinton, 'The A Priori and the Analytic', *Proceedings of the Aristotelian Society*, 64 (1963), 31–54, reprinted in *Necessary Truth*, ed. R. C. Sleigh (Englewood Cliffs, NJ: Prentice-Hall, 1972), pp. 89–109. For critical discussion see selection V by Putnam and selection VI by Chisholm.

[11] This position is suggested by Wittgenstein's *Philosophical Investigations* and *Remarks on the Foundations of Mathematics*, and is represented in selection IV by Stroud. Criticisms of the position can be found in selection V by Putnam.

[12] Chisholm takes this to be 'the traditional' conception of the a priori, and supports it in selection VI.

[13] This view is suggested in selection V by Putnam. For some relevant discussion see Manley Thompson, 'On A Priori Truth', *The Journal of Philosophy*, 78 (1981), 458–82.

[14] This position, with slight modification, is supported in selection IX by Swinburne. Notice that since this position does not appeal to rules of human language-use, it is not to be identified with Linguisticism as defined in (c) above.

generated by a reliable (i.e. truth-conducive) mechanism of belief-formation having the following feature: given any possible experience sufficient to enable humans (cognitively like us) to believe the proposition in question, that belief-forming mechanism would have been available to humans and, if exercised, would have produced true belief in that proposition.[15]

A fundamental task for a theory of a priori knowledge can be identified now as the project of adjudicating the conflict between the competing positions (a)–(h). A related task, furthermore, is the project of identifying any additional competing positions not entailed by (a)–(h). Whatever the ultimate outcome of these projects is, the epistemologist should begin by identifying what it is about a priori justification that demands the restriction of the class of propositions knowable a priori to the set of propositions delimited by a criterion such as one of (a)–(h). In beginning that way, the epistemologist will guarantee that his position on propositions knowable a priori is conceptually well motivated relative to the key epistemological concept of minimal a priori knowledge. As a further result, there will be minimal risk of conflating the trio of distinctions between the a priori and the a posteriori, the necessary and the contingent, and the analytic and the synthetic.

Most of the selections in this book represent efforts to support, or at least to criticize, one or another of the positions (a)–(h) on the distinctive character of propositions knowable a priori. In addition, many of the selections provide substantial clarification of the trio of distinctions we have been considering. Let us turn briefly to a more specific characterization of the following selections.

2. A SUMMARY OF THE SELECTIONS

In selection I, C. I. Lewis presents a pragmatic conception of the a priori, according to which a priori knowledge is knowledge of one's intent to employ a certain (conceptual) scheme of classification for

---

[15] A version of such reliabilism is outlined in selection X by Kitcher. See also Kitcher, 'A Priori Knowledge', *The Philosophical Review*, 76 (1980), 3–23. The distinctive feature of reliabilism is that it takes the notion of a priori justification to be analysable in terms of the notion of a truth conducive mechanism of belief-formation.

the organizing of experience. Lewis emphasizes that the way in which one constructs such a scheme is due to pragmatic considerations involving what suits one's needs. In addition, Lewis argues that all knowledge has a pragmatic a priori component in the aforementioned sense.

In selection II, A. J. Ayer defends a linguistic conception of the a priori, according to which the truths of logic and mathematics are a priori in the sense that we cannot abandon them without contradicting ourselves, i.e. without violating the rules governing our use of language. Ayer argues that the analyticity of the truths of logic and mathematics is the only good explanation of their apriority, and that there can be no a priori knowledge of empirical reality. Thus, Ayer's position rules out the possibility of a priori knowledge of synthetic truths.

In selection III, W. V. Quine attributes two dogmas to modern empiricism: (*a*) belief in a dichotomy between analytic and synthetic truths, and (*b*) belief in a sort of reductionism, according to which every meaningful sentence is equivalent to some sentence whose terms refer to immediate sensory experience. Quine surveys the prominent accounts of analyticity (up to 1951), and finds that each has serious shortcomings. In sections 5 and 6 of the selection, Quine focuses on the view that analytic truths are truths that are confirmed no matter what; in doing so, he considers an influential positivist view of apriority as epistemic irrevisability. Quine questions the actual epistemological significance of such apriority on the basis of the following consideration: any statement can be held true come what may, if we make drastic enough adjustments elsewhere in the system of accepted statements; conversely, by the same token, no statement is immune to revision. Thus we might plausibly interpret Quine as introducing a notion of *contextual* apriority as *system-relative* epistemic irrevisability. At any rate, a basic assumption of Quine's opposition to the two dogmas is that 'our statements about the external world face the tribunal of sense experience not individually but only as a corporate body'. Two important effects of Quine's rejection of the two dogmas are a weakening of the distinction between speculative metaphysics and empirical science and a moving toward the sort of pragmatism found in Dewey and James.

In selection IV, Barry Stroud argues that Wittgenstein's account of logically necessary truth cannot correctly be described as thoroughgoing conventionalism, according to which logical necessity is due solely to the individual decisions we happen to make regarding calculating, inferring, and so on. More specifically, Stroud contends that one of Wittgenstein's central aims was to formulate an account of necessity that steers a clear course between the Scylla of such conventionalism and the Charybdis of Platonism, according to which logical necessity is in no way dependent upon human logical and mathematical practices. Wittgenstein's intermediate position, according to Stroud, relies basically on the sort of anthropological conventionalism defined above in Part 1. The key assumption of the position is, roughly, that necessity and apriority are determined by human 'forms of life', i.e. human nature as determined by human biology and cultural history. An important implication of this assumption seems to be that if such forms of life preclude the genuine intelligibility of the denial of a proposition, then that proposition can be considered a necessary a priori truth. In any case, Stroud shows that Wittgenstein's position is definitely not thoroughgoing conventionalism.

In selection V, Hilary Putnam critically reacts to the positions of Ayer, Quine, and Wittgenstein represented in selections II–IV. Putnam begins with a critical discussion of (what he calls) 'a Wittgensteinian view' that the necessity of mathematical and logical truths is accounted for by the fact that, given our linguistic rules, we could not *count* anything as a counterexample to such truths. The problem with such a view, basically, is that the set of mathematical and logical truths is infinite, but the set of our linguistic rules is not; thus, the view in question must presuppose the notion of logical consequence that it aims to explain. Putnam also takes issue with the position I have called 'anthropological conventionalism', on the ground that human nature cannot explain the 'objective mathematical fact' of the consistency of a set of axioms, even if it can explain why we *accept* certain axioms. Putnam also provides a critical but constructive discussion of Quine's treatment of apriority. Specifically, he argues that Quine conflates the analytic and the a priori, and that (contrary to Quine) there are some truths that are a priori in the sense of being certified by the nature of human rationality:

e.g. not every statement is both true and false. Putnam finds it ultimately unexplainable, however, why the truths in question qualify as a priori; he finds such truths to be so basic that the notion of explanation collapses when we try to explain why they are true. Accordingly, Putnam rejects Ayer's view that the notion of linguistic convention can play an explanatory role here.

In selection VI, Roderick Chisholm argues for what he takes to be 'the traditional' conception of the a priori, according to which one mark of an a priori proposition is this: once we understand the proposition, we see that it is true. Chisholm's more refined analysis of the a priori relies on the notion of *certainty* and the notion of an *axiomatic proposition*; but in general his view is that with regard to an a priori proposition, our understanding it is all the evidence we need to see that it is true. In developing this view, Chisholm discusses Psychologism, Linguisticism, and certain relevant views of Leibniz, Kant, and Quine. One of Chisholm's main conclusions is that there is considerable support for the existence of synthetic a priori knowledge.

In selection VII, Saul Kripke begins with some clarification of the notions of apriority, analyticity, and necessity. After emphasizing that the notion of apriority is an epistemological (rather than a metaphysical) concept, Kripke takes up two controversial issues: (a) Can we have a priori knowledge of contingent truths? and (b) Is every necessarily true proposition knowable a priori by us? As noted above in Part I, Kripke argues that there can be a priori knowledge of contingent truths, on the ground that such knowledge can be exemplified by one's knowing the contingent truth that stick S is one metre long at a fixed time, where S is a certain stick in Paris that is used to fix the reference of the term 'one metre'. In addition, Kripke argues that there are necessarily true propositions that must be known a posteriori, if they are to be known at all. His main examples are true identity statements involving names, such as 'Hesperus is Phosphorus'. Kripke argues that such statements are necessarily true, but that they could not have been known a priori.

In selection VIII, Albert Casullo presents Kripke's case for the view that there are necessary a posteriori propositions and contingent a priori propositions, and argues that Kripke's case is at best inconclusive as a refutation of the traditional view that all a priori knowledge is of necessary propositions and that all necessary propositions are knowable a priori. Casullo grants that if there are essential properties of the sort identified by Kripke, then Kripke has shown that it is incorrect to hold that the truth value of all necessary propositions can be known a priori. However, Casullo resists the inference that the traditional view has been refuted, by means of an appeal to a distinction between knowledge of the *general* modal status of propositions and knowledge of the *specific* modal status of propositions. The former knowledge is knowledge of a proposition's being necessary or of its being contingent; whereas the latter knowledge is knowledge of its being necessarily true, necessarily false, contingently true, or contingently false. Regarding Kripke's case for contingent a priori propositions, Casullo focuses on Kripke's example of the proposition that stick S is one metre long (where S is the standard in Paris). His general argument is that if we distinguish sentences (*a*) S is one metre long, and (*b*) The length of S is one metre, and acknowledge the distinction between the attributive and the referential use of definite descriptions, there is no reason to suppose that Kripke has identified a case of a priori knowledge of a contingent proposition. Casullo concludes, accordingly, that Kripke has not refuted the traditional view that all a priori knowledge is of necessary propositions.

In selection IX, R. G. Swinburne aims generally to clarify the logical relations between analyticity, necessity, and apriority. He distinguishes three general ways of defining analyticity and three main senses of the a priori. In addition, he defends the view that a proposition is a priori if and only if it is analytic and can be known to be such. All a priori propositions are analytic, on Swinburne's view, in the sense that their negations are incoherent, i.e. entail self-contradictory propositions. Thus, Swinburne's view is basically equivalent to Necessity-Based Apriorism as defined above in Part 1. In the course of defending his view, Swinburne discusses the relevant positions of Ayer, Quine, and Kripke, and draws out the implications of his view for the impossibility of synthetic a priori knowledge.

In selection X, Philip Kitcher challenges the common assumption, apparently stemming from Kant, that the notions of apriority and necessity are equivalent in the sense that whatever proposition that is knowable a priori is also necessarily true and conversely. In broad agreement with Kripke, Kitcher argues against both the view that (*a*) If it is necessary that *p*, then *p* can be known a priori, and the view that (*b*) If *p* can be known a priori, then it is necessary that *p*. After distinguishing stronger and weaker versions of theses (*a*) and (*b*), Kitcher opposes a moderate version of (*b*) on the ground that one can know a priori the contingent truth that one actually exists, and he opposes a refined version of (*a*) with a *reductio* showing that it entails that, for any truth, someone can know that truth a priori. In the course of opposing (*a*) and (*b*), Kitcher interacts with the relevant arguments of Kripke and Keith Donnellan. In addition, his essay outlines a naturalistic reliabilist account of a priori knowledge that construes warrant as reliable belief-production.

The book concludes with a bibliography of important twentieth-century works relevant to philosophical issues about a priori knowledge.

I

A PRAGMATIC CONCEPTION OF THE

A PRIORI

C. I. LEWIS

THE conception of the a priori points to two problems which are perennial in philosophy: the part played in knowledge by the mind itself, and the possibility of 'necessary truth' or of knowledge 'independent of experience'. But traditional conceptions of the a priori have proved untenable. That the mind approaches the flux of immediacy with some godlike foreknowledge of principles which are legislative for experience, that there is any natural light or any innate ideas, it is no longer possible to believe.

Nor shall we find the clues to the a priori in any compulsion of the mind to incontrovertible truth or any peculiar kind of demonstration which establishes first principles. All truth lays upon the rational mind the same compulsion to belief; as Mr Bosanquet has pointed out, this character belongs to all propositions or judgments once their truth is established.

The difficulties of the conception are due, I believe, to two mistakes: whatever is a priori is necessary, but we have misconstrued the relation of necessary truth to mind; and the a priori is independent of experience, but in so taking it, we have misunderstood its relation to empirical fact. What is a priori is necessary truth not because it compels the mind's acceptance, but precisely because it does not. It is given experience, brute fact, the a posteriori element in knowledge which the mind must accept willy-nilly. The a priori represents an attitude in some sense freely taken, a stipulation of the mind itself, and a stipulation which might be made in some other way if it suited our bent or need. Such truth is necessary as opposed to contingent, not as opposed to voluntary. And the a

C. I. Lewis, 'A Pragmatic Conception of the A Priori', from *The Journal of Philosophy*, Vol. XX, No. 7 (March 27, 1923), pp. 169–77. Reprinted by permission of the Managing Editor.

priori is independent of experience not because it prescribes a form which the data of sense must fit, or anticipates some pre-established harmony of experience with the mind, but precisely because it prescribes nothing to experience. That is a priori which is true, no matter what. What it anticipates is not the given, but our attitude toward it: it concerns the uncompelled initiative of mind or, as Josiah Royce would say, our categorical ways of acting.

The traditional example of the a priori par excellence is the laws of logic. These cannot be derived from experience since they must first be taken for granted in order to prove them. They make explicit our general modes of classification. And they impose upon experience no real limitation. Sometimes we are asked to tremble before the spectre of the 'alogical', in order that we may thereafter rejoice that we are saved from this by the dependence of reality upon mind. But the 'alogical' is pure bogy, a word without a meaning. What kind of experience could defy the principle that everything must either be or not be, that nothing can both be and not be, or that if x is y and y is z, then x is z? If anything imaginable or unimaginable could violate such laws, then the ever-present fact of change would do it every day. The laws of logic are purely formal; they forbid nothing but what concerns the use of terms and the corresponding modes of classification and analysis. The law of contradiction tells us that nothing can be both white and not-white, but it does not and cannot tell us whether black is not-white, or soft or square is not-white. To discover *what contradicts what* we must always consult the character of experience. Similarly the law of the excluded middle formulates our decision that whatever is not designated by a certain term shall be designated by its negative. It declares our purpose to make, for every term, a complete dichotomy of experience, instead—as we might choose—of classifying on the basis of a tripartite division into opposites (as black and white) and the middle ground between the two. Our rejection of such tripartite division represents only our penchant for simplicity.

Further laws of logic are of similar significance. They are principles of procedure, the parliamentary rules of intelligent thought and speech. Such laws are independent of experience because they impose no limitations whatever upon it. They are legislative because they are addressed to ourselves—because definition, classification, and inference represent no operations of the objective world, but only our own categorical attitudes of mind.

And further, the ultimate criteria of the laws of logic are pragmatic. Those who suppose that there is, for example, *a* logic which everyone would agree to if he understood it and understood himself are more optimistic than those versed in the history of logical discussion have a right to be. The fact is that there are several logics, markedly different, each self-consistent in its own terms and such that whoever using it, if he avoids false premises, will never reach a false conclusion. Mr Russell, for example, bases *his* logic on an implication relation such that if twenty sentences be cut from a newspaper and put in a hat, and then two of these be drawn at random, one of them will certainly imply the other, and it is an even bet that the implication will be mutual. Yet upon a foundation so remote from ordinary modes of inference the whole structure of *Principia Mathematica* is built. This logic—and there are others even more strange—is utterly consistent and the results of it entirely valid. Over and above all questions of consistency, there are issues of logic which cannot be determined—nay, cannot even be argued—except on pragmatic grounds of conformity to human bent and intellectual convenience. That we have been blind to this fact, itself reflects traditional errors in the conception of the a priori.

We may note in passing one less important illustration of the a priori—the proposition 'true by definition'. Definitions and their immediate consequences, analytic propositions generally, are necessarily true, true under all possible circumstances. Definition is legislative because it is in some sense arbitrary. Not only is the meaning assigned to words more or less a matter of choice—that consideration is relatively trivial—but the manner in which the precise classifications which definition embodies shall be effected is something not dictated by experience. If experience were other than it is, the definition and its corresponding classification might be inconvenient, fantastic, or useless, but it could not be false. Mind makes classifications and determines meanings; in so doing it creates the a priori truth of analytic judgements. But that the manner of this creation responds to pragmatic considerations is so obvious that it hardly needs pointing out.

If the illustrations so far given seem trivial or verbal, that impression may be corrected by turning to the place which the a priori has in mathematics and in natural science. Arithmetic, for example, depends in toto upon the operation of counting or correlating, a procedure which can be carried out at will in any world containing identifiable things—even identifiable ideas—regardless of the further characters of experience. Mill challenged this a priori character of arithmetic. He asked us to suppose a demon sufficiently powerful and maleficent so that every time two things were brought together with two other things, this demon should always introduce a fifth. The implication which he supposed to follow is that under such circumstances $2 + 2 = 5$ would be a universal law of arithmetic. But Mill was quite mistaken. In such a world we should be obliged to become a little clearer than is usual about the distinction between arithmetic and physics; that is all. If two black marbles were put in the same urn with two white ones, the demon could take his choice of colors, but it would be evident that there were more black marbles or more white ones than were put in. The same would be true of all objects in any wise identifiable. We should simply find ourselves in the presence of an extraordinary physical law, which we should recognize as universal in our world, that whenever two things were brought into proximity with two others, an additional and similar thing was always created by the process. Mill's world would be physically most extraordinary. The world's work would be enormously facilitated if hats or locomotives or tons of coal could be thus multiplied by anyone possessed originally of two pairs. But the laws of mathematics would remain unaltered. It is because this is true that arithmetic is a priori. Its laws prevent *nothing*; they are compatible with anything which happens or could conceivably happen in nature. They would be true in any possible world. Mathematical addition is not a physical transformation. Physical changes which result in an increase or decrease of the countable things involved are matters of everyday occurrence. Such physical processes present us with phenomena in which the purely mathematical has to be separated out by abstraction. Those laws and those laws only have necessary truth which we are prepared to maintain, no matter what. It is because we shall always separate out that part of the phenomenon not in conformity with arithmetic and designate it by some other category—physical change, chemical reaction, optical illusion—that arithmetic is a priori.

The a priori element in science and in natural law is greater than might be supposed. In the first place, all science is based upon definitive concepts. The formulation of these concepts is, indeed, a matter determined by the commerce between our intellectual or our pragmatic interests and the nature of experience. Definition is classification. The scientific search is for such classification as will make it possible to correlate appearance and behaviour, to discover law, to penetrate to the 'essential nature' of things in order that behaviour may become predictable. In other words, if definition is unsuccessful, as early scientific definitions mostly have been, it is because the classification thus set up corresponds with no natural cleavage and does not correlate with any important uniformity of behaviour. A name itself must represent *some* uniformity in experience or it names nothing. What does not repeat itself or recur in intelligible fashion is not a thing. Where the definitive uniformity is a clue to other uniformities, we have successful scientific definition. Other definitions cannot be said to be false; they are merely useless. In scientific classification the search is, thus, for *things worth naming*. But the naming, classifying, defining activity is essentially prior to investigation. We cannot interrogate experience in general. Until our meaning is definite and our classification correspondingly exact, experience cannot conceivably answer our questions.

In the second place, the fundamental laws of any science—or those treated as fundamental—are a priori because they formulate just such definitive concepts or categorical tests by which alone investigation becomes possible. If the lightning strikes the railroad track at two places, *A* and *B*, how shall we tell whether these events are simultaneous?

We . . . require a definition of simultaneity such that this definition supplies us with the method by means of which . . . [we] can decide whether or not both the lightning strokes occurred simultaneously. As long as this requirement is not satisfied, I allow myself to be deceived as a physicist (and of course the same applies if I am not a physicist), when I imagine that I am able to attach a meaning to the statement of simultaneity. . . .

After thinking the matter over for some time you then offer the following suggestions with which to test simultaneity. By measuring along the rails, the connecting line AB should be measured up and an observer placed at the mid-point M of the distance AB. This observer should be supplied with an arrangement (e.g. two mirrors inclined at 90 degrees) which allows him visually to observe both places A and B at the same time. If the observer perceives the two flashes at the same time, then they are simultaneous.

I am very pleased with this suggestion, but for all that I cannot regard the matter as quite settled, because I feel constrained to raise the following objection: 'Your definition would certainly be right, if I only knew that the light by means of which the observer at M perceives the lightning flashes travels along the length A—M with the same velocity as along the length B—M. But an examination of this supposition would only be possible if we already had at our disposal the means of measuring time. It would thus appear as though we were moving here in a logical circle.'

After further consideration you cast a somewhat disdainful glance at me—and rightly so—and you declare: 'I maintain my previous definition, nevertheless, because in reality it assumes absolutely nothing about light. There is only *one* demand to be made of the definition of simultaneity, namely, that in every real case it must supply us with an empirical decision as to whether or not the conception which has to be defined is fulfilled. . . . That light requires the same time to traverse the path A—M as for the path B—M is in reality *neither a supposition nor a hypothesis* about the physical nature of light, but a *stipulation* which I can make of my own free will in order to arrive at a definition of simultaneity.' . . . We are thus led also to a definition of 'time' in physics.[1]

As this example from the theory of relativity well illustrates, we cannot even ask the questions which discovered law would answer until we have first by a priori stipulation formulated definitive criteria. Such concepts are not verbal definitions, nor classifications merely; they are themselves laws which prescribe a certain uniformity of behaviour to whatever is thus named. Such definitive laws are a priori; only so can we enter upon the investigation by which further laws are sought. Yet it should also be pointed out that such a priori laws are subject to abandonment if the structure which is built upon them does not succeed in simplifying our interpretation of phenomena. If, in the illustration given, the relation 'simultaneous with', as defined, should not prove transitive—if event A should

[1] Albert Einstein, *Relativity: The Special and General Theory*, trans. R. W. Lawson (New York, 1920), pp. 26–8; italics are the author's.

prove simultaneous with *B*, and *B* with *C*, but not *A* with *C*—this definition would certainly be rejected.

And thirdly, there is that a priori element in science—as in other human affairs—which constitutes the criteria of the real as opposed to the unreal in experience. An object itself is a uniformity. Failure to behave in certain categorical ways marks it as unreal. Uniformities of the type called 'natural law' are the clues to reality and unreality. A mouse which disappears where no hole is, is no real mouse; a landscape which recedes as we approach is but illusion. As the queen remarked in the episode of the wishing-carpet: 'if this were real, then it would be a miracle. But miracles do not happen. Therefore I shall wake presently.' That the uniformities of natural law are the only reliable criteria of the real is inescapable. But such a criterion is *ipso facto* a priori. No conceivable experience could dictate the alteration of a law so long as failure to obey that law marked the content of experience as unreal.

This is one of the puzzles of empiricism. We deal with experience: what any reality may be which underlies experience, we have to learn. What we desire to discover is natural law, the formulation of those uniformities which obtain amongst the real. But experience as it comes to us contains not only the real but all the content of illusion, dream, hallucination, and mistake. The *given* contains both real and unreal, confusingly intermingled. If we ask for uniformities of this unsorted experience, we shall not find them. Laws which characterize all experience, of real and unreal both, are non-existent and would in any case be worthless. What we seek are the uniformities of the *real*; but *until we have such laws, we cannot sift experience and segregate the real*.

The obvious solution is that the enrichment of experience, the separation of the real from the illusory or meaningless, and the formulation of natural law all grow up together. If the criteria of the real are a priori, that is not to say that no conceivable character of experience would lead to alteration of them. For example, spirits cannot be photographed. But if photographs of spiritistic phenomcna, taken under properly guarded conditions, should become sufficiently frequent, this a priori dictum would be called in question. What we should do would be to redefine our terms. Whether 'spook' was spirit or matter, whether the definition of 'spirit' or of 'matter' should be changed—all this would constitute one interrelated problem. We should reopen together the question of definition or classification, of criteria for this sort of real, and of natural law. And the solution of one of these would mean the solution of all. Nothing could *force* a redefinition of spirit or of matter. A sufficiently fundamental relation to human bent, to human interests, would guarantee continuance unaltered even in the face of unintelligible and baffling experiences. In such problems, the mind finds itself uncompelled save by its own purposes and needs. I *may* categorize experience as I will; but *what* categorical distinctions will best serve my interests and objectify my own intelligence? What the mixed and troubled experience shall be— that is beyond me. But what I shall do with it—that is my own question, when the character of experience is sufficiently before me. I am coerced only by my own need to understand.

It would indeed be inappropriate to characterize as a priori a law which we are wholly prepared to alter in the light of further experience, even though in an isolated case we should discard as illusory any experience which failed to conform. But the crux of the situation lies in this: beyond such principles as those of logic, which we seem fully prepared to maintain no matter what, there must be further and more particular criteria of the real prior to any investigation of nature whatever. We cannot even interrogate experience without a network of categories and definitive concepts. And we must further be prepared to say what experimental findings will answer what questions, and how. Without tests which represent anterior principle, there is no question which experience could answer at all. Thus the most fundamental laws in any category—or those which we regard as most fundamental—are a priori, even though continued failure to render experience intelligible in such terms might result eventually in the abandonment of that category altogether. Matters so comparatively small as the behaviour of Mercury and of starlight passing the sun's limb may, if there be persistent failure to bring them within the field of previously accepted modes of explanation, result in the abandonment of the independent categories of space and time. But without the definitions, fundamental principles, and tests of the type which constitute such categories, no experience whatever could prove or disprove anything. And to that mind which should find independent space and time absolutely necessary conceptions, no possible experiment could prove the principles of relativity. 'There must be some error in the experimental findings, or some law not yet discovered', represents an attitude which can never be rendered impossible. And the only sense in which it could be proved unreasonable would be the pragmatic one of comparison with another method of categorical analysis which more successfully reduced all such experience to order and law.

At the bottom of all science and all knowledge are categories and definitive concepts which represent fundamental habits of thought and deep-lying attitudes which the human mind has taken in the light of its total experience. But a new and wider experience may bring about some alteration of these attitudes, even though by themselves they dictate nothing as to the content of experience, and no experience can conceivably prove them invalid.

Perhaps some will object to this conception on the ground that only such principles should be designated a priori as the human mind *must* maintain, no matter what; that if, for example, it is shown possible to arrive at a consistent doctrine of physics in terms of relativity even by the most arduous reconstruction of our fundamental notions, then the present conceptions are by that fact shown not to be a priori. Such objection is especially likely from those who would conceive the a priori in terms of an absolute mind or an absolutely universal human nature. We should readily agree that a decision by popular approval or a congress of scientists or anything short of such a test as would bring to bear the full weight of human capacity and interest would be ill-considered as having to do with the a priori. But we wish to emphasize two facts: first, that in the field of those conceptions and principles which have altered in human history, there are those which could neither be proved nor disproved by any experience, but represent the uncompelled initiative of human thought—that without this uncompelled initiative no growth of science, nor any science at all, would be conceivable; and second, that the difference between such conceptions as are, for example, concerned in the decision of relativity versus absolute space and time, and those more permanent attitudes such as are vested in the laws of logic, there is only a difference of degree. The dividing line between the a priori and the a posteriori is that between principles and definitive concepts which *can* be maintained in the face of all experience and those genuinely empirical generalizations which *might* be proven flatly false. The thought which both rationalism and empiricism have missed is that there are principles, representing the initiative of mind, which impose upon experience no limitations whatever, but that such conceptions are still subject to alteration on pragmatic grounds when the expanding boundaries of experience reveal their infelicity as intellectual instruments.

Neither human experience nor the human mind has a character which is universal, fixed, and absolute. 'The human mind' does not exist at all save in the sense that all humans are very much alike in fundamental respects, and that the language habit and the enormously important exchange of ideas has greatly increased our likeness in those respects which are here in question. Our categories and definitions are peculiarly social products, reached in the light of experiences which have much in common, and beaten out, like other pathways, by the coincidence of human purposes and the exigencies of human co-operation. Concerning the a priori there need be neither universal agreement nor complete historical continuity. Conceptions, such as those of logic, which are least likely to be affected by the opening of new ranges of experience, represent the most stable of our categories; but none of them is beyond the possibility of alteration.

Mind contributes to experience the element of order, of classification, categories, and definition. Without such, experience would be unintelligible. Our knowledge of the validity of these is simply consciousness of our own fundamental ways of acting and our own intellectual intent. Without this element, knowledge is impossible, and it is here that whatever truths are necessary and independent of experience must be found. But the commerce between our categorical ways of acting, our pragmatic interests, and the particular character of experience is closer than we have realized. No explanation of any one of these can be complete without consideration of the other two.

Pragmatism has sometimes been charged with oscillating between two contrary notions: the one, that experience is 'through and through malleable to our purpose'; the other, that facts are 'hard' and uncreated by the mind. We here offer a mediating conception: through all our knowledge runs the element of the a priori, which is indeed malleable to our purpose and responsive to our need. But throughout, there is also that other element of experience which is 'hard', 'independent', and unalterable to our will.

II

THE A PRIORI

A. J. AYER

THE view of philosophy which we have adopted may, I think, fairly be described as a form of empiricism. For it is characteristic of an empiricist to eschew metaphysics, on the ground that every factual proposition must refer to sense-experience. And even if the conception of philosophizing as an activity of analysis is not to be discovered in the traditional theories of empiricists, we have seen that it is implicit in their practice. At the same time, it must be made clear that, in calling ourselves empiricists, we are not avowing a belief in any of the psychological doctrines which are commonly associated with empiricism. For, even if these doctrines were valid, their validity would be independent of the validity of any philosophical thesis. It could be established only by observation, and not by the purely logical considerations upon which our empiricism rests.

Having admitted that we are empiricists, we must now deal with the objection that is commonly brought against all forms of empiricism; the objection, namely, that it is impossible on empiricist principles to account for our knowledge of necessary truths. For, as Hume conclusively showed, no general proposition whose validity is subject to the test of actual experience can ever be logically certain. No matter how often it is verified in practice, there still remains the possibility that it will be confuted on some future occasion. The fact that a law has been substantiated in $n-1$ cases affords no logical guarantee that it will be substantiated in the nth case also, no matter how large we take n to be. And this means that no general proposition referring to a matter of fact can ever be shown to be necessarily and universally true. It can at best be a

A. J. Ayer, 'The A Priori', from *Language, Truth and Logic*, 2nd ed., pp. 71–87. Copyright 1946 A. J. Ayer. Reprinted by permission of Victor Gollancz Ltd.

probable hypothesis. And this, we shall find, applies not only to general propositions, but to all propositions which have a factual content. They can none of them ever become logically certain. This conclusion, which we shall elaborate later on, is one which must be accepted by every consistent empiricist. It is often thought to involve him in complete scepticism; but this is not the case. For the fact that the validity of a proposition cannot be logically guaranteed in no way entails that it is irrational for us to believe it. On the contrary, what is irrational is to look for a guarantee where none can be forthcoming; to demand certainty where probability is all that is obtainable. We have already remarked upon this, in referring to the work of Hume. And we shall make the point clearer when we come to treat of probability, in explaining the use which we make of empirical propositions. We shall discover that there is nothing perverse or paradoxical about the view that all the 'truths' of science and common sense are hypotheses; and consequently that the fact that it involves this view constitutes no objection to the empiricist thesis.

Where the empiricist does encounter difficulty is in connection with the truths of formal logic and mathematics. For whereas a scientific generalization is readily admitted to be fallible, the truths of mathematics and logic appear to everyone to be necessary and certain. But if empiricism is correct no proposition which has a factual content can be necessary or certain. Accordingly, the empiricist must deal with the truths of logic and mathematics in one of the two following ways: he must say either that they are not necessary truths, in which case he must account for the universal conviction that they are; or he must say that they have no factual content, and then he must explain how a proposition which is empty of all factual content can be true and useful and surprising.

If neither of these courses proves satisfactory, we shall be obliged to give way to rationalism. We shall be obliged to admit that there are some truths about the world which we can know independently of experience; that there are some properties which we can ascribe to all objects, even though we cannot conceivably observe that all objects have them. And we shall have to accept it as a mysterious inexplicable fact that our thought has this power to reveal to us authoritatively the nature of objects which we have never observed.

Or else we must accept the Kantian explanation which, apart from the epistemological difficulties which we have already touched on, only pushes the mystery a stage further back.

It is clear that any such concession to rationalism would upset the main argument of my book. For the admission that there were some facts about the world which could be known independently of experience would be incompatible with our fundamental contention that a sentence says nothing unless it is empirically verifiable. And thus the whole force of our attack on metaphysics would be destroyed. It is vital, therefore, for us to be able to show that one or other of the empiricist accounts of the propositions of logic and mathematics is correct. If we are successful in this, we shall have destroyed the foundations of rationalism. For the fundamental tenet of rationalism is that thought is an independent source of knowledge, and is moreover a more trustworthy source of knowledge than experience; indeed some rationalists have gone so far as to say that thought is the only source of knowledge. And the ground for this view is simply that the only necessary truths about the world which are known to us are known through thought and not through experience. So that if we can show either that the truths in question are not necessary or that they are not 'truths about the world' we shall be taking away the support on which rationalism rests. We shall be making good the empiricist contention that there are no 'truths of reason' which refer to matters of fact.

The course of maintaining that the truths of logic and mathematics are not necessary or certain was adopted by Mill. He maintained that these propositions were inductive generalizations based on an extremely large number of instances. The fact that the number of supporting instances was so very large accounted, in his view, for our believing these generalizations to be necessarily and universally true. The evidence in their favour was so strong that it seemed incredible to us that a contrary instance should ever arise. Nevertheless, it was in principle possible for such generalizations to be confuted. They were highly probable, but, being inductive generalizations, they were not certain. The difference between them and the hypotheses of natural science was a difference in degree and not in kind. Experience gave us very good reason to suppose that a 'truth' of mathematics or logic was true universally;

but we were not possessed of a guarantee. For these 'truths' were only empirical hypotheses which had worked particularly well in the past; and, like all empirical hypotheses, they were theoretically fallible.

I do not think that this solution of the empiricist's difficulty with regard to the propositions of logic and mathematics is acceptable. In discussing it, it is necessary to make a distinction which is perhaps already enshrined in Kant's famous dictum that, although there can be no doubt that all our knowledge begins with experience, it does not follow that it all arises out of experience.[1] When we say that the truths of logic are known independently of experience, we are not of course saying that they are innate, in the sense that we are born knowing them. It is obvious that mathematics and logic have to be learned in the same way as chemistry and history have to be learned. Nor are we denying that the first person to discover a given logical or mathematical truth was led to it by an inductive procedure. It is very probable, for example, that the principle of the syllogism was formulated not before but after the validity of syllogistic reasoning had been observed in a number of particular cases. What we are discussing, however, when we say that logical and mathematical truths are known independently of experience, is not a historical question concerning the way in which these truths were originally discovered, nor a psychological question concerning the way in which each of us comes to learn them, but an epistemological question. The contention of Mill's which we reject is that the propositions of logic and mathematics have the same status as empirical hypotheses; that their validity is determined in the same way. We maintain that they are independent of experience in the sense that they do not owe their validity to empirical verification. We may come to discover them through an inductive process; but once we have apprehended them we see that they are necessarily true, that they hold good for every conceivable instance. And this serves to distinguish them from empirical generalizations. For we know that a proposition whose validity depends upon experience cannot be seen to be necessarily and universally true.

In rejecting Mill's theory, we are obliged to be somewhat dog-

---

[1] *Critique of Pure Reason*, 2nd edn., Introduction, sect. i.

matic. We can do no more than state the issue clearly and then trust that his contention will be seen to be discrepant with the relevant logical facts. The following considerations may serve to show that of the two ways of dealing with logic and mathematics which are open to the empiricist, the one which Mill adopted is not the one which is correct.

The best way to substantiate our assertion that the truths of formal logic and pure mathematics are necessarily true is to examine cases in which they might seem to be confuted. It might easily happen, for example, that when I came to count what I had taken to be five pairs of objects, I found that they amounted only to nine. And if I wished to mislead people I might say that on this occasion twice five was not ten. But in that case I should not be using the complex sign '2×5=10' in the way in which it is ordinarily used. I should be taking it not as the expression of a purely mathematical proposition, but as the expression of an empirical generalization, to the effect that whenever I counted what appeared to me to be five pairs of objects I discovered that they were ten in number. This generalization may very well be false. But if it proved false in a given case, one would not say that the mathematical proposition '2×5=10' had been confuted. One would say that I was wrong in supposing that there were five pairs of objects to start with, or that one of the objects had been taken away while I was counting, or that two of them had coalesced, or that I had counted wrongly. One would adopt as an explanation whatever empirical hypothesis fitted in best with the accredited facts. The one explanation which would in no circumstances be adopted is that ten is not always the product of two and five.

To take another example: if what appears to be a Euclidean triangle is found by measurement not to have angles totalling 180 degrees, we do not say that we have met with an instance which invalidates the mathematical proposition that the sum of the three angles of a Euclidean triangle is 180 degrees. We say that we have measured wrongly, or, more probably, that the triangle we have been measuring is not Euclidean. And this is our procedure in every case in which a mathematical truth might appear to be confuted. We always preserve its validity by adopting some other explanation of the occurrence.

The same thing applies to the principles of formal logic. We may take an example relating to the so-called law of excluded middle, which states that a proposition must be either true or false, or, in other words, that it is impossible that a proposition and its contradictory should neither of them be true. One might suppose that a proposition of the form '*x* has stopped doing *y*' would in certain cases constitute an exception to this law. For instance, if my friend has never yet written to me, it seems fair to say that it is neither true nor false that he has stopped writing to me. But in fact one would refuse to accept such an instance as an invalidation of the law of excluded middle. One would point out that the proposition 'My friend has stopped writing to me' is not a simple proposition, but the conjunction of the two propositions 'My friend wrote to me in the past' and 'My friend does not write to me now'; and, furthermore, that the proposition 'My friend has not stopped writing to me' is not, as it appears to be, contradictory to 'My friend has stopped writing to me', but only contrary to it. For it means 'My friend wrote to me in the past, and he still writes to me.' When, therefore, we say that such a proposition as 'My friend has stopped writing to me' is sometimes neither true nor false, we are speaking inaccurately. For we seem to be saying that neither it nor its contradictory is true. Whereas what we mean, or anyhow should mean, is that neither it nor its apparent contradictory is true. And its apparent contradictory is really only its contrary. Thus we preserve the law of excluded middle by showing that the negating of a sentence does not always yield the contradictory of the proposition originally expressed.

There is no need to give further examples. Whatever instance we care to take, we shall always find that the situations in which a logical or mathematical principle might appear to be confuted are accounted for in such a way as to leave the principle unassailed. And this indicates that Mill was wrong in supposing that a situation could arise which would overthrow a mathematical truth. The principles of logic and mathematics are true universally simply because we never allow them to be anything else. And the reason for this is that we cannot abandon them without contradicting ourselves, without sinning against the rules which govern the use of language, and so making our utterances self-stultifying. In other words, the truths of logic and mathematics are analytic propositions or tautologies. In saying this we are making what will be held to be an extremely controversial statement, and we must now proceed to make its implications clear.

The most familiar definition of an analytic proposition, or judgement, as he called it, is that given by Kant. He said[2] that an analytic judgement was one in which the predicate B belonged to the subject A as something which was covertly contained in the concept of A. He contrasted analytic with synthetic judgements, in which the predicate B lay outside the subject A, although it did stand in connection with it. Analytic judgements, he explains, 'add nothing through the predicate to the concept of the subject, but merely break it up into those constituent concepts that have all along been thought in it, although confusedly.' Synthetic judgements, on the other hand, 'add to the concept of the subject a predicate which has not been in any wise thought in it, and which no analysis could possibly extract from it.' Kant gives 'all bodies are extended' as an example of an analytic judgement, on the ground that the required predicate can be extracted from the concept of 'body', 'in accordance with the principle of contradiction'; as an example of a synthetic judgement, he gives 'all bodies are heavy'. He refers also to '$7+5=12$' as a synthetic judgement, on the ground that the concept of twelve is by no means already thought in merely thinking the union of seven and five. And he appears to regard this as tantamount to saying that the judgement does not rest on the principle of contradiction alone. He holds, also, that through analytic judgements our knowledge is not extended as it is through synthetic judgements. For in analytic judgements 'the concept which I already have is merely set forth and made intelligible to me.'

I think that this is a fair summary of Kant's account of the distinction between analytic and synthetic propositions, but I do not think that it succeeds in making the distinction clear. For even if we pass over the difficulties which arise out of the use of the vague term 'concept', and the unwarranted assumption that every judgement, as well as every German or English sentence, can be said to have a subject and a predicate, there remains still this crucial defect. Kant does not give one straightforward criterion for distinguishing between analytic and synthetic propositions; he gives two distinct

[2] *Critique of Pure Reason*, 2nd edn., Introduction, sect. iv and v.

criteria, which are by no means equivalent. Thus his ground for holding that the proposition '7+5=12' is synthetic is, as we have seen, that the subjective intension of '7+5' does not comprise the subjective intension of '12'; whereas his ground for holding that 'all bodies are extended' is an analytic proposition is that it rests on the principle of contradiction alone. That is, he employs a psychological criterion in the first of these examples, and a logical criterion in the second, and takes their equivalence for granted. But, in fact, a proposition which is synthetic according to the former criterion may very well be analytic according to the latter. For, as we have already pointed out, it is possible for symbols to be synonymous without having the same intensional meaning for anyone; and accordingly, from the fact that one can think of the sum of seven and five without necessarily thinking of twelve, it by no means follows that the proposition '7+5=12' can be denied without self-contradiction. From the rest of his argument, it is clear that it is this logical proposition, and not any psychological proposition, that Kant is really anxious to establish. His use of the psychological criterion leads him to think that he has established it, when he has not.

I think that we can preserve the logical import of Kant's distinction between analytic and synthetic propositions, while avoiding the confusions which mar his actual account of it, if we say that a proposition is analytic when its validity depends solely on the definitions of the symbols it contains, and synthetic when its validity is determined by the facts of experience. Thus, the proposition 'There are ants which have established a system of slavery' is a synthetic proposition. For we cannot tell whether it is true or false merely by considering the definitions of the symbols which constitute it. We have to resort to actual observation of the behaviour of ants. On the other hand, the proposition 'either some ants are parasitic or none are' is an analytic proposition. For one need not resort to observation to discover that there either are or are not ants which are parasitic. If one knows what is the function of the words 'either', 'or', and 'not', then one can see that any proposition of the form 'Either *p* is true or *p* is not true' is valid, independently of experience. Accordingly, all such propositions are analytic.

It is to be noticed that the proposition 'Either some ants are parasitic or none are' provides no information whatsoever about the behaviour of ants, or, indeed, about any matter of fact. And this applies to all analytic propositions. They none of them provide any information about any matter of fact. In other words, they are entirely devoid of factual content. And it is for this reason that no experience can confute them.

When we say that analytic propositions are devoid of factual content, and consequently that they say nothing, we are not suggesting that they are senseless in the way that metaphysical utterances are senseless. For, although they give us no information about any empirical situation, they do enlighten us by illustrating the way in which we use certain symbols. Thus if I say, 'Nothing can be coloured in different ways at the same time with respect to the same part of itself', I am not saying anything about the properties of any actual thing; but I am not talking nonsense. I am expressing an analytic proposition, which records our determination to call a colour expanse which differs in quality from a neighbouring colour expanse a different part of a given thing. In other words, I am simply calling attention to the implications of a certain linguistic usage. Similarly, in saying that if all Bretons are Frenchmen, and all Frenchmen Europeans, then all Bretons are Europeans, I am not describing any matter of fact. But I am showing that in the statement that all Bretons are Frenchmen, and all Frenchmen Europeans, the further statement that all Bretons are Europeans is implicitly contained. And I am thereby indicating the convention which governs our usage of the words 'if' and 'all'.

We see, then, that there is a sense in which analytic propositions do give us new knowledge. They call attention to linguistic usages, of which we might otherwise not be conscious, and they reveal unsuspected implications in our assertions and beliefs. But we can see also that there is a sense in which they may be said to add nothing to our knowledge. For they tell us only what we may be said to know already. Thus, if I know that the existence of May Queens is a relic of tree-worship, and I discover that May Queens still exist in England, I can employ the tautology 'If p implies q, and p is true, q is true' to show that there still exists a relic of tree-worship in England. But in saying that there are still May Queens in England, and that the existence of May Queens is a relic of tree-worship, I have already asserted the existence in England of a relic of tree-worship. The use of the tautology does, indeed, enable me to make this concealed assertion explicit. But it does not provide me with any new knowledge, in the sense in which empirical evidence that the election of May Queens had been forbidden by law would provide me with new knowledge. If one had to set forth all the information one possessed, with regard to matters of fact, one would not write down any analytic propositions. But one would make use of analytic propositions in compiling one's encyclopaedia, and would thus come to include propositions which one would otherwise have overlooked. And, besides enabling one to make one's list of information complete, the formulation of analytic propositions would enable one to make sure that the synthetic propositions of which the list was composed formed a self-consistent system. By showing which ways of combining propositions resulted in contradictions, they would prevent one from including incompatible propositions and so making the list self-stultifying. But in so far as we had actually used such words as 'all' and 'or' and 'not' without falling into self-contradiction, we might be said already to know what was revealed in the formulation of analytic propositions illustrating the rules which govern our usage of these logical particles. So that here again we are justified in saying that analytic propositions do not increase our knowledge.

The analytic character of the truths of formal logic was obscured in the traditional logic through its being insufficiently formalized. For in speaking always of judgements, instead of propositions, and introducing irrelevant psychological questions, the traditional logic gave the impression of being concerned in some specially intimate way with the workings of thought. What it was actually concerned with was the formal relationship of classes, as is shown by the fact that all its principles of inference are subsumed in the Boolean class-calculus, which is subsumed in its turn in the propositional calculus of Russell and Whitehead.[3] Their system, expounded in *Principia Mathematica*, makes it clear that formal logic is not concerned with the properties of men's minds, much less with the properties of material objects, but simply with the possibility of combining propositions by means of logical particles into analytic propositions,

[3] See Karl Menger, 'Die Neue Logik', *Krise und Neuaufbau in den Exakten Wissenschaften*, pp. 94–6; and Lewis and Langford, *Symbolic Logic*, ch. 5.

and with studying the formal relationship of these analytic propositions, in virtue of which one is deducible from another. Their procedure is to exhibit the propositions of formal logic as a deductive system, based on five primitive propositions, subsequently reduced in number to one. Hereby the distinction between logical truths and principles of inference, which was maintained in the Aristotelian logic, very properly disappears. Every principle of inference is put forward as a logical truth and every logical truth can serve as a principle of inference. The three Aristotelian 'laws of thought', the law of identity, the law of excluded middle, and the law of non-contradiction, are incorporated in the system, but they are not considered more important than the other analytic propositions. They are not reckoned among the premises of the system. And the system of Russell and Whitehead itself is probably only one among many possible logics, each of which is composed of tautologies as interesting to the logician as the arbitrarily selected Aristotelian 'laws of thought'.[4]

A point which is not sufficiently brought out by Russell, if indeed it is recognized by him at all, is that every logical proposition is valid in its own right. Its validity does not depend on its being incorporated in a system, and deduced from certain propositions which are taken as self-evident. The construction of systems of logic is useful as a means of discovering and certifying analytic propositions, but it is not in principle essential even for this purpose. For it is possible to conceive of a symbolism in which every analytic proposition could be seen to be analytic in virtue of its form alone.

The fact that the validity of an analytic proposition in no way depends on its being deducible from other analytic propositions is our justification for disregarding the question whether the propositions of mathematics are reducible to propositions of formal logic, in the way that Russell supposed.[5] For even if it is the case that the definition of a cardinal number as a class of classes similar to a given class is circular, and it is not possible to reduce mathematical notions to purely logical notions, it will still remain true that the propositions of mathematics are analytic propositions. They will form a special class of analytic propositions, containing special

---

[4] Lewis and Langford, *Symbolic Logic*, ch. 7, for an elaboration of this point.
[5] See *Introduction to Mathematical Philosophy*, ch. 2.

terms, but they will be none the less analytic for that. For the criterion of an analytic proposition is that its validity should follow simply from the definition of the terms contained in it, and this condition is fulfilled by the propositions of pure mathematics.

The mathematical propositions which one might most pardonably suppose to be synthetic are the propositions of geometry. For it is natural for us to think, as Kant thought, that geometry is the study of the properties of physical space, and consequently that its propositions have factual content. And if we believe this, and also recognize that the truths of geometry are necessary and certain, then we may be inclined to accept Kant's hypothesis that space is the form of intuition of our outer sense, a form imposed by us on the matter of sensation, as the only possible explanation of our a priori knowledge of these synthetic propositions. But while the view that pure geometry is concerned with the physical space was plausible enough in Kant's day, when the geometry of Euclid was the only geometry known, the subsequent invention of non-Euclidean geometries has shown it to be mistaken. We see now that the axioms of a geometry are simply definitions, and that the theorems of a geometry are simply the logical consequences of these definitions.[6] A geometry is not in itself about physical space; in itself it cannot be said to be 'about' anything. But we can use a geometry to reason about physical space. That is to say, once we have given the axioms a physical interpretation, we can proceed to apply the theorems to the objects which satisfy the axioms. Whether a geometry can be applied to the actual physical world or not, is an empirical question which falls outside the scope of the geometry itself. There is no sense, therefore, in asking which of the various geometries known to us are false and which are true. In so far as they are all free from contradiction, they are all true. What one can ask is which of them is the most useful on any given occasion, which of them can be applied most easily and most fruitfully to an actual empirical situation. But the proposition which states that a certain application of a geometry is possible is not itself a proposition of that geometry. All that the geometry itself tells us is that if anything can be brought under the definitions, it will also satisfy the theorems. It is therefore a purely logical system, and its propositions are purely analytic propositions.

[6] Cf. H. Poincaré, *La Science et l'Hypothèse*, Pt. II, ch. 3.

It might be objected that the use made of diagrams in geometrical treatises shows that the geometrical reasoning is not purely abstract and logical, but depends on our intuition of the properties of figures. In fact, however, the use of diagrams is not essential to completely rigorous geometry. The diagrams are introduced as an aid to our reason. They provide us with a particular application of the geometry, and so assist us to perceive the more general truth that the axioms of the geometry involve certain consequences. But the fact that most of us need the help of an example to make us aware of those consequences does not show that the relation between them and the axioms is not a purely logical relation. It shows merely that our intellects are unequal to the task of carrying out very abstract processes of reasoning without the assistance of intuition. In other words, it has no bearing on the nature of geometrical propositions, but is simply an empirical fact about ourselves. Moreover, the appeal to intuition, though generally of psychological value, is also a source of danger to the geometer. He is tempted to make assumptions which are accidentally true of the particular figure he is taking as an illustration, but do not follow from his axioms. It has, indeed, been shown that Euclid himself was guilty of this, and consequently that the presence of the figure is essential to some of his proofs.[7] This shows that his system is not, as he presents it, completely rigorous, although of course it can be made so. It does not show that the presence of the figure is essential to a truly rigorous geometrical proof. To suppose that it did would be to take as a necessary feature of all geometries what is really only an incidental defect in one particular geometrical system.

We conclude, then, that the propositions of pure geometry are analytic. And this leads us to reject Kant's hypothesis that geometry deals with the form of intuition of our outer sense. For the ground for this hypothesis was that it alone explained how the propositions of geometry could be both true a priori and synthetic; and we have seen that they are not synthetic. Similarly, our view that the propositions of arithmetic are not synthetic but analytic leads us to reject the Kantian hypothesis[8] that arithmetic is concerned with our

---

[7] Cf. M. Black, *The Nature of Mathematics*, p. 154.
[8] This hypothesis is not mentioned in the *Critique of Pure Reason*, but was maintained by Kant at an earlier date.

pure intuition of time, the form of our inner sense. And thus we are able to dismiss Kant's transcendental aesthetic without having to bring forward the epistemological difficulties which it is commonly said to involve. For the only argument which can be brought in favour of Kant's theory is that it alone explains certain 'facts'. And now we have found that the 'facts' which it purports to explain are not facts at all. For while it is true that we have a priori knowledge of necessary propositions, it is not true, as Kant supposed, that any of these necessary propositions are synthetic. They are without exception analytic propositions, or, in other words, tautologies.

We have already explained how it is that these analytic propositions are necessary and certain. We saw that the reason why they cannot be confuted in experience is that they do not make any assertion about the empirical world. They simply record our determination to use words in a certain fashion. We cannot deny them without infringing the conventions which are presupposed by our very denial, and so falling into self-contradiction. And this is the sole ground of their necesssity. As Wittgenstein puts it, our justification for holding that the world could not conceivably disobey the laws of logic is simply that we could not say of an unlogical world how it would look.[9] And just as the validity of an analytic proposition is independent of the nature of the external world; so it is independent of the nature of our minds. It is perfectly conceivable that we should have employed different linguistic conventions from those which we actually do employ. But whatever these conventions might be, the tautologies in which we recorded them would always be necessary. For any denial of them would be self-stultifying.

We see, then, that there is nothing mysterious about the apodeictic certainty of logic and mathematics. Our knowledge that no observation can ever confute the proposition '7+5=12' depends simply on the fact that the symbolic expression '7+5' is synonymous with '12', just as our knowledge that every oculist is an eye-doctor depends on the fact that the symbol 'eye-doctor' is synonymous with 'oculist'. And the same explanation holds good for every other a priori truth.

What is mysterious at first sight is that these tautologies should on occasion be so surprising, that there should be in mathematics and

[9] *Tractatus Logico-Philosophicus*, 3·031.

logic the possibility of invention and discovery. As Poincaré says: 'If all the assertions which mathematics puts forward can be derived from one another by formal logic, mathematics cannot amount to anything more than an immense tautology. Logical inference can teach us nothing essentially new, and if everything is to proceed from the principle of identity, everything must be reducible to it. But can we really allow that these theorems which fill so many books serve no other purpose than to say in a roundabout fashion "$A = A$"?'[10] Poincaré finds this incredible. His own theory is that the sense of invention and discovery in mathematics belongs to it in virtue of mathematical induction, the principle that what is true for the number 1×2, and true for $n + 1 \times 2$ when it is true for n, is true for all numbers. And he claims that this is a synthetic a priori principle. It is, in fact, a priori, but it is not synthetic. It is a defining principle of the natural numbers, serving to distinguish them from such numbers as the infinite cardinal numbers, to which it cannot be applied.[11] Moreover, we must remember that discoveries can be made, not only in arithmetic, but also in geometry and formal logic, where no use is made of mathematical induction. So that even if Poincaré were right about mathematical induction, he would not have provided a satisfactory explanation of the paradox that a mere body of tautologies can be so interesting and so surprising.

The true explanation is very simple. The power of logic and mathematics to surprise us depends, like their usefulness, on the limitations of our reason. A being whose intellect was infinitely powerful would take no interest in logic and mathematics.[12] For he would be able to see at a glance everything that his definitions implied, and accordingly, could never learn anything from logical inference which he was not fully conscious of already. But our intellects are not of this order. It is only a minute proportion of the consequences of our definitions that we are able to detect at a glance. Even so simple a tautology as '$91 \times 79 = 7189$' is beyond the scope of our immediate apprehension. To assure ourselves that

---

[10] *La Science et l'Hypothèse*, Pt. I, ch. 1.

[11] Cf. B. Russell's *Introduction to Mathematical Philosophy*, ch. 3, p. 27.

[12] Cf. Hans Hahn, 'Logik, Mathematik und Naturerkennen', *Einheitswissenschaft*, Pt II, p. 18. 'Ein allwissendes Wesen braucht keine Logik und keine Mathematik'.

'7189' is synonymous with '91 × 79' we have to resort to calculation, which is simply a process of tautological transformation—that
is, a process by which we change the form of expressions without
altering their significance. The multiplication tables are rules for
carrying out this process in arithmetic, just as the laws of logic are
rules for the tautological transformation of sentences expressed in
logical symbolism or in ordinary language. As the process of
calculation is carried out more or less mechanically, it is easy for us
to make a slip and so unwittingly contradict ourselves. And this
accounts for the existence of logical and mathematical 'falsehoods',
which otherwise might appear paradoxical. Clearly the risk of error
in logical reasoning is proportionate to the length and the complexity of the process of calculation. And in the same way, the more
complex an analytic proposition is, the more chance it has of
interesting and surprising us.

It is easy to see that the danger of error in logical reasoning can be
minimized by the introduction of symbolic devices, which enable us
to express highly complex tautologies in a conveniently simple
form. And this gives us an opportunity for the exercise of invention
in the pursuit of logical enquiries. For a well-chosen definition will
call our attention to analytic truths, which would otherwise have
escaped us. And the framing of definitions which are useful and
fruitful may well be regarded as a creative act.

Having thus shown that there is no inexplicable paradox involved
in the view that the truths of logic and mathematics are all of them
analytic, we may safely adopt it as the only satisfactory explanation
of their a priori necessity. And in adopting it we vindicate the
empiricist claim that there can be no a priori knowledge of reality.
For we show that the truths of pure reason, the propositions which
we know to be valid independently of all experience, are so only in
virtue of the lack of factual content. To say that a proposition is true
a priori is to say that it is a tautology. And tautologies, though they
may serve to guide us in our empirical search for knowledge, do not
in themselves contain any information about any matter of fact.

III

TWO DOGMAS OF EMPIRICISM

W. V. QUINE

MODERN empiricism has been conditioned in large part by two dogmas. One is a belief in some fundamental cleavage between truths which are *analytic*, or grounded in meanings independently of matters of fact, and truths which are *synthetic*, or grounded in fact. The other dogma is *reductionism*: the belief that each meaningful statement is equivalent to some logical construct upon terms which refer to immediate experience. Both dogmas, I shall argue, are ill-founded. One effect of abandoning them is, as we shall see, a blurring of the supposed boundary between speculative metaphysics and natural science. Another effect is a shift toward pragmatism.

I. BACKGROUND FOR ANALYTICITY

Kant's cleavage between analytic and synthetic truths was foreshadowed in Hume's distinction between relations of ideas and matters of fact, and in Leibniz's distinction between truths of reason and truths of fact. Leibniz spoke of the truths of reason as true in all possible worlds. Picturesqueness aside, this is to say that the truths of reason are those which could not possibly be false. In the same vein we hear analytic statements defined as statements whose denials are self-contradictory. But this definition has small explanatory value; for the notion of self-contradictoriness, in the quite broad sense needed for this definition of analyticity, stands in exactly the same need of clarification as does the notion of analyticity itself. The two notions are the two sides of a single dubious coin.

Kant conceived of an analytic statement as one that attributes to

W. V. Quine, 'Two Dogmas of Empiricism', reprinted by permission of the publishers from *A Logical Point of View*, 2nd. Edition, Rev., by W. V. Quine, Cambridge, Massachusetts: Harvard University Press, © 1953, 1961, 1980 by the President and Fellows of Harvard College; © 1981 by W. V. Quine.

its subject no more than is already conceptually contained in the subject. This formulation has two shortcomings: it limits itself to statements of subject-predicate form, and it appeals to a notion of containment which is left at a metaphorical level. But Kant's intent, evident more from the use he makes of the notion of analyticity than from his definition of it, can be restated thus: a statement is analytic when it is true by virtue of meanings and independently of fact. Pursuing this line, let us examine the concept of *meaning* which is presupposed.

Meaning, let us remember, is not to be identified with naming. Frege's example of 'Evening Star' and 'Morning Star', and Russell's of 'Scott' and 'the author of *Waverley*', illustrate that terms can name the same thing but differ in meaning. The distinction between meaning and naming is no less important at the level of abstract terms. The terms '9' and 'the number of the planets' name one and the same abstract entity but presumably must be regarded as unlike in meaning; for astronomical observation was needed, and not mere reflection on meanings, to determine the sameness of the entity in question.

The above examples consist of singular terms, concrete and abstract. With general terms, or predicates, the situation is somewhat different but parallel. Whereas a singular term purports to name an entity, abstract or concrete, a general term does not; but a general term is *true* of an entity, or of each of many, or of none. The class of all entities of which a general term is true is called the *extension* of the term. Now paralleling the contrast between the meaning of a singular term and the entity named, we must distinguish equally between the meaning of a general term and its extension. The general terms 'creature with a heart' and 'creature with kidneys', for example, are perhaps alike in extension but unlike in meaning.

Confusion of meaning with extension, in the case of general terms, is less common than confusion of meaning with naming in the case of singular terms. It is indeed a commonplace in philosophy to oppose intension (or meaning) to extension, or, in a variant vocabulary, connotation to denotation.

The Aristotelian notion of essence was the forerunner, no doubt, of the modern notion of intension or meaning. For Aristotle it was essential in men to be rational, accidental to be two-legged. But there is an important difference between this attitude and the doctrine of meaning. From the latter point of view it may indeed be conceded (if only for the sake of argument) that rationality is involved in the meaning of the word 'man' while two-leggedness is not; but two-leggedness may at the same time be viewed as involved in the meaning of 'biped' while rationality is not. Thus from the point of view of the doctrine of meaning it makes no sense to say of the actual individual, who is at once a man and a biped, that his rationality is essential and his two-leggedness accidental or vice versa. Things had essences, for Aristotle, but only linguistic forms have meanings. Meaning is what essence becomes when it is divorced from the object of reference and wedded to the word.

For the theory of meaning a conspicuous question is the nature of its objects: what sort of things are meanings? A felt need for meant entities may derive from an earlier failure to appreciate that meaning and reference are distinct. Once the theory of meaning is sharply separated from the theory of reference, it is a short step to recognizing as the primary business of the theory of meaning simply the synonymy of linguistic forms and the analyticity of statements; meanings themselves, as obscure intermediary entities, may well be abandoned.

The problem of analyticity then confronts us anew. Statements which are analytic by general philosophical acclaim are not, indeed, far to seek. They fall into two classes. Those of the first class, which may be called *logically true*, are typified by:

(1) No unmarried man is married.

The relevant feature of this example is that it not merely is true as it stands, but remains true under any and all reinterpretations of 'man' and 'married'. If we suppose a prior inventory of *logical* particles, comprising 'no', 'un-', 'not', 'if', 'then', 'and', etc., then in general a logical truth is a statement which is true and remains true under all reinterpretations of its components other than the logical particles.

But there is also a second class of analytic statements, typified by:

(2) No bachelor is married.

The characteristic of such a statement is that it can be turned into a logical truth by putting synonyms for synonyms; thus (2) can be turned into (1) by putting 'unmarried man' for its synonym 'bachelor'. We still lack a proper characterization of this second class of analytic statements, and therewith of analyticity generally, inasmuch as we have had in the above description to lean on a notion of 'synonymy' which is no less in need of clarification than analyticity itself.

In recent years Carnap has tended to explain analyticity by appeal to what he calls state-descriptions.[1] A state-description is any exhaustive assignment of truth values to the atomic, or non-compound, statements of the language. All other statements of the language are, Carnap assumes, built up of their component clauses by means of the familiar logical devices, in such a way that the truth value of any complex statement is fixed for each state-description by specifiable logical laws. A statement is then explained as analytic when it comes out true under every state-description. This account is an adaptation of Leibniz's 'true in all possible worlds'. But note that this version of analyticity serves its purpose only if the atomic statements of the language are, unlike 'John is a bachelor' and 'John is married', mutually independent. Otherwise there would be a state-description which assigned truth to 'John is a bachelor' and to 'John is married', and consequently 'No bachelors are married' would turn out synthetic rather than analytic under the proposed criterion. Thus the criterion of analyticity in terms of state-descriptions serves only for languages devoid of extra-logical synonym-pairs, such as 'bachelor' and 'unmarried man'—synonym-pairs of the type which give rise to the 'second class' of analytic statements. The criterion in terms of state-descriptions is a reconstruction at best of logical truth, not of analyticity.

I do not mean to suggest that Carnap is under any illusions on this point. His simplified model language with its state-descriptions is aimed primarily not at the general problem of analyticity but at another purpose, the clarification of probability and induction. Our problem, however, is analyticity; and here the major difficulty lies not in the first class of analytic statements, the logical truths, but

---

[1] Carnap (3), pp. 9 ff; (4), pp. 70 ff.

rather in the second class, which depends on the notion of synonymy.

2. DEFINITION

There are those who find it soothing to say that the analytic statements of the second class reduce to those of the first class, the logical truths, by *definition*; 'bachelor', for example, is *defined* as 'unmarried man'. But how do we find that 'bachelor' is defined as 'unmarried man'? Who defined it thus, and when? Are we to appeal to the nearest dictionary, and accept the lexicographer's formulation as law? Clearly this would be to put the cart before the horse. The lexicographer is an empirical scientist, whose business is the recording of antecedent facts; and if he glosses 'bachelor' as 'unmarried man' it is because of his belief that there is a relation of synonymy between those forms, implicit in general or preferred usage prior to his own work. The notion of synonymy presupposed here has still to be clarified, presumably in terms relating to linguistic behaviour. Certainly the 'definition' which is the lexicographer's report of an observed synonymy cannot be taken as the ground of the synonymy.

Definition is not, indeed, an activity exclusively of philologists. Philosophers and scientists frequently have occasion to 'define' a recondite term by paraphrasing it into terms of a more familiar vocabulary. But ordinarily such a definition, like the philologist's, is pure lexicography, affirming a relation of synonymy antecedent to the exposition in hand.

Just what it means to affirm synonymy, just what the interconnections may be which are necessary and sufficient in order that two linguistic forms be properly describable as synonymous, is far from clear; but, whatever these interconnections may be, ordinarily they are grounded in usage. Definitions reporting selected instances of synonymy come then as reports upon usage.

There is also, however, a variant type of definitional activity which does not limit itself to the reporting of pre-existing synonymies. I have in mind what Carnap calls *explication*—an activity to which philosophers are given, and scientists also in their more philosophical moments. In explication the purpose is not merely to paraphrase the definiendum into an outright synonym, but actually to improve upon the definiendum by refining or supplementing its meaning. But even explication, though not merely reporting a pre-existing synonymy between definiendum and definiens, does rest, nevertheless, on *other* pre-existing synonymies. The matter may be viewed as follows. Any word worth explicating has some contexts which, as wholes, are clear and precise enough to be useful; and the purpose of explication is to preserve the usage of these favoured contexts while sharpening the usage of other contexts. In order that a given definition be suitable for purposes of explication, therefore, what is required is not that the definiendum in its antecedent usage be synonymous with the definiens, but just that each of these favoured contexts of the definiendum, taken as a whole in its antecedent usage, be synonymous with the corresponding context of the definiens.

Two alternative definientia may be equally appropriate for the purposes of a given task of explication and yet not be synonymous with each other; for they may serve interchangeably within the favoured contexts but diverge elsewhere. By cleaving to one of these definientia rather than the other, a definition of explicative kind generates, by fiat, a relation of synonymy between definiendum and definiens which did not hold before. But such a definition still owes its explicative function, as seen, to pre-existing synonymies.

There does, however, remain still an extreme sort of definition which does not hark back to prior synonymies at all: namely, the explicitly conventional introduction of novel notations for purposes of sheer abbreviation. Here the definiendum becomes synonymous with the definiens simply because it has been created expressly for the purpose of being synonymous with the definiens. Here we have a really transparent case of synonymy created by definition; would that all species of synonymy were as intelligible. For the rest, definition rests on synonymy rather than explaining it.

The word 'definition' has come to have a dangerously reassuring sound, owing no doubt to its frequent occurrence in logical and mathematical writings. We shall do well to digress now into a brief appraisal of the role of definition in formal work.

In logical and mathematical systems either of two mutually

antagonistic types of economy may be striven for, and each has its peculiar practical utility. On the one hand, we may seek economy of practical expression—ease and brevity in the statement of multifarious relations. This sort of economy calls usually for distinctive concise notations for a wealth of concepts. Second, however, and oppositely, we may seek economy in grammar and vocabulary; we may try to find a minimum of basic concepts such that, once a distinctive notation has been appropriated to each of them, it becomes possible to express any desired further concept by mere combination and iteration of our basic notations. This second sort of economy is impractical in one way, since a poverty in basic idioms tends to a necessary lengthening of discourse. But it is practical in another way: it greatly simplifies theoretical discourse *about* the language, through minimizing the terms and the forms of construction wherein the language consists.

Both sorts of economy, though prima facie incompatible, are valuable in their separate ways. The custom has consequently arisen of combining both sorts of economy by forging in effect two languages, the one a part of the other. The inclusive language, though redundant in grammar and vocabulary, is economical in message lengths, while the part, called primitive notation, is economical in grammar and vocabulary. Whole and part are correlated by rules of translation whereby each idiom not in primitive notation is equated to some complex built up of primitive notation. These rules of translation are the so-called *definitions* which appear in formalized systems. They are best viewed not as adjuncts to one language but as correlations between two languages, the one a part of the other.

But these correlations are not arbitrary. They are supposed to show how the primitive notations can accomplish all purposes, save brevity and convenience, of the redundant language. Hence the definiendum and its definiens may be expected, in each case, to be related in one or another of the three ways lately noted. The definiens may be a faithful paraphrase of the definiendum into the narrower notation, preserving a direct synonymy[2] as of antecedent

---

[2] According to an important variant sense of 'definition', the relation preserved may be the weaker relation of mere agreement in reference. But definition in this sense is better ignored in the present connection, being irrelevant to the question of synonymy.

usage; or the definiens may, in the spirit of explication, improve upon the antecedent usage of the definiendum; or finally, the definiendum may be a newly created notation, newly endowed with meaning here and now.

In formal and informal work alike, thus, we find that definition—except in the extreme case of the explicitly conventional introduction of new notations—hinges on prior relations of synonymy. Recognizing then that the notion of definition does not hold the key to synonymy and analyticity, let us look further into synonymy and say no more of definition.

3. INTERCHANGEABILITY

A natural suggestion, deserving close examination, is that the synonymy of two linguistic forms consists simply in their interchangeability in all contexts without change of truth value—interchangeability, in Leibniz's phrase, *salva veritate*.[3] Note that synonyms so conceived need not even be free from vagueness, as long as the vaguenesses match.

But it is not quite true that the synonyms 'bachelor' and 'unmarried man' are everywhere interchangeable *salva veritate*. Truths which become false under substitution of 'unmarried man' for 'bachelor' are easily constructed with the help of 'bachelor of arts' or 'bachelor's buttons'; also with the help of quotation, thus:

'Bachelor' has less than ten letters.

Such counter-instances can, however, perhaps be set aside by treating the phrases 'bachelor of arts' and 'bachelor's buttons' and the quotation ' "bachelor" ' each as a single indivisible word and then stipulating that the interchangeability *salva veritate* which is to be the touchstone of synonymy is not supposed to apply to fragmentary occurrences inside of a word. This account of synonymy, supposing it acceptable on other counts, has indeed the drawback of appealing to a prior conception of 'word' which can be counted on to present difficulties of formulation in its turn. Nevertheless, some progress might be claimed in having reduced the problem of

---

[3] Cf. Lewis (1), p. 373.

synonymy to a problem of wordhood. Let us pursue this line a bit, taking 'word' for granted.

The question remains whether interchangeability *salva veritate* (apart from occurrences within words) is a strong enough condition for synonymy, or whether, on the contrary, some heteronymous expressions might be thus interchangeable. Now let us be clear that we are not concerned here with synonymy in the sense of complete identity in psychological associations or poetic quality; indeed no two expressions are synonymous in such a sense. We are concerned only with what may be called *cognitive* synonymy. Just what this is cannot be said without successfully finishing the present study; but we know something about it from the need which arose for it in connection with analyticity in §1. The sort of synonymy needed there was merely such that any analytic statement could be turned into a logical truth by putting synonyms for synonyms. Turning the tables and assuming analyticity, indeed, we could explain cognitive synonymy of terms as follows (keeping to the familiar example): to say that 'bachelor' and 'unmarried man' are cognitively synonymous is to say no more nor less than that the statement:

(3) All and only bachelors are unmarried men

is analytic.[4]

What we need is an account of cognitive synonymy not presupposing analyticity—if we are to explain analyticity conversely with help of cognitive synonymy as undertaken in §1. And indeed such an independent account of cognitive synonymy is at present up for consideration, namely, interchangeability *salva veritate* everywhere except within words. The question before us, to resume the thread at last, is whether such interchangeability is a sufficient condition for cognitive synonymy. We can quickly assure ourselves that it is, by examples of the following sort. The statement:

(4) Necessarily all and only bachelors are bachelors

is evidently true, even supposing 'necessarily' so narrowly con-

---

[4] This is cognitive synonymy in a primary, broad sense. Carnap ((3), pp. 56 ff.) and Lewis ((2), pp. 83 ff.) have suggested how, once this notion is at hand, a narrower sense of cognitive synonymy which is preferable for some purposes can in turn be derived. But this special ramification of concept-building lies aside from the present purposes and must not be confused with the broad sort of cognitive synonymy here concerned.

strued as to be truly applicable only to analytic statements. Then, if 'bachelor' and 'unmarried man' are interchangeable *salva veritate*, the result:

(5) Necessarily all and only bachelors are unmarried men

of putting 'unmarried man' for an occurrence of 'bachelor' in (4) must, like (4), be true. But to say that (5) is true is to say that (3) is analytic, and hence that 'bachelor' and 'unmarried man' are cognitively synonymous.

Let us see what there is about the above argument that gives it its air of hocus-pocus. The condition of interchangeability *salva veritate* varies in its force with variations in the richness of the language at hand. The above argument supposes we are working with a language rich enough to contain the adverb 'necessarily', this adverb being so construed as to yield truth when and only when applied to an analytic statement. But can we condone a language which contains such an adverb? Does the adverb really make sense? To suppose that it does is to suppose that we have already made satisfactory sense of 'analytic'. Then what are we so hard at work on right now?

Our argument is not flatly circular, but something like it. It has the form, figuratively speaking, of a closed curve in space.

Interchangeability *salva veritate* is meaningless until relativized to a language whose extent is specified in relevant respects. Suppose now we consider a language containing just the following materials. There is an indefinitely large stock of one-place predicates (for example, 'F' where 'Fx' means that x is a man) and many-place predicates (for example, 'G' where 'Gxy' means that x loves y), mostly having to do with extra-logical subject-matter. The rest of the language is logical. The atomic sentences consist each of a predicate followed by one or more variables 'x', 'y', etc.; and the complex sentences are built up of the atomic ones by truth functions ('not', 'and', 'or', etc.) and quantification. In effect such a language enjoys the benefits also of descriptions and indeed singular terms generally, these being contextually definable in known ways. Even abstract singular terms naming classes, classes of classes, etc., are contextually definable in case the assumed stock of predicates includes the two-place predicate of class membership. Such a language can be adequate to classical mathematics and indeed to scientific discourse generally, except in so far as the latter involves debatable devices such as contrary-to-fact conditionals or modal adverbs like 'necessarily'. Now a language of this type is extensional, in this sense: any two predicates which agree extensionally (that is, are true of the same objects) are interchangeable *salva veritate*.[5]

In an extensional language, therefore, interchangeability *salva veritate* is no assurance of cognitive synonymy of the desired type. That 'bachelor' and 'unmarried man' are interchangeable *salva veritate* in an extensional language assures us of no more than that (3) is true. There is no assurance here that the extensional agreement of 'bachelor' and 'unmarried man' rests on meaning rather than merely on accidental matters of fact, as does the extensional agreement of 'creature with a heart' and 'creature with kidneys'.

For most purposes extensional agreement is the nearest approximation to synonymy we need care about. But the fact remains that extensional agreement falls far short of cognitive synonymy of the type required for explaining analyticity in the manner of §1. The type of cognitive synonymy required there is such as to equate the synonymy of 'bachelor' and 'unmarried man' with the analyticity of (3), not merely with the truth of (3).

So we must recognize that interchangeability *salva veritate*, if construed in relation to an extensional language, is not a sufficient condition of cognitive synonymy in the sense needed for deriving analyticity in the manner of §1. If a language contains an intensional adverb 'necessarily' in the sense lately noted, or other particles to the same effect, then interchangeability *salva veritate* in such a language does afford a sufficient condition of cognitive synonymy; but such a language is intelligible only in so far as the notion of analyticity is already understood in advance.

The effort to explain cognitive synonymy first, for the sake of deriving analyticity from it afterward as in §1, is perhaps the wrong approach. Instead we might try explaining analyticity somehow without appeal to cognitive synonymy. Afterward we could doubtless derive cognitive synonymy from analyticity satisfactorily enough if desired. We have seen that cognitive synonymy of

---

[5] This is the substance of Quine (1), *121.

'bachelor' and 'unmarried man' can be explained as analyticity of (3). The same explanation works for any pair of one-place predicates, of course, and it can be extended in obvious fashion to many-place predicates. Other syntactical categories can also be accommodated in fairly parallel fashion. Singular terms may be said to be cognitively synonymous when the statement of identity formed by putting '=' between them is analytic. Statements may be said simply to be cognitively synonymous when their biconditional (the result of joining them by 'if and only if') is analytic.[6] If we care to lump all categories into a single formulation, at the expense of assuming again the notion of 'word' which was appealed to early in this section, we can describe any two linguistic forms as cognitively synonymous when the two forms are interchangeable (apart from occurrences within 'words') *salva* (no longer *veritate* but) *analyticitate*. Certain technical questions arise, indeed, over cases of ambiguity or homonymy; let us not pause for them, however, for we are already digressing. Let us rather turn our backs on the problem of synonymy and address ourselves anew to that of analyticity.

4. SEMANTICAL RULES

Analyticity at first seemed most naturally definable by appeal to a realm of meanings. On refinement, the appeal to meanings gave way to an appeal to synonymy or definition. But definition turned out to be a will-o'-the-wisp, and synonymy turned out to be best understood only by dint of a prior appeal to analyticity itself. So we are back at the problem of analyticity.

I do not know whether the statement 'Everything green is extended' is analytic. Now does my indecision over this example really betray an incomplete understanding, an incomplete grasp of the 'meanings', of 'green' and 'extended'? I think not. The trouble is not with 'green' or 'extended', but with 'analytic'.

It is often hinted that the difficulty in separating analytic statements from synthetic ones in ordinary language is due to the vagueness of ordinary language and that the distinction is clear when we have a precise artificial language with explicit 'semantical

[6] The 'if and only if' itself is intended in the truth functional sense. See Carnap (3), p. 14.

rules'. This, however, as I shall now attempt to show, is a confusion.

The notion of analyticity about which we are worrying is a purported relation between statements and languages: a statement *S* is said to be *analytic* for a language *L*, and the problem is to make sense of this relation generally, that is, for variable '*S*' and '*L*'. The gravity of this problem is not perceptibly less for artificial languages than for natural ones. The problem of making sense of the idiom '*S* is analytic for *L*', with variable '*S*' and '*L*', retains its stubbornness even if we limit the range of the variable '*L*' to artificial languages. Let me now try to make this point evident.

For artificial languages and semantical rules we look naturally to the writings of Carnap. His semantical rules take various forms, and to make my point I shall have to distinguish certain of the forms. Let us suppose, to begin with, an artificial language L_0 whose semantical rules have the form explicitly of a specification, by recursion or otherwise, of all the analytic statements of L_0. The rules tell us that such and such statements, and only those, are the analytic statements of L_0. Now here the difficulty is simply that the rules contain the word 'analytic', which we do not understand! We understand what expressions the rules attribute analyticity to, but we do not understand what the rules attribute to those expressions. In short, before we can understand a rule which begins 'A statement *S* is analytic for language L_0 if and only if . . .', we must understand the general relative term 'analytic for'; we must understand '*S* is analytic for *L*' where '*S*' and '*L*' are variables.

Alternatively we may, indeed, view the so-called rule as a conventional definition of a new simple symbol 'analytic-for-L_0', which might better be written untendentiously as '*K*' so as not to seem to throw light on the interesting word 'analytic'. Obviously any number of classes *K*, *M*, *N*, etc. of statements of L_0 can be specified for various purposes or for no purpose; what does it mean to say that *K*, as against *M*, *N*, etc., is the class of the 'analytic' statements of L_0?

By saying what statements are analytic for L_0 we explain 'analytic-for-L_0' but not 'analytic', not 'analytic for'. We do not begin to explain the idiom '*S* is analytic for *L*' with variable '*S*' and '*L*' even if we are content to limit the range of '*L*' to the realm of artificial languages.

Actually we do know enough about the intended significance of 'analytic' to know that analytic statements are supposed to be true. Let us then turn to a second form of semantical rule, which says not that such and such statements are analytic but simply that such and such statements are included among the truths. Such a rule is not subject to the criticism of containing the un-understood word 'analytic'; and we may grant for the sake of argument that there is no difficulty over the broader term 'true'. A semantical rule of this second type, a rule of truth, is not supposed to specify all the truths of the language; it merely stipulates, recursively or otherwise, a certain multitude of statements which, along with others unspecified, are to count as true. Such a rule may be conceded to be quite clear. Derivatively, afterward, analyticity can be demarcated thus: a statement is analytic if it is (not merely true but) true according to the semantical rule.

Still there is really no progress. Instead of appealing to an unexplained word 'analytic', we are now appealing to an unexplained phrase 'semantical rule'. Not every true statement which says that the statements of some class are true can count as a semantical rule—otherwise *all* truths would be 'analytic' in the sense of being true according to semantical rules. Semantical rules are distinguishable, apparently, only by the fact of appearing on a page under the heading 'Semantical Rules'; and this heading is itself then meaningless.

We can say indeed that a statement is *analytic-for-L_0* if and only if it is true according to such and such specifically appended 'semantical rules', but then we find ourselves back at essentially the same case which was originally discussed: '*S* is analytic-for-L_0 if and only if. . . .' Once we seek to explain '*S* is analytic for *L*' generally for variable '*L*' (even allowing limitation of '*L*' to artificial languages), the explanation 'true according to the semantical rules of *L*' is unavailing; for the relative term 'semantical rule of' is as much in need of clarification, at least, as 'analytic for'.

It may be instructive to compare the notion of semantical rule with that of postulate. Relative to a given set of postulates, it is easy to say what a postulate is: it is a member of the set. Relative to a given set of semantical rules, it is equally easy to say what a semantical rule is. But given simply a notation, mathematical or otherwise, and indeed as thoroughly understood a notation as you please in point of the translations or truth conditions of its statements, who can say which of its true statements rank as postulates? Obviously the question is meaningless—as meaningless as asking which points in Ohio are starting-points. Any finite (or effectively specifiable infinite) selection of statements (preferably true ones, perhaps) is as much *a* set of postulates as any other. The word 'postulate' is significant only relative to an act of enquiry; we apply the word to a set of statements just in so far as we happen, for the year or the moment, to be thinking of those statements in relation to the statements which can be reached from them by some set of transformations to which we have seen fit to direct our attention. Now the notion of semantical rule is as sensible and meaningful as that of postulate, if conceived in a similarly relative spirit—relative, this time, to one or another particular enterprise of schooling unconversant persons in sufficient conditions for truth of statements of some natural or artificial language L. But from this point of view no one signalization of a subclass of the truths of L is intrinsically more a semantical rule than another; and, if 'analytic' means 'true by semantical rules', no one truth of L is analytic to the exclusion of another.[7]

It might conceivably be protested that an artificial language L (unlike a natural one) is a language in the ordinary sense *plus* a set of explicit semantical rules—the whole constituting, let us say, an ordered pair; and that the semantical rules of L then are specifiable simply as the second component of the pair L. But, by the same token and more simply, we might construe an artificial language L outright as an ordered pair whose second component is the class of its analytic statements; and then the analytic statements of L become specifiable simply as the statements in the second component of L. Or better still, we might just stop tugging at our bootstraps altogether.

Not all the explanations of analyticity known to Carnap and his readers have been covered explicitly in the above considerations, but the extension to other forms is not hard to see. Just one additional factor should be mentioned which sometimes enters:

[7] The foregoing paragraph was not part of the present essay as originally published; it was prompted by Martin (see Bibliography).

sometimes the semantical rules are in effect rules of translation into ordinary language, in which case the analytic statements of the artificial language are in effect recognized as such from the analyticity of their specified translations in ordinary language. Here certainly there can be no thought of an illumination of the problem of analyticity from the side of the artificial language.

From the point of view of the problem of analyticity the notion of an artificial language with semantical rules is a *feu follet par excellence*. Semantical rules determining the analytic statements of an artificial language are of interest only in so far as we already understand the notion of analyticity; they are of no help in gaining this understanding.

Appeal to hypothetical languages of an artificially simple kind could conceivably be useful in clarifying analyticity, if the mental or behavioural or cultural factors relevant to analyticity—whatever they may be—were somehow sketched into the simplified model. But a model which takes analyticity merely as an irreducible character is unlikely to throw light on the problem of explicating analyticity.

It is obvious that truth in general depends on both language and extra-linguistic fact. The statement 'Brutus killed Caesar' would be false if the world had been different in certain ways, but it would also be false if the word 'killed' happened rather to have the sense of 'begat'. Thus one is tempted to suppose in general that the truth of a statement is somehow analysable into a linguistic component and a factual component. Given this supposition, it next seems reasonable that in some statements the factual component should be null; and these are the analytic statements. But, for all its a priori reasonableness, a boundary between analytic and synthetic statements simply has not been drawn. That there is such a distinction to be drawn at all is an unempirical dogma of empiricists, a metaphysical article of faith.

5. THE VERIFICATION THEORY AND REDUCTIONISM

In the course of these sombre reflections we have taken a dim view first of the notion of meaning, then of the notion of cognitive synonymy, and finally of the notion of analyticity. But what, it may be asked, of the verification theory of meaning? This phrase has established itself so firmly as a catchword of empiricism that we should be very unscientific indeed not to look beneath it for a possible key to the problem of meaning and the associated problems.

The verification theory of meaning, which has been conspicuous in the literature from Peirce onward, is that the meaning of a statement is the method of empirically confirming or infirming it. An analytic statement is that limiting case which is confirmed no matter what.

As urged in §1, we can as well pass over the question of meanings as entities and move straight to sameness of meaning, or synonymy. Then what the verification theory says is that statements are synonymous if and only if they are alike in point of method of empirical confirmation or infirmation.

This is an account of cognitive synonymy not of linguistic forms generally, but of statements.[8] However, from the concept of synonymy of statements we could derive the concept of synonymy for other linguistic forms, by considerations somewhat similar to those at the end of §3. Assuming the notion of 'word', indeed, we could explain any two forms as synonymous when the putting of the one form for an occurrence of the other in any statement (apart from occurrences within 'words') yields a synonymous statement. Finally, given the concept of synonymy thus for linguistic forms generally, we could define analyticity in terms of synonymy and logical truth as in §1. For that matter, we could define analyticity more simply in terms of just synonymy of statements together with logical truth; it is not necessary to appeal to synonymy of linguistic forms other than statements. For a statement may be described as analytic simply when it is synonymous with a logically true statement.

So, if the verification theory can be accepted as an adequate

---

[8] The doctrine can indeed be formulated with terms rather than statements as the units. Thus Lewis describes the meaning of a term as '*a criterion in mind*, by reference to which one is able to apply or refuse to apply the expression in question in the case of presented, or imagined, things or situations' ((2), p. 133). For an instructive account of the vicissitudes of the verification theory of meaning, centred however on the question of meaning*fulness* rather than synonymy and analyticity, see Hempel.

account of statement synonymy, the notion of analyticity is saved after all. However, let us reflect. Statement synonymy is said to be likeness of method of empirical confirmation or infirmation. Just what are these methods which are to be compared for likeness? What, in other words, in the nature of the relation between a statement and the experiences which contribute to or detract from its confirmation?

The most naive view of the relation is that it is one of direct report. This is *radical reductionism*. Every meaningful statement is held to be translatable into a statement (true or false) about immediate experience. Radical reductionism, in one form or another, well antedates the verification theory of meaning explicitly so called. Thus Locke and Hume held that every idea must either originate directly in sense experience or else be compounded of ideas thus originating; and taking a hint from Tooke we might rephrase this doctrine in semantical jargon by saying that a term, to be significant at all, must be either a name of a sense datum or a compound of such names or an abbreviation of such a compound. So stated, the doctrine remains ambiguous as between sense data as sensory events and sense data as sensory qualities; and it remains vague as to the admissible ways of compounding. Moreover, the doctrine is unnecessarily and intolerably restrictive in the term-by-term critique which it imposes. More reasonably, and without yet exceeding the limits of what I have called radical reductionism, we may take full statements as our significant units—thus demanding that our statements as wholes be translatable into sense-datum language, but not that they be translatable term by term.

This emendation would unquestionably have been welcome to Locke and Hume and Tooke, but historically it had to await an important reorientation in semantics—the reorientation whereby the primary vehicle of meaning came to be seen no longer in the term but in the statement. This reorientation, explicit in Frege ((1), §60), underlies Russell's concept of incomplete symbols defined in use; also it is implicit in the verification theory of meaning, since the objects of verification are statements.

Radical reductionism, conceived now with statements as units, set itself the task of specifying a sense-datum language and showing how to translate the rest of significant discourse, statement by statement, into it. Carnap embarked on this project in the *Aufbau*.

The language which Carnap adopted as his starting-point was not a sense-datum language in the narrowest conceivable sense, for it included also the notations of logic, up through higher set theory. In effect, it included the whole language of pure mathematics. The ontology implicit in it (that is, the range of values of its variables) embraced not only sensory events but classes, classes of classes, and so on. Empiricists there are who would boggle at such prodigality. Carnap's starting-point is very parsimonious, however, in its extra-logical or sensory part. In a series of constructions in which he exploits the resources of modern logic with much ingenuity, Carnap succeeds in defining a wide array of important additional sensory concepts which, but for his constructions, one would not have dreamed were definable on so slender a basis. He was the first empiricist who, not content with asserting the reducibility of science to terms of immediate experience, took serious steps toward carrying out the reduction.

If Carnap's starting-point is satisfactory, still his constructions were, as he himself stressed, only a fragment of the full programme. The construction of even the simplest statements about the physical world was left in a sketchy state. Carnap's suggestions on this subject were, despite their sketchiness, very suggestive. He explained spatio-temporal point-instants as quadruples of real numbers and envisaged assignment of sense qualities to point-instants according to certain canons. Roughly summarized, the plan was that qualities should be assigned to point-instants in such a way as to achieve the laziest world compatible with our experience. The principle of least action was to be our guide in constructing a world from experience.

Carnap did not seem to recognize, however, that his treatment of physical objects fell short of reduction not merely through sketchiness, but in principle. Statements of the form 'Quality q is at point-instant $x;y;z;t$' were, according to his canons, to be apportioned truth values in such a way as to maximize and minimize certain overall features, and with growth of experience the truth values were to be progressively revised in the same spirit. I think this is a good schematization (deliberately over-simplified, to be sure) of what science really does; but it provides no indication, not even the sketchiest, of how a statement of the form 'Quality q is at $x;y;z;t$' could ever be translated into Carnap's initial language of sense data and logic. The connective 'is at' remains an added undefined connective; the canons counsel us in its use but not in its elimination.

Carnap seems to have appreciated this point afterward; for in his later writings he abandoned all notion of the translatability of statements about the physical world into statements about immediate experience. Reductionism in its radical form has long since ceased to figure in Carnap's philosophy.

But the dogma of reductionism has, in a subtler and more tenuous form, continued to influence the thought of empiricists. The notion lingers that to each statement, or each synthetic statement, there is associated a unique range of possible sensory events such that the occurrence of any of them would add to the likelihood of truth of the statement, and that there is associated also another unique range of possible sensory events whose occurrence would detract from that likelihood. This notion is of course implicit in the verification theory of meaning.

The dogma of reductionism survives in the supposition that each statement, taken in isolation from its fellows, can admit of confirmation or infirmation at all. My counter-suggestion, issuing essentially from Carnap's doctrine of the physical world in the *Aufbau*, is that our statements about the external world face the tribunal of sense experience not individually but only as a corporate body.[9]

The dogma of reductionism, even in its attenuated form, is intimately connected with the other dogma—that there is a cleavage between the analytic and the synthetic. We have found ourselves led, indeed, from the latter problem to the former through the verification theory of meaning. More directly, the one dogma clearly supports the other in this way: as long as it is taken to be significant in general to speak of the confirmation and infirmation of a statement, it seems significant to speak also of a limiting kind of statement which is vacuously confirmed, *ipso facto*, come what may; and such a statement is analytic.

[9] This doctrine was well argued by Duhem, pp. 303–28. Or see Lowinger, pp. 132–40.

The two dogmas are, indeed, at root identical. We lately reflected that in general the truth of statements does obviously depend both upon language and upon extra-linguistic fact; and we noted that this obvious circumstance carries in its train, not logically but all too naturally, a feeling that the truth of a statement is somehow analysable into a linguistic component and a factual component. The factual component must, if we are empiricists, boil down to a range of confirmatory experiences. In the extreme case where the linguistic component is all that matters, a true statement is analytic. But I hope we are now impressed with how stubbornly the distinction between analytic and synthetic has resisted any straightforward drawing. I am impressed also, apart from prefabricated examples of black and white balls in an urn, with how baffling the problem has always been of arriving at any explicit theory of the empirical confirmation of a synthetic statement. My present suggestion is that it is nonsense, and the root of much nonsense, to speak of a linguistic component and a factual component in the truth of any individual statement. Taken collectively, science has its double dependence upon language and experience; but this duality is not significantly traceable into the statements of science taken one by one.

The idea of defining a symbol in use was, as remarked, an advance over the impossible term-by-term empiricism of Locke and Hume. The statement, rather than the term, came with Frege to be recognized as the unit accountable to an empiricist critique. But what I am now urging is that even in taking the statement as unit we have drawn our grid too finely. The unit of empirical significance is the whole of science.

6. EMPIRICISM WITHOUT THE DOGMAS

The totality of our so-called knowledge or beliefs, from the most casual matters of geography and history to the profoundest laws of atomic physics or even of pure mathematics and logic, is a man-made fabric which impinges on experience only along the edges. Or, to change the figure, total science is like a field of force whose boundary conditions are experience. A conflict with experience at the periphery occasions readjustments in the interior of the field.

Truth values have to be redistributed over some of our statements. Re-evaluation of some statements entails re-evaluation of others, because of their logical interconnections—the logical laws being in turn simply certain further statements of the system, certain further elements of the field. Having re-evaluated one statement we must re-evaluate some others, which may be statements logically connected with the first or may be the statements of logical connections themselves. But the total field is so underdetermined by its boundary conditions, experience, that there is much latitude of choice as to what statements to re-evaluate in the light of any single contrary experience. No particular experiences are linked with any particular statements in the interior of the field, except indirectly through considerations of equilibrium affecting the field as a whole.

If this view is right, it is misleading to speak of the empirical content of an individual statement—especially if it is a statement at all remote from the experiential periphery of the field. Furthermore, it becomes folly to seek a boundary between synthetic statements, which hold contingently on experience, and analytic statements, which hold come what may. Any statement can be held true come what may, if we make drastic enough adjustments elsewhere in the system. Even a statement very close to the periphery can be held true in the face of recalcitrant experience by pleading hallucination or by amending certain statements of the kind called logical laws. Conversely, by the same token, no statement is immune to revision. Revision even of the logical law of the excluded middle has been proposed as a means of simplifying quantum mechanics; and what difference is there in principle between such a shift and the shift whereby Kepler superseded Ptolemy, or Einstein Newton, or Darwin Aristotle?

For vividness I have been speaking in terms of varying distances from a sensory periphery. Let me try now to clarify this notion without metaphor. Certain statements, though *about* physical objects and not sense experience, seem peculiarly germane to sense experience—and in a selective way: some statements to some experiences, others to others. Such statements, especially germane to particular experiences, I picture as near the periphery. But in this relation of 'germaneness' I envisage nothing more than a loose association reflecting the relative likelihood, in practice, of our choosing one statement rather than another for revision in the event of recalcitrant experience. For example, we can imagine recalcitrant experiences to which we would surely be inclined to accommodate our system by re-evaluating just the statement that there are brick houses on Elm Street, together with related statements on the same topic. We can imagine other recalcitrant experiences to which we would be inclined to accommodate our system by re-evaluating just the statement that there are no centaurs, along with kindred statements. A recalcitrant experience can, I have urged, be accommodated by any of various alternative re-evaluations in various alternative quarters of the total system; but, in the cases which we are now imagining, our natural tendency to disturb the total system as little as possible would lead us to focus our revisions upon these specific statements concerning brick houses or centaurs. These statements are felt, therefore, to have a sharper empirical reference than highly theoretical statements of physics or logic or ontology. The latter statements may be thought of as relatively centrally located within the total network, meaning merely that little preferential connection with any particular sense data obtrudes itself.

As an empiricist I continue to think of the conceptual scheme of science as a tool, ultimately, for predicting future experience in the light of past experience. Physical objects are conceptually imported into the situation as convenient intermediaries—not by definition in terms of experience, but simply as irreducible posits comparable, epistemologically, to the gods of Homer. For my part I do, *qua* lay physicist, believe in physical objects and not in Homer's gods; and I consider it a scientific error to believe otherwise. But in point of epistemological footing the physical objects and the gods differ only in degree and not in kind. Both sorts of entities enter our conception only as cultural posits. The myth of physical objects is epistemologically superior to most in that it has proved more efficacious than other myths as a device for working a manageable structure into the flux of experience.

Positing does not stop with macroscopic physical objects. Objects at the atomic level are posited to make the laws of macroscopic objects, and ultimately the laws of experience, simpler and more manageable; and we need not expect or demand full definition of atomic and subatomic entities in terms of macroscopic ones, any more than definition of macroscopic things in terms of sense data. Science is a continuation of common sense, and it continues the common-sense expedient of swelling ontology to simplify theory.

Physical objects, small and large, are not the only posits. Forces are another example; and indeed we are told nowadays that the boundary between energy and matter is obsolete. Moreover, the abstract entities which are the substance of mathematics— ultimately classes and classes of classes and so on up—are another posit in the same spirit. Epistemologically these are myths on the same footing with physical objects and gods, neither better nor worse except for differences in the degree to which they expedite our dealings with sense experiences.

The overall algebra of rational and irrational numbers is under-determined by the algebra of rational numbers, but is smoother and more convenient; and it includes the algebra of rational numbers as a jagged or gerrymandered part. Total science, mathematical and natural and human, is similarly but more extremely under-determined by experience. The edge of the system must be kept squared with experience; the rest, with all its elaborate myths or fictions, has as its objective the simplicity of laws.

Ontological questions, under this view, are on a par with questions of natural science.[10] Consider the question whether to countenance classes as entities. This, as I have argued elsewhere,[11] is the question whether to quantify with respect to variables which take classes as values. Now Carnap (6) has maintained that this is a question not of matters of fact but of choosing a convenient language form, a convenient conceptual scheme or framework for science. With this I agree, but only on the proviso that the same be conceded regarding scientific hypotheses generally. Carnap ((6), p. 32 n) has recognized that he is able to preserve a double standard for ontological questions and scientific hypotheses only by assuming an absolute distinction between the analytic and the synthetic; and I

[10] 'L'ontologie fait corps avec la science elle-même et ne peut en être separée.' Meyerson, p. 439.
[11] See Quine, *From a Logical Point of View*, 2nd edn. (Cambridge: Harvard University Press, 1961), pp. 12 f., 102 ff.

need not say again that this is a distinction which I reject.[12]

The issue over there being classes seems more a question of convenient conceptual scheme; the issue over there being centaurs, or brick houses on Elm Street, seems more a question of fact. But I have been urging that this difference is only one of degree, and that it turns upon our vaguely pragmatic inclination to adjust one strand of the fabric of science rather than another in accommodating some particular recalcitrant experience. Conservatism figures in such choices, and so does the quest for simplicity.

Carnap, Lewis, and others take a pragmatic stand on the question of choosing between language forms, scientific frameworks; but their pragmatism leaves off at the imagined boundary between the analytic and the synthetic. In repudiating such a boundary I espouse a more thorough pragmatism. Each man is given a scientific heritage plus a continuing barrage of sensory stimulation; and the considerations which guide him in warping his scientific heritage to fit his continuing sensory promptings are, where rational, pragmatic.

BIBLIOGRAPHICAL REFERENCES

Carnap, Rudolf (1), *Der logische Aufbau der Welt* (Berlin, 1928).

—— (2), *The Logical Syntax of Language* (New York: Harcourt Brace, and London: Kegan Paul, 1937). Translation, with extensions, of *Logische Syntax der Sprache* (Vienna: Springer, 1934).

—— (3), *Meaning and Necessity* (Chicago: University of Chicago Press, 1947).

—— (4), *Logical Foundations of Probability* (Chicago: University of Chicago Press, 1950).

—— (5), 'Testability and Meaning', *Philosophy of Science*, 3 (1936), 419–71; 4 (1937), 1–40 (reprinted, New Haven: Graduate Philosophy Club, Yale University, 1950).

—— (6), 'Empiricism, Semantics, and Ontology', *Revue internationale de philosophie*, 4 (1950), 20–40. Reprinted in Linsky.

Duhem, Pierre, *La Théorie physique: son objet et sa structure* (Paris, 1906).

Frege, Gottlob (1), *Foundations of Arithmetic* (New York: Philosophical Library, 1950). Reprint of *Grundlagen der Arithmetik* (Breslau, 1884) with English translation in parallel.

[12] For an effective expression of further misgivings over this distinction, see White (1).

Hempel, C. G. (1), 'Problems and Changes in the Empiricist Criterion of Meaning', *Revue internationale de philosophie*, 4 (1950), 41–63. Reprinted in Linsky.

—— (2), 'The Concept of Cognitive Significance: A Reconsideration', *Proceedings of American Academy of Arts and Sciences*, 80 (1951), 61–77.

Lewis, C. I. (1), *A Survey of Symbolic Logic* (Berkeley, 1918).

—— (2), *An Analysis of Knowledge and Valuation* (LaSalle, Ill.: Open Court, 1946).

Linsky, Leonard (ed.), *Semantics and the Philosophy of Language* (Urbana: University of Illinois Press, 1952).

Lowinger, Armand, *The Methodology of Pierre Duhem* (New York: Columbia University Press, 1941).

Martin, R. M., 'On "analytic" ', *Philosophical Studies*, 3 (1952), 42–7.

Meyerson, Émile, *Identité et realité*. (Paris, 1908; 4th edn., 1932).

Quine, W. V. (1), *Mathematical Logic* (New York: Norton, 1940; Cambridge: Harvard University Press, 1947; rev. edn., Cambridge: Harvard University Press, 1951).

Tooke, J. H. Ἔπεα πτερόεντα; or, *The Diversions of Purley*. 2 vols. (London, 1786, 1805, 1829; Boston, 1806).

White, Morton (1), 'The Analytic and the Synthetic: an Untenable Dualism', in Sidney Hook (ed.), *John Dewey: Philosopher of Science and Freedom* (New York: Dial Press, 1950), pp. 316–30. Reprinted in Linsky.

WITTGENSTEIN AND LOGICAL NECESSITY

BARRY STROUD

MICHAEL DUMMETT has described Wittgenstein's account of logical necessity as a 'full-blooded conventionalism'.[1] On this view, the source of the necessity of any necessary statement is 'our having expressly decided to treat that very statement as unassailable'. (p. 329.) Even faced with a rigorous mathematical proof:

> at each step we are free to choose to accept or reject the proof; there is nothing in our formulation of the axioms and of the rules of inference, and nothing in our minds when we accepted these before the proof was given, which of itself shows whether we shall accept the proof or not; and hence there is nothing which *forces* us to accept the proof. If we accept the proof, we confer necessity on the theorem proved; we 'put it in the archives' and will count nothing as telling against it. In doing this we are making a new decision, and not merely making explicit a decision we had already made implicitly. (p. 330.)

This implies that it is possible for someone to accept the axioms and the rules of inference and yet to reject the proof, without having failed to understand those axioms or rules. But, Dummett objects:

> We want to say that we do not know what it would be like for someone who, by ordinary criteria, already understood the concepts employed, to reject this proof. . . . The examples given in Wittgenstein's book are—amazingly

Barry Stroud, 'Wittgenstein and Logical Necessity' from *The Philosophical Review* 74, (1965), 504–18. Reprinted by permission of the Managing Editor and the author.
[1] Michael Dummett, 'Wittgenstein's Philosophy of Mathematics', *Philosophical Review*, 68 (1959), 324 ff. Page numbers alone in parentheses in the text always refer to this article. References to Wittgenstein's writings always contain an abbreviation of the title of the book in question. '*PI*' will refer to Wittgenstein's *Philosophical Investigations* (New York, 1953), and unless otherwise indicated, parenthetical references will be to the numbered sections of Pt. I. '*RFM*' will refer to *Remarks on the Foundations of Mathematics* (Oxford, 1956).

for him—thin and unconvincing. I think that this is a fairly sure sign that there is something wrong with Wittgenstein's account. (p. 333.)

Dummett is obviously on strong ground here—it seems impossible to understand this alleged possibility—but I think Wittgenstein would agree. His examples are not designed to show that we do understand this. What is important for the problem of logical necessity is to explain what makes the denial of a necessary truth 'impossible' or 'unintelligible'. It is not enough to say that it is 'logically impossible', since an explanation of logical necessity is just what is in question. Dummett appears to agree with this (pp. 328–9). In the rest of this paper I shall try to say what, according to Wittgenstein, is responsible for the unintelligibility in such cases.

In defending the claim that he is not committed to saying that everybody could infer in any way at all, Wittgenstein points out that it is essential to inferring, calculating, counting, and so forth, that not just any result is allowed as correct. If everybody continues the series as he likes, or infers just any way at all, then 'we shan't call it "continuing the series" and also presumably not "inference" ' (*RFM* I. 116). General agreement among people as to the correct results of inferences or calculations and general agreement in the results that one gets oneself at different times are both necessary in order for there to be inferring or calculating at all (*RFM* II. 6, 73). The same holds for counting, continuing a series, and so on. These are all activities in which the possibility of different results at different times and places is not left open. It is just here that a calculation differs from an experiment, where people at different times and places can get different results.

These remarks suggest that the source of necessity in inferring or calculating is simply that any activity in which just any results were allowed would not be *called* 'inferring', 'calculating', and so forth. In the case of drawing logical conclusions:

The steps which are not brought in question are logical inferences. But the reason why they are not brought in question is not that they 'certainly correspond to the truth'—or something of the sort—no, it is just this that is called 'thinking', 'speaking', 'inferring', 'arguing'. (*RFM* I. 155.)

This looks like the standard claim that all necessity finds its source in definitions or in the meanings of words. In inferring, one must write down 'q' after '$p \supset q$' and 'p' because to do otherwise is to cease to infer correctly, and correct inference is just 'defined' by the laws of logic. That is what we call correct inference. This would presumably mean that, since it is possible for something else to be meant by 'correct inference', it would also be possible for something else to be the conclusion. Despite suggestions of this 'standard conventionalism' in Wittgenstein, I agree with Dummett that he does not hold such a view, although it is not always easy to see how what he says differs from it.

The main target of Wittgenstein's writings on necessity is the Platonism of Frege and the early Russell. In this respect he and the logical positivists are alike. According to Platonism it would be impossible for someone, when given the order 'Add 2', to write down all the same numerals as we do up to '1000' and then to go on '1004, 1008, . . .', and still be able to justify his going on in that way. It would be impossible because it is simply wrong, in continuing the series '+ 2', to write down '1004' right after '1000'; that is not, in fact, the next member of the series. So the pupil must either have misunderstood the instructions or have made a mistake. Anyone who puts anything other than '1002' is wrong and should be declared an idiot or an incorrigible if he persists in his perversity. As Frege puts it: 'here we have a hitherto unknown kind of insanity.'[2]

The conventionalist's opposition to Platonism consists primarily in showing that our present ways of inferring, counting, calculating, and so forth, are not the only possible ones. But the standard conventionalist would also reject the alleged possibility on the grounds that the description of such a state of affairs is contradictory. If the person has understood the instructions, if he has just written down '1000', and if he is to continue following the instructions, then he *must* write down '1002'. Of course, he is free not to continue the series at all, or to claim that he has been following instructions like 'Add 2 up to 1000, 4 up to 2000', and so forth, but it is logically impossible (involves a contradiction) for him to have understood the instructions correctly and to write down '1004' right after '1000'. His claiming that '1004' is the correct step is a sufficient condition of his having abandoned the ordinary sense attached to

<hr>

[2] G. Frege, *Grundgesetze der Arithmetik* (Jena, 1903), p. xvi.

the order 'Add 2'. That it is correct to write '1002' is already contained in the meaning of those instructions, and once one has agreed to follow them, then because they mean what they do there are certain steps which one logically must take.

The crucial notion in this conventionalistic theory is that of understanding the meaning of a word or a rule, and this is something to which Wittgenstein devotes a great deal of attention. Part of his interest in it is in the sense, if any, in which someone's having understood the instructions somehow logically guarantees that he will write down '1002' right after '1000'. If this is logically guaranteed, then it would seem that his going on '1004, 1008, . . .' could be due only to misunderstanding or to a mistake; in any event, he could not have understood correctly. But what is it to understand correctly? What determines which move is the correct one at a given point? The answer would appear to be that the way the order was meant, or what was meant by the person giving the order, determines which steps are correct. But again, Wittgenstein asks, what shows which way the order was meant? It is not the case that the teacher very quickly thought of each particular step which he wanted the pupil to take, and even if he did, that would not show that 'meaning 1002, 1004, . . .' meant 'thinking of 1002, 1004, . . .' (*PI* 692). Rather, what the order means will be shown in the ways we use it, in what we do in following it, in the ways we are taught to use it, and so on (*RFM* I. 2).

If someone who had learned to continue various series just as we do began to differ from us when he went beyond any point he had reached in his training, would it follow that he simply had not understood the instructions? If he continued to do this, must we say that he is unintelligent, perhaps idiotic? Wittgenstein tries as follows to suggest negative answers to these questions:

If my reply is: 'Oh yes of course, *that* is how I was applying it!' or: 'Oh! That's how I ought to have applied it!'; then I am playing your game. But if I simply reply: 'Different?—But this surely *isn't* different!'—what will you do? That is: somebody may reply like a rational person and yet not be playing our game. (*RFM* I. 115.)

He tries to show that not all cases of deviating from what we expect or from what we all do in continuing the series can be put down to simple misunderstanding, stupidity, or deliberate perversity on the part of the pupil. It is almost certain in any particular case we come across that some discoverable mistake has occurred, and that the pupil will come to recognize this. But *must* he do so? Is there no possibility other than those mentioned above? The example is intended to suggest that there is. But the important, and difficult, problem is to say exactly what this alleged possibility comes to. Although Frege said it would be a new kind of insanity, 'he never said what this "insanity" would really be like' (*RFM* I. 151). To see what it would be like is to understand on what our being compelled in inferring, calculating, counting, and so forth, rests.

The person who continues the series '1004, 1008, . . .' is described as 'finding it natural' to go on in that way; it 'strikes him as the same' as he has done earlier. In trying to get such a person to continue the series as we do it would no longer be useful for us to go through the training and give him the old explanations over again. And providing him with a rule precisely formulated in mathematical terms would not avoid the difficulties, since it is just the possibility of his understanding such a rule that is in question.

In such a case we might say, perhaps: It comes natural to this person to understand our order with our explanations as *we* should understand the order: 'Add 2 up to 1000, 4 up to 2000, 6 up to 3000, and so on.'
Such a case would present similarities with one in which a person naturally reacted to the gesture of pointing with the hand by looking in the direction of the line from fingertip to wrist, not from wrist to fingertip. (*PI* 185.)

For Wittgenstein, it will not be enough to object that, if we are patient and careful, surely we could eventually get the pupil to see that he is to make the same move after '1000' as before—that he is not to change the size of the steps. He is convinced that he is making the same move, and 'who says what "change" and "remaining the same" mean here' (*RFM* I. 113)? One is inclined to reply, I think, that nobody *says* what is the same and what is different; it is just a fact that the pupil is wrong in supposing that going on '1004, 1008, . . .' is doing the same as he was in writing down '2, 4, 6, . . .' But is there some discoverable fact of which we are aware, and which he is missing? What sort of fact is it, and how could he be brought to acknowledge it? Trying to explain to him that he has not gone on in the same way would be like trying to teach someone how to carry out the order 'Go this way' when I point in a particular direction. If that person naturally reacted to the gesture of pointing by looking in the direction of the line from fingertip to wrist, it would not be enough to say to him, 'If I point this way (pointing with my right hand) I mean that you should go *this* way (pointing with my left hand in the same direction).' Isn't every explanation of how someone should follow an arrow in the position of another arrow (*BB* p. 97)?

Or, to choose another example, suppose we come across some people who find it natural to sell wood, not by cubic measure or board feet as we do, but at a price proportionate to the area covered by the pile of wood, and they pay no attention to the height of the pile.

How could I show them that—as I should say—you don't really buy more wood if you buy a pile covering a bigger area?—I should, for instance, take a pile which was small by their ideas and, by laying the logs around, change it into a 'big' one. This *might* convince them—but perhaps they would say: 'Yes, now it's a *lot* of wood and costs more'—and that would be the end of the matter. (*RFM* I. 149.)

This case is analogous to that of trying to get the deviant pupil to see that the next step after '1000' is really '1002'.[3] But can we describe what these people do as 'selling wood the wrong way'? Is it a way whose 'incorrectness' we could point out to them? And surely it is not logically impossible for there to be such people: the example does not contain a hidden contradiction.

The natural reply to this example is that it shows only that such

---

[3] There are some important features of the two cases as presented which are not analogous. We are imagining a single pupil who makes a single deviant move after having done exactly as we had expected up till now, whereas the example of the wood-sellers is presented from the outset as one in which we come across a whole, flourishing society. Consequently, what appears to be a sudden and inexplicable change, or an individual aberration, in the former case is not present in the latter. Furthermore, and crucially, the society of wood-sellers is not our own, but the strange pupil has apparently sprung up right in our midst. I think that these and other disanalogies can be avoided by presenting both cases in the same way from the beginning, although Wittgenstein never does this. (Some of the difficulties which these differences appear to create for the later stages of my argument were pointed out to me by Professor Stanley Cavell.)

people mean by 'a lot of wood' and 'a little wood' something different from what we mean by it, and similarly, as Dummett suggests, anyone who agrees with us in accepting all the steps in a proof but who then refuses to accept what we all accept as the conclusion must be blind to the meaning that has already been given to the words in the premisses or in previous proofs. It seems as if he could not remain faithful to the meanings of those words and still reject the conclusion. Dummett concludes from this that he is simply *deciding* to accept some particular statement as necessary in complete isolation from everything else he has accepted. This is why Wittgenstein is called a 'full-blooded' conventionalist. The strange people Wittgenstein describes differ from us only in having 'adopted different conventions'. But does it follow from the case which Wittgenstein tries to construct that the deviant pupil simply chooses to write '1004' and that his choice makes that the correct step? Can the people in Wittgenstein's examples properly be said to differ from us only in having adopted different conventions? I think the answer is 'No'. One thing implied by saying that we have adopted, or are following, a convention is that there are alternatives which we could adopt in its place. But in the case of writing '1002' right after '1000' there appear to be no alternatives open to us. It seems impossible to understand how we could 'adopt the convention' that writing '998, 1000, 1004, . . .' is going on in the same way, or taking steps of the same size. Surely if writing '998, 1000, 1002, . . .' is not taking steps of the same size, then nothing is.

I have been trying to suggest so far that for Wittgenstein such 'alternatives' are not inconceivable or unimaginable because they involve or lead to a logical contradiction. Just as there is no logical contradiction involved in the supposition that people might sell wood, and defend their doing so, in the way described earlier, so there is no logical contradiction involved in supposing that someone might agree with us in all uses of words or in all steps of a proof up to the present, and that he should now accept something different from what we all accept as the conclusion, without being simply idiotic or deliberately perverse. Wittgenstein's examples are designed to show this; it is part of the attack on Platonism. But as long as such alternatives are inconceivable in whatever sense, it looks as if Dummett is right in pointing out that 'we do not know what it would be like for someone who, by ordinary criteria, already understood the concepts employed, to reject the proof'. And if we do not know what this would be like, how can we find at all plausible Wittgenstein's purported examples of someone who 'replies like a rational person' and yet is not 'playing our game'? So it appears that, as Dummett says, Wittgenstein's examples are 'thin and unconvincing', as they presumably must be if they are supposed to be examples of something that is unimaginable or inconceivable.

This seems to present the interpreter of Wittgenstein with a choice between two alternatives. Either Wittgenstein has not succeeded in giving any clear or intelligible examples of people whose ways of calculating, and so forth, are radically different from ours, and therefore he has not begun to support his anti-Platonistic account of logical necessity; or else he has succeeded in giving intelligible, perhaps even convincing, examples which commit him to a 'full-blooded conventionalism'. And if the latter is the case, then Dummett's successful attack on radical conventionalism will be equally successful against Wittgenstein. But this choice is not an exhaustive one. There can be plausible examples to show the possibility of ways of counting, inferring, calculating, and so forth, different from ours, but which do not imply that our doing these things as we do is solely a result of our abiding by, or having adopted, certain more or less arbitrary conventions to which there are clear and intelligible alternatives. Nor do such examples imply that 'at each step we are free to accept or reject the proof' or that 'a statement's being necessarily true is solely a result of our having decided to treat that very statement as unassailable'. But at one point Wittgenstein says:

So much is clear: when someone says: 'If you follow the rule, it *must* be like this', he has not any *clear* concept of what experience would correspond to the opposite.
    Or again: he has not any clear concept of what it would be like for it to be otherwise. And this is very important. (*RFM* III. 29.)

If this is true, how can he hope to be successful in giving examples of what it would be like for it to be otherwise, while still maintaining that there is logical necessity in such cases? How can he have it both ways? The solution to this dilemma is to be found in the explanation of why we do not have any clear concept of the opposite in the case of logical necessity, and why Wittgenstein speaks of our not having a *clear* concept here. How could we have any concept at all?

Wittgenstein gives many examples of people whose ways of inferring, counting, calculating, and so forth, are different in significant ways from ours. As well as the woodsellers mentioned earlier, there might be others who sell wood at a price equal to the labour of felling the timber, measured by the age and strength of the woodman. Or perhaps each buyer pays the same however much he takes (*RFM* I. 147). Also, there might be people who measured with soft rubber rulers, or with rulers which expanded to an extraordinary extent when slightly heated (*RFM* I. 5). Or suppose that people in their calculations sometimes divided by '$(n\text{-}n)$' and yet were not bothered by the results. They would be like people who did not prepare lists of names systematically (for example, alphabetically), and so in some lists some names would appear more than once, but they accept this without worrying (*RFM* V. 8). Or there might be people who count, but when they want to know numbers for various practical purposes ask certain other people who, having had the practical problem explained to them, shut their eyes and let the appropriate number come to them (*RFM* V. 14). There are many more such examples, merely mentioned or briefly discussed, throughout Wittgenstein's *Remarks*.[4] They are all intended to be analogous in various ways to the 'possibility' that someone might go on '1004' right after '1000' in continuing the series '+ 2'.

When first presented with these examples it seems that we can understand them, and that we can come to know what such people would be like. We do not happen to do things in these strange ways, but, it seems, we could. If these examples represent clear alternatives, then why doesn't it follow that our calculating, counting, measuring, and so forth, as we do is purely a matter of convention? If this is not a matter of convention, how can these examples be perfectly intelligible to us? In suggesting answers to these questions I shall have begun to show how Wittgenstein can escape between the horns of the above dilemma.

[4] E.g., *RFM* I. 136, 139, 152, 168; II. 76, 78, 81, 84; III. 15, 17; IV. 5; V. 6, 12, 27, 29, 36, 42, 43, 44.

When we look more closely at the examples, are they really as intelligible as they seemed at first? For instance, consider the people who sell wood at a price proportionate to the area covered by the pile of wood and who defend their doing so in the way described earlier. Surely they would have to believe that a one-by-six-inch board all of a sudden increased in size or quantity when it was turned from resting on its one-inch edge to resting on its six-inch side. And what would the relation between quantity and weight possibly be for such people? A man could buy as much wood as he could possibly lift, only to find, upon dropping it, that he had just lifted more wood than he could possibly lift. Or is there more wood, but the same weight? Or perhaps these people do not understand the expressions 'more' and 'less' at all. They must, if they can say, 'Now it's a lot of wood, and costs more'. And do these people think of themselves as shrinking when they shift from standing on both feet to standing on one? Also, it would be possible for a house that is twice as large as another built on exactly the same plan to contain much less wood. How much wood is bought need have no connection with how much wood is needed for building the house. And so on. Problems involved in understanding what it would be like to sell wood in this way can be multiplied indefinitely.

If so, then so far we do not really know what it would be like for us to sell wood, and to try to justify our doing so, in the way Wittgenstein has described. And we have already noted the difficulties in trying to understand the example of continuing the series '+ 2'. I think the initial intelligibility and strength of Wittgenstein's examples derive from their being severely isolated or restricted. We think we can understand and accept them as representing genuine alternatives only because the wider-reaching consequences of counting, calculating, and so forth, in these deviant ways are not brought out explicitly. When we try to trace out the implications of behaving like that consistently and quite generally, our understanding of the alleged possibilities diminishes. I suspect that this would happen with most, if not all, of Wittgenstein's examples, but I do not need to prove this in general, since if my interpretation is right these examples will fulfil their intended role whether or not this point holds.

The reason for this progressive decrease in intelligibility, I think, is that the attempt to get a clearer understanding of what it would be like to be one of these people and to live in their world inevitably leads us to abandon more and more of our own familiar world and the ways of thinking about it upon which our understanding rests. The more successful we are in projecting ourselves into such a world, the less we shall have left in terms of which we can find it intelligible. In trying to understand these alleged possibilities, we constantly come across more and more difficulties, more and more questions which must be answered before we can understand them. But this is not to say that we do not understand them because they are 'meaningless' or 'contradictory', or because what they purport to represent is 'logically impossible'.

Wittgenstein's examples are intended to oppose Platonism by showing that calculating, counting, inferring, and so forth, might have been done differently. But this implies no more than that the inhabitants of the earth might have engaged in those practices in accordance with rules which are different from those we actually follow. It is in that sense a contingent fact that calculating, inferring, and so forth, are carried out in the ways that they are—just as it is a contingent fact that there is such a thing as calculating or inferring at all. But we can understand and acknowledge the contingency of this fact, and hence the possibility of different ways of calculating, and so forth, without understanding what those different ways might have been. If so, then it does not follow that those rules by which calculating, and so forth, might have been carried out constitute a set of genuine alternatives open to us among which we could choose, or even among which we could have chosen. The only sense that has been given to the claim that 'somebody may reply like a rational person and yet not be playing our game' is that there might have been different sorts of beings from us, that the inhabitants of the earth might have come to think and behave in ways different from their actual ones. But this does not imply that we are free to put whatever we like after '1000' when given the instructions 'Add 2', or that our deciding to put '1002' is what makes that the correct step. Consequently, Wittgenstein's examples do not commit him to a 'radical conventionalism' in Dummett's sense. In trying to explain more fully why he is not committed to this I will return to the sense in which he can be called a 'conventionalist'.

In several places Wittgenstein describes what he is doing in some such way as this:

What we are supplying are really remarks on the natural history of man: not curiosities however, but rather observations on facts which no one has doubted, and which have only gone unremarked because they are always before our eyes. (*RFM* I. 141.)

What facts does he have in mind here, and what role do they play in his account of logical necessity? The reason for calling them 'facts of our natural history' is to emphasize both what I have called their contingency—that is, that they might not have obtained—and the fact that they are somehow 'constitutive' of mankind—that is, their obtaining is what is responsible for human nature's being what it is.

Part of human behaviour consists of calculating sums, distances, quantities, of making inferences, drawing conclusions, and so forth. It is a fact that we engage in such practices: 'mathematics is after all an anthropological phenomenon' (*RFM* V. 26). There are various facts which make it possible for calculating to occur at all. For example, our memories are generally good enough for us not to take numbers twice in counting up to 12, and not to leave any out (*RFM* V. 2); in correlating two groups of five strokes we practically always can do so without remainder (*RFM* I. 64); somebody who has learned to calculate never goes on getting different results, in a given multiplication, from what is in the arithmetic books (*RFM* I. 112); and so on. The inhabitants of the earth might have lacked these and other simple abilities, and if so there would be no such thing as calculating at all. In that way the possibility of calculating depends on such contingent facts. These are examples of what Wittgenstein calls the 'physical', 'psychological', and 'physiological' facts which make activities such as calculating possible (*RFM* V. 1, 15).

A contingent fact which is responsible for our calculating as we actually do is the fact that we take '1002, 1004, . . .' to be going on in the same way as putting down '996, 998, 1000, . . .'. It is a fact that we naturally go on in this way, but people might not have done so. Since they might naturally have followed the rule in a different way, our rules alone do not logically guarantee that they will not be taken or understood in deviant ways. A rule itself does not make 'strange' ways of following it impossible, since a rule is not something which stands apart from our understanding of it, and which mysteriously contains within it all of its future applications. How we naturally understand and follow the rule determines which applications of it are correct, and the way a rule is followed will depend in part on what we take to be 'going on in the same way'. 'The use of the word "rule" and the use of the word "same" are interwoven' (*PI* 225). It is because people might not share our natural reactions, or might not be in accord with us in their 'judgements of sameness' that their understanding the instructions does not rule out their taking a different step from ours at some point while still finding what they have done to be in accord with the rule. So understanding the rule in the way we do depends on such things as finding it natural to go on to '1002' right after '1000'. That we take just the step we do here is a contingent fact, but it is not the result of a decision; it is not a convention to which there are alternatives among which we could choose. And that we share any such 'judgements' at all (whatever they might be) is also a contingent fact, but without this agreement there would be no understanding of any rules at all.

If language is to be a means of communication there must be agreement not only in definitions but also (queer as this may sound) in judgements. This seems to abolish logic, but does not do so. (*PI* 242.)

Those described as 'not playing our game' are the people who are not in accord with us in the 'judgements' on which the possibility of language and communication rests. Wittgenstein's examples of the possibility of people like this serve to bring out the contingency of the fact that, as things are, we are in accord in these 'judgements'. Anyone who did not go on as we do need not be simply continuing a different series (for example, 'Add 2 up to 1000, 4 up to 2000', and so forth), and in that way be 'playing a game' different from the one we happen to be playing; nor need he have misunderstood the instructions in a way that can be pointed out to him by more careful explanations. But someone like this would not be fully intelligible to us. Our relation to him would be like our relation to people who naturally reacted to the gesture of pointing by looking in the direction of the line from fingertip to wrist, or who sold wood in the way described earlier. It is not simply that they happen to have chosen to do things one way, and we happen to have chosen to do them differently, but that they would be different sorts of beings from us, beings which we could not understand and with which we could not enter into meaningful communication. They would ultimately be unfathomable to us (compare, for example, *RFM* I. 34, 61, 66, 152). In order to have a 'clear concept' of what it would be like to think and behave as they do we would have to be able to abandon many, if not all, of those 'judgements' on which our being able to think or conceive of anything at all rests.

What I have been saying will explain what would otherwise be a puzzling distinction which Wittgenstein makes in a well-known passage:

I am not saying: if such-and-such facts of nature were different people would have different concepts (in the sense of a hypothesis). But: if anyone believes that certain concepts are absolutely the correct ones, and that having different ones would mean not realizing something that we realize— then let him imagine certain very general facts of nature to be different from what we are used to, and the formation of concepts different from the usual ones will become intelligible to him. (*PI* p. 230.)

The point of Wittgenstein's examples of people who do not 'play our game' is only to show that our having the concepts and practices we have is dependent upon certain facts which might not have obtained. They show only that 'the formation of concepts different from the usual ones' is intelligible to us; but it does not follow from this that those concepts themselves are intelligible to us. And since the intelligibility of alternative concepts and practices is required by the thesis of radical conventionalism which Dummett ascribes to Wittgenstein, I think that thesis is not borne out by Wittgenstein's examples.

The 'shared judgements' (for example, of sameness) upon which our being able to communicate rests, and which are responsible for our calculating, inferring, and so forth, as we do are not properly seen, then, as the results of free decisions in the manner of the logical positivists. They might have been different and, if they had been, then calculating, inferring, and so forth, would have been done differently. But this does not make them conventions in the positivists' sense. In defending the claim that we had made the

correct move after '1000' in following the rule 'Add 2' we could
ultimately get back to something like our 'shared judgement' that
putting down '1002' is doing the same as we were doing earlier.
There is nothing further we could appeal to. These 'judgements'
represent the limits of our knowledge, and thus they have a role
similar to the explicit conventions of the positivists.

From what has been said so far it might still look as if our 'sharing
judgements' is nothing more than our all agreeing that certain
propositions are true or unassailable. But the 'agreement' of which
Wittgenstein speaks here is not the unanimous acceptance of a
particular truth or set of truths.

'So you are saying that human agreement decides what is true and what is
false?'—It is what human beings *say* that is true and false; and they agree in
the *language* they use. That is not agreement in opinions but in form of life.
(*PI* 241.)

This 'agreement' is the universal accord of human beings in behaving in certain ways—those 'natural reactions' which we all share, or
those human practices the engaging in which makes a creature
human. Those are the 'facts of our natural history' which he is
appealing to. The correctness of steps in calculating is not ultimately
established on the basis of their agreeing with or being entailed by
certain truths which we have accepted without foundation, or which
are 'self-evident':

The limits of empiricism are not assumptions unguaranteed, or intuitively
known to be correct: they are ways in which we make comparisons and in
which we act. (*RFM* V. 18.)

This distinguishes Wittgenstein both from the Platonist and from
the standard conventionalist. I shall comment on only one other
aspect of this difference.

I have said that it is a 'fact of our natural history' in Wittgenstein's
sense that we agree in finding certain steps in following a rule 'doing
the same'. In some cases we all naturally go on in the same way from
the steps which have already been taken. This is what makes it
possible for us to follow any rules at all.

And does this mean e.g. that the definition of 'same' would be this: same is what all or most human beings with one voice take for the same?—Of course not.

For of course I don't make use of the agreement of human beings to affirm identity. What criterion do you use, then? None at all. (*RFM* V. 33.)

But if there is no criterion for the truth of assertions of identity, how can we know they are true? Without a proof to the contrary, might not all human beings, for all their agreement, be wrong in supposing that writing '1002' is going on in the same way as writing '1000' after '998'? Wittgenstein replies that 'to use a word without a justification does not mean to use it wrongfully' (*RFM* V. 33). And in this case, at this stage, there is no 'justification' of the sort the empiricist seeks. But why not?

The correctness of particular calculations, inferences, and so forth, is decided by appeal to the rules, but can't we also ask whether those rules themselves are correct, whether our techniques of calculation, inference, and so forth, are the correct ones?

The danger here, I believe, is one of giving a justification of our procedure when there is no such thing as a justification and we ought simply to have said: *that's how we do it*. (*RFM* II. 74.)

The ultimate appeal in seeking a 'foundation' for our procedures of calculating, inferring, and so forth, can only be to 'ways in which we make comparisons and in which we act'. That is all that an account of the 'foundation' or 'source' of logical necessity can achieve. This perhaps helps to explain the point of passages like this:

What has to be accepted, the given, is—so one could say—*forms of life*. (*PI* p. 226.)

Because these procedures cannot be given a 'justification' it does not follow that they are shaky or unreliable, or that we are courting trouble if we decide to engage in them. We do not decide to accept or reject them at all, any more than we decide to be human beings as opposed to trees. To ask whether our human practices or forms of life themselves are 'correct' or 'justified' is to ask whether we are 'correct' or 'justified' in being the sorts of things we are.

At the end of his paper Dummett recommends interposing

between the Platonist and constructivist pictures of thought and reality an intermediate picture

> of objects springing into being in response to our probing. We do not *make* the objects but must accept them as we find them (this corresponds to the proof imposing itself on us); but they were not already there for our statements to be true or false of before we carried out the investigations which brought them into being. (p. 348.)

As far as I understand this, it seems to be just the picture to be derived from Wittgenstein if my interpretation is in general correct. Logical necessity, he says, is not like rails that stretch to infinity and compel us always to go in one and only one way; but neither is it the case that we are not compelled at all. Rather, there are the rails we have already travelled, and we can extend them beyond the present point only by depending on those that already exist. In order for the rails to be navigable they must be extended in smooth and natural ways; how they are to be continued is to that extent determined by the route of those rails which are already there. I have been primarily concerned to explain the sense in which we are 'responsible' for the ways in which the rails are extended, without destroying anything that could properly be called their objectivity.

V

ANALYTICITY AND APRIORITY: BEYOND WITTGENSTEIN AND QUINE

HILARY PUTNAM

BOTH Wittgenstein and Quine have had important insights in connection with the nature of mathematical and logical 'necessity', and both have written things that have transformed the discussion of this topic. But it is the burden of this paper to show that the views of both are unacceptable as they stand. I hope that a short and sharp statement of why both sorts of views will not do may help take us to a new stage in the discussion.

PART I: WHY MATHEMATICAL NECESSITY IS NOT EXPLAINED BY HUMAN NATURE, 'FORMS OF LIFE', ETC.

Wittgensteinian Views

Just *what* Wittgenstein's contention is, in connection with philosophers' opinions, theories, and arguments on the topic of 'mathematical necessity', has been a subject of considerable controversy. Clearly he thinks the whole discussion is nonsensical and confused; but *why* (in his view) it is nonsensical and confused, and whether he offers any explanation at all of why we *think* there is such a thing as mathematical necessity and of what the difference is between mathematical and empirical statements, is a subject on which there seems to be a great deal of disagreement among his interpreters.

I shall not attempt to do any textual exegesis here. I know what the (several) views of *Wittgensteinians* are, even if I do not know for sure which, if any, was Wittgenstein's; and what I shall try to show is

Hilary Putnam, 'Analyticity and Apriority: Beyond Wittgenstein and Quine', from *Midwest Studies in Philosophy*, Vol. 4, pp. 423–41, ed. P. French et al., 1979. Reprinted by permission of the University of Minnesota Press and the author.

that not even the most sophisticated of these 'Wittgensteinian' views is tenable.

Here is a first approximation to Wittgenstein's view: when we make a mathematical assertion, say '2 + 2 = 4', the 'necessity' of this assertion is accounted for by the fact that we would not *count* anything as a counterexample to the statement. The statement is not a 'description' of any fact, but a 'rule of description': i.e. a directive to the effect that cases in which we *seem* to add two things to two things and get five, or whatever, are to be explained away (e.g. by saying that a fifth thing must have been produced by the interaction). In a terminology employed by other philosophers, the statement is *analytic*.

The problem with such views—a problem Wittgenstein himself clearly points out, which is why the above cannot be more than a first approximation to Wittgenstein's view—is that the set of theorems of mathematics is infinite (or appears to be infinite: I shall explain the reservation shortly). Only a finite number of mathematical truths, such as '2 + 2 = 4', 'every number has a successor', can possibly be *primitive* rules of description (be what Carnap called 'meaning postulates'); most mathematical truths are not *directly* meaning stipulations, or 'rules of description', or whatever, but only *consequences* of 'rules of description'.

Now, the thesis that every theorem of mathematics is either true by convention (a meaning postulate, in Carnap's sense, or a 'rule of description' in Wittgenstein's) or else a *consequence* of statements that are true by convention has often been advanced as an *epistemologically explanatory thesis* (e.g. by Ayer in *Language, Truth, and Logic* and Carnap in the *Foundations of Logic and Mathematics*), but it cannot really explain the truth of the theorems of mathematics (*other* than the ones in the finite set that are *directly* 'true by convention') at all, for a reason pointed out by both Wittgenstein and Quine: namely, *it takes logic to derive the consequences from the conventions*. The 'exciting' thesis that logic is true by convention reduces to the unexciting claim that *logic is true by conventions plus logic*. No real advance has been made.

What then was Wittgenstein's view? Call the Wittgenstein who held (or seemed to hold) that '2 + 2 = 4' is true by convention (a 'rule of description') 'Wittgenstein$_1$'. Call the Wittgenstein who pointed out the emptiness of the Ayer–Carnap position 'Wittgenstein$_2$'. What could Wittgenstein$_2$'s position have been? (Not to mention Wittgenstein$_3$, Wittgenstein$_4$,. . .)

Michael Dummett (1959) suggested a daring possibility: namely, that Wittgenstein was a *radical conventionalist*. That is, Wittgenstein was a conventionalist who held not just that some finite set of meaning postulates is true by convention, but that whenever we accept what we call a 'proof' in logic or mathematics, an *act of decision* is involved: a decision to *accept* the proof. This decision, on Dummett's reading, is never *forced* on us by some prior thing called the 'concepts' or 'the meaning of the words'; even given these *as they have previously been specified*, it is still *up to us* whether we shall accept the proof as a valid deployment of those concepts or not. The decision to accept the proof is a *further* meaning stipulation: the 'theorems of mathematics and logic' that we actually prove and accept are not just *consequences* of conventions, but *individually* conventional. Such a 'radical' conventionalism, Dummett pointed out, would be immune to the Quine–Wittgenstein objection to the Ayer–Carnap sort of conventionalism.

In response, Barry Stroud (1965) pointed out[1] that the position Dummett calls 'radical conventionalism' cannot possibly be Wittgenstein's. A convention, in the literal sense, is something we can legislate either way. Wittgenstein does not anywhere say or suggest that the mathematician providing a theorem is *legislating* that it shall be a theorem (and the mathematician would get into a lot of trouble, to put it mildly, if he tried to 'legislate' it the opposite way).

Basing himself on a good deal of textual evidence, Stroud suggested that Wittgenstein's position was that it is not *convention* or *legislation* but our *forms of life* (i.e. our human nature as determined by our biology-plus-cultural-history) that cause us to accept certain proofs *as* proofs. And Stroud's reply to Dummett's interpretation appears to have been generally accepted by Wittgenstein scholars.

The Consistency Objection

It appears to me that Stroud's reply, while correct as a response to Dummett's interpretation, does not speak to the real philosophical

[1] For a related discussion see Canfield (1975).

point Dummett was making. The real point is that if *either* Dummett *or* Stroud is right, then Wittgenstein is claiming that mathematical truth and necessity *arise in us*, that it is human nature and forms of life that *explain* mathematical truth and necessity. If this is right, then it is the greatest philosophical discovery of all time. Even if it is wrong, it is an astounding philosophical claim. If Stroud does not dispute that Wittgenstein advanced this claim— and he does not seem to dispute it—then *his* interpretation of Wittgenstein is a revision of Dummett's rather than a total rejection of it.

Unfortunately, there seems to be a devastating objection to Wittgenstein's position (i.e. to 'Wittgenstein$_2$') if Stroud has really got him right: consider number theory (Peano arithmetic) in any of its standard formalizations. Even if our acceptance of the Peano axioms is just the acceptance of a bunch of *meaning determinations* (whether these be *stipulations*, i.e. acts of legislation, as on the 'conventionalist' interpretation, or fixed by our 'forms of life', as on Stroud's interpretation), still they are not *logically arbitrary* determinations, for they are, after all, required to be *consistent*. Our nature, our forms of life, etc., may explain why we *accept* the Peano axioms *as opposed to some other consistent set*; but our nature cannot possibly make an *inconsistent* set of axioms *true*. And consistency is an *objective mathematical fact*, not an *empirical* fact. Thus, there is at least *one* mathematical fact—namely the consistency of the meaning determinations themselves, *whatever* these be produced by—which is *not* explained by our nature or 'forms of life' in any intelligible sense.

Sometimes the reply to this is merely the textual point that Wittgenstein pooh-poohed consistency ('Why this *one* bug-a-boo?'), pointed out that an inconsistent system could still be usable (if one avoids drawing the contradiction), etc. But these remarks do not speak to the objection. Wittgenstein had better have something *better* than this to say in response to the objection or he is done for (as a philosopher of logic and mathematics).

And he does have something better than this to say. His *real* response to the consistency objection goes to the very depths of his philosophy, and without drawing it out, one cannot begin to do justice to his thought.

Wittgenstein on 'following a rule'

Suppose I have a certain concept in my mind. Whatever introspectible *signs* there may be that I have the concept, whatever mental presentations I am able to call up in connection with the concept, cannot specify the *content* of the concept, as Wittgenstein argued in the famous sections of *Philosophical Investigations* which concern 'following a rule': say the rule 'add one'. For, if two species in two possible worlds (I state the argument in *most* un-Wittgensteinian terminology!) have the same mental signs in connection with the expression 'add one', it is still possible that their *practice* might diverge; and it is the practice, as Wittgenstein shows, that fixes the *interpretation*; signs do not interpret themselves—not even mental signs (or, one might add for the benefit of physicalists like Hartry Field or David Lewis, signs in the brain). To take a simple example—a variant of Wittgenstein's own 'add one' example— even if someone *pictures* the relation '*C* is the ponential of *A* and *B*' (i.e. *C* follows from *A* and *B* by *modus ponens*) in his mind just as we do and has agreed with us on finitely many cases (e.g. that *q* is the ponential of $(p \vee r) \supset q$ and $(p \vee r)$), still he may have a divergent interpretation of 'ponential of' which will only reveal itself in some future cases (even if he agrees with us in his 'theory', i.e. what he *says* about 'ponential of', for he may have a divergent interpretation of the whole theory, as the Skolem–Löwenheim theorem shows).

The relevance of this to philosophy of mathematics is immediate. First of all, there is the question of *finitism*: human practice, actual and potential, only extends finitely far. We cannot 'go on counting forever', even if we say we can, not really. If there are possible *divergent extensions of our practice,* then there are possible *divergent interpretations of even the natural number sequence*: our practice, our mental representations, etc., do not (in set-theoretic terminology) single out a unique 'standard model' or even the natural number sequence. We are tempted to think they do because we easily shift from 'we could go on counting' to 'an *ideal machine* could go on counting' (or 'an *ideal mind* could go on counting'); but talk of ideal machines (or minds) is very different, Wittgenstein reminds us, from talk of *actual* machines and persons. Talk of what an ideal machine could do is talk *within* mathematics; it cannot fix the interpretation *of* mathematics.

Second, if Wittgenstein is right (and I am presently inclined to think that he is), then the statement 'there are seven consecutive sevens in the decimal expansion of π' may have *no* truth value: speaking set-theoretically, it may be true in some models that fit our practice and false in others. And similarly, and for the same reason, 'Peano arithmetic is consistent' may have *no* truth value: for this statement too talks about an infinite sequence (the sequence of *all* theorems of Peano arithmetic), and the sequence may not really be determinate.

Still, assuming some number—say 10^{20}—is small enough so that we could collectively and over time (perhaps several generations) examine all proofs with fewer than that number of symbols, the question 'Is Peano arithmetic 10^{20}-consistent?' should have a determinate answer even on Wittgenstein's view.

Why Wittgenstein's View does not Work

To see why Wittgenstein's view does not work, it is necessary to resolve an ambiguity in the view. It is true (and, as we have conceded, it is also a profound observation) that even so simple an operation as *modus ponens* is not 'fixed' once and for all by our mental representation of the operation; it is our actual 'unpacking' of the mental representation in action, our *de facto* dispositions which determine what we *mean* by 'ponential of'. But there are two 'scenarios' as to *how* our dispositions might determine the extension of 'ponential of'. *Scenario* 1: Given a putative proof (with less than 10^{20} symbols) one checks it by going down by line, verifying that each line with *ax* next to it is an axiom, and that each line with two numbers (n) (m) next to it is the ponential of the lines numbered (n), (m) respectively. If the last line is '$1 = 0$', one announces 'Peano arithmetic has turned out to be inconsistent'. *Scenario* 2: Given a putative proof (with less than 10^{20} symbols) one proceeds as in scenario 1 *except that* if *any* line is '$1 = 0$' (or anything verifiably false by just elementary calculation and truth-functional logic), then one *modifies what counts as ponential* so that the line in question is said *not* to be the ponential of the relevant lines (n), (m).

Both scenarios are logically possible. And if our actual dispositions *were* as described in scenario 2, then Peano arithmetic would certainly be consistent in the absolute sense, and this consistency would *arise from us*, be explained by our nature (our dispositions) in a clear sense. But the actual scenario, the scenario that describes the dispositions we actually *have*, is scenario 1. And *that* scenario does not 'build in' absolute consistency. Perhaps 'ponential of' is only defined 'finitistically' in the way we described in the preceding section; perhaps the extension of 'ponential of' is not *fixed* in the case of proofs and formulas that are beyond human and machine reach; certainly, in the cases where it *is* fixed, it is fixed only by our dispositions and not just by the thought-signs in our minds or the representations in our brains; *but the 10^{20}-consistency of Peano arithmetic is still not an artefact of this dispositionally fixed interpretation.*

Note that I am *not* denying that mathematical truth is 'perspectival' in the sense of depending for its very *content* on our actual existential natures and dispositions (think of how many different things could be *meant* by the words, thought-signs, etc., that we use to represent Peano arithmetic to ourselves and each other; imagine different possible worlds in which the words, thought-signs, etc., are the same but the *practice* diverges from ours at various points). *All* truth is perspectival in this sense, and I agree with Wittgenstein that this makes nonsense of metaphysical talk of our representations 'copying' reality. But perspectival facts are still facts. The content of the judgement that there is a large mountain ash on my property depends on our 'forms of life', *granted*; the fact that there is a mountain ash on my property is in that sense, perspectival, *granted*; but it is *not an artefact of the way we use the words* that there is a large mountain ash on my property. And no more is it an *artefact of the way we use the words* that Peano arithmetic is 10^{20}-consistent. The truth of the judgement that there is a mountain ash on my property depends on our nature, but also on more than our nature; it is not a truth that is *explained* by facts about human nature; it does not *arise from us*. And similarly, the fact that Peano arithmetic is 10^{20}-consistent depends on our nature, but also on more than our nature; it similarly is not a truth that is *explained* by facts about human nature; it too does not *arise from us*. Only if our dispositions were described in scenario 2 would they *explain* the truth of the consistency statement.

Another Wittgensteinian Move

There is a move that may also have been in Wittgenstein's mind which we shall briefly consider here. One might hold that it is a presupposition of, say, '2 + 2 = 4', that we shall never *meet* a situation we would count as a counterexample (this is an *empirical* fact); and one might claim that the appearance of a 'factual' element in the statement '2 + 2 = 4' arises from *confusing* the mathematical assertion (which has *no* factual content, it is claimed) with the empirical assertion first mentioned.

This move, however, depends heavily on overlooking or denying the circumstance that an empirical fact can have a partly mathematical *explanation*. Thus, let T be an actual (physically instantiated) Turing machine so programmed that if it is started scanning the input '111', it never halts. Suppose we start T scanning the input '111', let T run for two weeks, and then turn T off. In the course of the two-week run, T did not halt. Is it not the case that the *explanation* of the fact that T did not halt is simply the *mathematical* fact that a Turing machine with that programme never halts on the input, *together with* the empirical fact that T instantiates that programme (and continued to do so throughout the two weeks)?

Similarly, if human beings spend millions of years searching through all the proofs with less than 10^{20} symbols in Peano arithmetic and they never find a proof of '1 = 0', is not the *explanation* of this fact simply that, as a matter of *mathematical* fact, Peano arithmetic is 10^{20}-consistent, *and* the human beings took sufficient care so that the putative proofs they examined during the long search really *were* proofs in Peano arithmetic?

As for the case of the statement '2 + 2 = 4': suppose that on five thousand occasions two things are added to two other things (using some physical operation of combination) and the resulting group is counted. Suppose that 4,800 times the result of the count is '4'; that 198 times the result is '5'; and that 2 times the result is '3'. Suppose a careful investigation is made, and it is found that in the 198 cases in which the result was '5', some interaction (e.g. sexual reproduction) added an individual to the group, and that in the two cases in which the result was '3', some interaction destroyed a member of the group. Is not the explanation of the fact that in the remaining 4,800 cases the result of the count was '4' just the fact that in *those* cases no individual involved in the combining process was destroyed or otherwise removed from the group counted at the end; that no individuals were added to the final group by any interactions; and that, as a matter of simple arithmetic fact, $2 + 2 = 4$?

If this is merely something we *say* then, *granted* that that explains what we say about these 4,800 cases, how is it that we actually *found* (as opposed to just *posited*) an explanation of what went wrong in the deviant 200 cases? If one says that it is just a *surd* empirical fact that one *does* find such explanations in such cases, then is one not abandoning the whole world view of science since Newton for a very strange metaphysics? On the scientific view, *many* facts have partly mathematical explanations (and much of the business of science consists in giving them); on the alternative metaphysical picture, there are just all these surd empirical facts *and* a way we *talk* about them. We do not often come up with apparent counterexamples to '$2 + 2 = 4$', but it is not *because* two and two *do* make four that we do not. Rather, on the picture just suggested, it is *because* we do not often come up with apparent counterexamples that we say '$2 + 2 = 4$'. Why should anyone believe this?

Perhaps if the world were such that we regularly came up with apparent counterexamples to '$2 + 2 = 4$' in some context (say, counting bosons), then the best language-cum-theory might be one that said that in some cases two and two make five. If such a case could be coherently described, this would be reason to think that *arithmetic is empirical*; but it still would not be reason to think that arithmetic is not *factual*.

The Conceivability of the Mathematically Impossible

What I have argued is that 'Peano arithmetic is 10^{20}-consistent' and 'Turing machine T will not halt if run for so-and-so many operations on input "111"' are *mathematical facts*, and that these facts are not explained by our 'natures' or 'forms of life'. It is not that these statements are true because we have a disposition to *protect* them from what would otherwise be falsifiers; we have no such disposition. What I want to consider in the present section is the nature of such mathematical facts.

Unlike '2 + 2 = 4', which certainly seems a priori, the two facts just mentioned have a quasi-empirical character. We can conceive of their being false, whereas we doubt we can conceive of '2 + 2 = 4' being false; it may be, in the case of the second fact, that there is no *proof* that Turing machine *T* won't halt on the given input in so-and-so many steps which does not amount to *running* the machine, or a calculation which exactly simulates the operations of the machine, *through* so-and-so many steps (some combinatorial facts seem 'brute'); both statements can be overthrown by a well-attested *calculation*.

But is there *really* a sense of 'conceivable' (of any philosophical importance) in which the *falsity* of these *mathematically true* statements is *conceivable*? How can the *mathematically impossible* be conceivable?

The answer is that there is no part of our language in which it is more wrong to think of our understanding of the sentences as consisting in a sort of Cartesian 'clear and distinct idea' of the *conditions under which they are true* than mathematics. We do not understand Fermat's last theorem by having a 'clear and distinct idea' of the conditions under which it is true: how could we? Our mastery of mathematical language resides, at least in part, in our knowledge of *proof conditions* as opposed to *truth conditions*, in our knowledge of the *conditions of verification* holistically associated with the sentences by mathematical practice. But part of the notion of a *verification condition* in both mathematical science and empirical science is this: verification conditions are conditions that correspond to a certain *skill*: the skill of being able to tell when a sentence has been proved (or, in empirical science, confirmed). It is part of the notion of such a skill that one can have it without knowing in advance whether the sentence in question *will* be proved or disproved (confirmed or disconfirmed).

Understanding Fermat's last theorem, for example, consists at least in part of being able to recognize a proof or at least a counterexample; the weird view is the view of Ayer and Carnap according to which *all* true mathematical assertions have 'the same meaning' and it requires a *psychological* explanation (allegedly) to say why we do not *recognize* that Fermat's last theorem has the same meaning (assuming it is true) as '$2 + 2 = 4$'. *Only* the supposition that the meaning is the *truth conditions* could have led to such a view (and then only on a view according to which grasp of the truth conditions is something like an eidetic image of all the worlds in which they obtain).

In short, we can understand 'T will halt', although, in fact, it may be *mathematically impossible* for T to halt, because we are not mathematically omniscient, because our *understanding* of most mathematical sentences has to consist (in part) in a skill of recognizing whether they are proved or disproved, and because *this* kind of understanding *never* involves *knowing in advance* whether the statement *will be proved or disproved*. In this respect, '$2 + 2 = 4$' may be different; knowing that '$2 + 2 = 4$' may be involved in knowing the arithmetical language; but knowing whether Peano arithmetic is 10^{20}-consistent or not is *not* presupposed by knowing the arithmetical language. I *understand* the statement 'Peano arithmetic is *not* 10^{20}-consistent', even though it is in fact *mathematically false*, because I have a skill (or participate in a society that has that skill!). I (we) could *tell* if we found a proof that Peano arithmetic is inconsistent. The fact that the *specification* of that ability is possible *independently* of whether the proposition to be understood *can* be proved or not should not surprise us; if it were *not* the case we could *understand* only those mathematical statements that are already decided!

The 'Revisability' of Mathematics

The remarks I have been making have a connection with a curious fact which I now wish to point out: although *all* mathematical truths are 'metaphysically necessary', i.e. true in all possible worlds, simply because nothing that violates a truth of mathematics *counts* as a *description* of a 'possible world', *some* mathematical truths are 'epistemically contingent'. What I have in mind is the following: there may be no way in which we can *know* that a certain abstract structure is consistent other than by seeing it instantiated either in mental images or in some physical representation. For example, the only way to convince myself that it is possible to make n triangles using m rigid bars of equal length (for certain values of n and m) may be to actually produce the figure; the only way to show that a certain Turing machine halts may be to run it (or simulate its running on paper) until it halts; the only way to know that a certain formal system is inconsistent may be to *derive* the contradiction in it. Now the statement that *these m* matches (or whatever) are arranged so as to form *n* triangles is certainly an a posteriori statement. It is even an *empirical* statement. Yet my rational confidence in the mathematically necessary statement 'it is possible to form *n* triangles with *m* rigid bars' is *no greater* than my confidence in the empirical statement. If I come to doubt the empirical statement, then, unless I have some *other* example that establishes the truth of the mathematical statement, I will come to doubt the mathematical statement too. Nor need there be any way in which I could 'in principle' *know* the truth of the mathematical statement without depending on some such empirical statement about mental or physical objects, diagrams, calculations, etc.

If this point has not been very much appreciated in the past (although Descartes was clearly aware of this problem) it is because of the tendency, we remarked, to think that a fully rational ('ideally rational') being should be mathematically omniscient: should be able to 'just know' all mathematical truths *without proof*. (Perhaps by surveying all the integers, all the real numbers, etc., in his head.) This is just forgetting, once again, that we *understand* mathematical language *through* being able to recognize *proofs* (plus, of course, certain empirical applications, e.g. *counting*). It is not irrational to need a *proof* before one believes, for example, Fermat's last theorem—quite the contrary.

Of course, the status of '2 + 2 = 4' is quite different. We do not need a *proof* for this statement (barring epistemological catastrophe, e.g. coming to doubt *all* our past *counting*: but it is not clear what becomes of the concept of rationality itself when there is an epistemological catastrophe). Perhaps '2 + 2 = 4' is rationally unrevisable (or, at least, rationally unrevisable as long as 'universal hallucination', 'all my past memories are a delusion', and the like are not in the field). But, if we consider that '2 + 2 = 4' can sometimes be part of an *explanation*, is the fact (if it is a fact) that a rational being could not believe the denial of '2 + 2 = 4' (barring epistemological catastrophe) an explanation of the *truth* of '2 + 2 = 4'? Or is it rather just a fact about *rationality*?

Putting this question aside, like the hot potato it is, let us briefly consider the status of such mathematical truths as 'Peano arithmetic is consistent' and the principle of mathematical induction. These are not like the singular or purely existential combinatorial statements lately considered ('This formal system is inconsistent', 'There exists a way of forming m triangles with n matches', 'This Turing machine halts in less than N steps'). Certainly our beliefs in the consistency of Peano arithmetic and in induction are not epistemically contingent in the way that my belief that one can form m triangles using n matches (imagine I have just convinced myself by finding the arrangement) is epistemically contingent. I believe that arithmetic is consistent because I believe the axioms are true, and I believe that from true premises one cannot derive a contradiction; I have also studied and taught the Gentzen consistency proof; and these are a priori reasons. Yet there are still circumstances under which I would abandon my belief that Peano arithmetic is consistent; I would abandon that belief *if I discovered a contradiction*.

Many philosophers will feel that this remark is 'cheating'. They would say 'But you *could not* discover a contradiction.' True, it is mathematically impossible (and even 'metaphysically impossible', in the recently fashionable jargon) that there should be a contradiction in Peano arithmetic. But, as I remarked above, it *is not epistemically impossible*. We can conceive of finding a contradiction in Peano arithmetic, and we can make sense of the question 'What would you do if you came across a contradiction in Peano arithmetic?' ('Restrict the induction schema,' would be my answer.)

As a matter of fact, there are circumstances in which it would be rational to believe that Peano arithmetic was inconsistent *even though it was not*.

Thus, suppose I am caused to hallucinate by some marvellous process (say, by making me a 'brain in a vat' without my knowing it, and controlling all my sensory inputs superscientifically), and the content of the hallucination is that the whole logical community learns of a contradiction in Peano arithmetic (Saul Kripke discovers it). The proof is checked by famous logicians and even by machine, and it holds up. Perhaps I do not have time to check the proof myself; but I would believe, and rationally so, I contend, that Peano arithmetic *is* inconsistent on such evidence. And this shows that even 'Peano arithmetic is consistent' is not a fully rationally unrevisable statement. (Neither is full first-order induction, since an inconsistency in Peano arithmetic would make it rational to suppose that unrestricted induction was contradictory.)

This is messy. Clearly, philosophy of mathematics is *hard*. But the Wittgensteinian views that (1) mathematical statements do not express objective facts; and (2) their truth and necessity (or appearance of necessity) arise from and are explained by *our* nature, cannot be right.

If *our* nature explains why we shall never come across a contradiction in Peano arithmetic then, in exactly the same sense and to the same degree, it explains why there is a mountain ash in my yard. Both facts are dependent on my conceptual lenses; but neither fact is an artefact of these lenses. I do not create the properties of individual proofs in Peano arithmetic any more than I create the berries on the mountain ash.

PART 2: RE QUINE

Introduction

These criticisms of Wittgenstein are grist for Quine's mill. Quine, at least as early as Wittgenstein, criticized the moderate conventionalist position for emptiness. But, whereas Wittgenstein departed from moderate conventionalism in the direction of radical conventionalism (which holds that the truth of the theorems as well as that of the axioms arises from us), Quine departed from moderate conventionalism in the direction of *empiricism*. In Quine's view, the unrevisability of mathematical statements is greater in degree than that of, say, the three-dimensionality of space or the conservation of energy, but not absolute. Truths of mathematics are partly empirical and partly 'conventional' like *all* truths; mathematics is as factual as physics, only better 'protected'.

Everything I said against Wittgenstein's view is consonant with these views of Quine. But Quine's views, like Wittgenstein's, will not do as they stand.

The problem with Wittgenstein's views is that they exaggerate the unrevisability of mathematics and logic. The problem with Quine's views is that they underestimate it. The view I wish to defend is not that classical logic and mathematics are a priori; I myself have argued elsewhere that logic is revisable, and that a form of modular logic ('quantum logic') should be adopted for the purpose of formalizing physical theory, and not classical logic. What I think (I blush to confess) is that what is a priori is that *most* statements obey certain logical laws. This will very likely offend both Platonistically minded and constructively minded philosophers (and both Wittgensteinians and Quinians); nevertheless, I shall try to make it plausible.

Quine and the A Priori

Are there a priori truths? In other words, are there true statements which (1) it is rational to accept (at least if the right arguments occur to me), and (2) which it would never subsequently be rational to reject no matter how the world turns out (epistemically) to be? More simply, are there statements whose truth we would not be justified in denying in any *epistemically* possible world? Or is it rather the case that for *every* statement s there is an epistemically possible world in which it is fully rational to believe that not-s?

It is easy to see that this question depends crucially on the notion of a *statement*. *Statement* and not *sentence*: since for any *sentence* ϕ we can imagine a circumstance in which it would be rational to deny ϕ by just imagining a world in which it is rational to *change the meanings* of the words in ϕ in some suitable way (as those meanings are given by a standard translation manual connecting the language to which ϕ belongs at the two different times to some neutral language). So no one can possibly hold that there are unrevisable *sentences*. Accordingly, one response to the question for a philosopher who denies, as Quine does, that *synonymy* makes any sense—i.e. a philosopher who denies that there is any clear sense to the question 'does ϕ express the same statement at the two different times?'—is simply to say that apriority is a meaningless notion. The notion of apriority presupposes the notion of synonymy as much as the notion of analyticity does, and is meaningless for the same reason that the notion of synonymy is meaningless.

There is one trouble with this argument, and that is that it has not the slightest persuasive force for someone who is unconvinced, as I am unconvinced, that no sense can be made of the notion of *synonymy*. To my way of thinking, any philosophical claim that rests on the contention that no reasonable standard of synonymy exists at all, not even an interest-relative one, founders in absurdity. It may well be, of course, that Quine would not wish to deny the existence of an *interest-relative* standard of synonymy; however, if there is such a standard, then it makes sense to ask whether there are any sentences ϕ such that (1) *given the way we presently interpret them*, no fully rational being could deny them; and/or (2) if the world turns out to be such that a fully rational being *does* subsequently deny ϕ, then that will be because the *meaning* of ϕ, as specified by the way *we* translate ϕ into our present language, given *our* interests, will have changed. In short, if there is something— something useful and important, even if, in a sense, 'relative'—to the notion of synonymy, then why should there not be *as much* to the notion of apriority?

As I have pointed out elsewhere, however, Quine has another argument against apriority, one that does not depend at all upon his attacks on synonymy and on a 'linguistic' notion of analyticity. As Quine puts the argument, in the form of a rhetorical question,

Any statement can be held true come what may if we make drastic enough adjustments elsewhere in the system. Even a statement very close to the periphery can be held true in the face of recalcitrant experience by pleading hallucination or by amending certain statements of the kind called logical laws. Conversely, by the same token, no statement is immune to revision. Revision even of the logical law of the excluded middle has been proposed as a means of simplifying quantum mechanics; and what difference is there in principle between such a shift and a shift whereby Kepler superseded Ptolemy, or Einstein Newton, or Darwin Aristotle? (Quine, 1951, p. 43.) [Also reprinted in this volume, p. 63.]

The revisions from which statements are not immune in the cases Quine describes are not changes of reference but of belief. To say, 'Einstein changed the meaning of "straight line" ' would not explain away the appearance of a revision of belief; for how can we now say which paths were straight 'in the old sense' if the space-like geodesics of our space–time aren't? Something we thought to be a priori impossible turned out to be true.

In 'Carnap and Logical Truth', where he employs a similar argument, Quine draws the moral explicitly: 'We had been trying to make sense of the role of convention in a priori knowledge. Now the very distinction between a priori and empirical begins to waver and dissolve, at least as a distinction between sentences. (It could of course still hold as a distinction between factors in one's adoption of a sentence, but both factors might be operative everywhere.)' (Quine, 1966, p. 115).

It is this *argument from the history of science* that I challenge.

Here is a simple counter-example:

Could a fully rational being deny that *not every statement is both true and false*? To fix our ideas, let us specify that by a statement we mean simply a *belief or possible belief*, either one's own or someone else's, and that the term 'statement' is not intended to presuppose that beliefs are or are not 'propositions' as distinct from 'sentences' or even 'inscriptions'. Could someone, then, think all his own beliefs (and everyone else's) were both true and false? Let us also stipulate that we do not presuppose any particular account of 'truth' (e.g. that truth is or is not distinct from maximum warranted assertibility). If you do not like 'true', could someone believe that all his own beliefs (and everyone else's), and all possible beliefs, for that matter, are both fully warrantedly assertible and that their negations are fully warrantedly assertible as well?

At first blush, the answer is clearly 'no'. By *our* lights, to believe that all one's beliefs are both true and false (or whatever) is to give up *both* the notions of *belief* and *truth* (or warranted assertibility). In short, to believe *all* statements are correct (which is what we are talking about) would be to have no notion of rationality. At least *one* statement is a priori, because to deny that statement would be to forfeit rationality itself.

One a priori truth. It is, of course, possible to be sceptical about the existence of rationality itself. What I have in mind is not the possibility of total scepticism or relativism; what I am rather thinking of is the possibility that 'rational' or 'rationally acceptable' or 'warrantedly assertible' may not be the right notions for epistemology/methodology. Perhaps one should not say that statements are warrantedly assertible, but that they have a certain numerical 'degree of confirmation', as Carnap urged, or perhaps one should use some notion that is not thought of yet. But then the question, whether some statements (and some rules of inference) are such that it is always rational to accept (deny) them, will have an analogue in terms of the new notion of degree of confirmation, or whatever. The question *'Are there any a priori truths?'* is a question *within* the theory of rationality; as long as we accept the theory, or the prospect of such a theory, we cannot justify rejecting or accepting any particular answer by the consideration that the theory of rationality itself may need recasting. What we are trying to answer by our lights (and by who else's lights should we try to answer it?—a question Quine is fond of asking) is whether an ideal theory of rationality would have certain features: we can speculate about this just as physicists speculate about whether an ideal physical theory would have certain features, while recognizing, just as they do, that our answer itself is a provisional one and that the true shape of future theory will be different in many unforeseen ways from what we now envisage.

This being said, it does seem, as we remarked, that there is at least one a priori truth: that not every statement is both true (or fully correct to assert) and at the same time false (or fully correct to deny). But, of course, this statement itself admits of more than one interpretation. To bring out more clearly the interpretation I have in mind, let me speak of the rule: *infer every statement from every premiss and from every set of premisses, including the empty set* as the absolutely inconsistent rule (AIR). It is clear from the notion of rationality itself that to accept the AIR would be to abandon rationality. And the interpretation of 'Not every statement is both true and false' (or, more simply, 'Not every statement is true') that I have in mind is simply the interpretation under which to affirm this statement is simply to *reject* the AIR. In particular, acceptance of this statement, like rejection of the AIR, does not commit one to any particular view of what truth and falsity are (or what correctness is, or what inference is). It assumes what we may call the *generic* notions of truth (or correctness) and falsity (or incorrectness), and not the particular philosophical notions (e.g. the realist notion of truth, or the notion of warranted assertibility) which arise when one *refines* or *philosophically* analyses the generic notions. I take it that there is a clear enough sense to the notions of rejecting the AIR, and of denying that every statement is both true and false. What I suggest is that it cannot seriously be maintained that there is an epistemically possible world in which acceptance of the AIR would be fully rational and warranted; and, further, I maintain that the point that acceptance of the AIR would involve abandonment of rationality itself is one that a fully rational mind should be able to see in any world. In short, the AIR is a priori rejectable.

The reader may wonder why I stated the principle of contradiction in such a weak form. Why did I not take 'not both p and not-p' as my example of an a priori truth? The answer is that our intuitions about what is true of *every* statement are much hazier than our intuitions about typical or normal statements. Consider the Russell antinomy: 'There is a set Z such that Z has as members all and only those sets that do not have themselves as members.' Suppose some future logical genius discovers a very elegant way of avoiding the antinomy without paying the usual price of stratifying the universe into types by admitting that some statements—in particular the 'paradoxical' ones, such as the Russell antinomy—are *both true and false*. Is this *really* ruled out a priori?

The reader may reply that this would not work because it is well known that from even one instance of 'p & $\sim p$' one can derive every statement. But this assumes that certain rules of propositional calculus are retained; perhaps the new scheme would depend on relevance logic (in which *it is not* true that 'every statement follows from a contradiction'). It seems to me that this is not something we can rule out a priori. Rather, this is just the sort of case in which we want to look at the complete proposal in the whole theoretical context before deciding. Perhaps there are epistemically possible worlds in which it is rational to believe that the Russell antinomy is both true and false. But this does not affect our argument that it would be an abandonment of rationality to believe that *every* statement was both true and false (or to believe that *typically* statements are both true and false).

Again, it may be objected that 'Normally statements are not both true and false' contains the vague term 'normally'. And also, even the statement 'Not every statement is both true and false' involves rather vague (I called them 'generic') notions of 'statement', 'truth', and 'falsity'. If *all* a priori truths contain such vague notions, then it may be that apriority is a phenomenon that affects only our ordinary language; that in the canonical, regimented, totally precise notation that Quine refers to in *Word and Object* as 'our first class conceptual system', there are indeed no a priori truths.

But the fact is that most of science and metascience cannot even be expressed in a perfectly precise notation (and all the more so if one includes philosophy under the rubric 'metascience' as Quine does). Words such as 'normally', 'typically', etc., are indispensable in biology and economics, not to mention law, history, sociology, etc.; while 'broad spectrum' notions such as 'cause' and 'factor' are indispensable for the introduction of new theoretical notions, even if they do not appear in 'finished science', if there is such a thing. Philosophy cannot be limited to commentary upon a supposed 'first-class conceptual system' which scarcely exists and whose expressive resources cover only a tiny fragment of what we care about.

So far the picture that is emerging from our discussion looks like this: there are some a priori truths, truths certified by the theory of rationality itself; but they have the character of *maxims*—general principles that are not, or at least may not be, exceptionless, and they involve 'generic', or somewhat pre-theoretical, notions rather than the (supposedly) perfectly precise notions of an ideal theory in the exact sciences. That, barring a new treatment of very exceptional cases such as the Russell antinomy, a statement is not both true and false (in the ordinary pre-theoretic sense of 'true' and 'false') is an example.

Apriority and Analyticity

The argument I have given for the apriority of 'not every statement is true' and 'not every statement is both true and false' suggests another argument, an argument based on meaning theory rather than theory of rationality. This argument goes as follows: if someone accepts 'All statements are true', then, by the principle of universal instantiation (which we may take to be involved in the *meaning* of the universal quantifier), he is committed to '*Snow is white*' *is true*, to '*Snow is not white*' *is true*, to '*My hand has five fingers' is true*, to '*My hand does not have five fingers' is true*, etc. In short, given the rule of universal instantiation, acceptance of 'Every statement is true' (and of one's various beliefs and candidate beliefs and their negations as 'statements', in the relevant sense) commits one to acceptance of the AIR. And this is why the statement must be rejected.

Even if this argument is correct, it does not wholly avoid the theory of rationality, for the argument depends on the fact that one cannot accept the AIR, and this is based on considerations about rationality rather than upon considerations about meaning. It might be suggested, however, that if we agree that the *meaning* of the universal quantifier requires us to accept universal instantiation, then we can *immediately* give an example of an a priori (in fact, of an *analytic*) truth, namely, any suitable instance of 'If for every x, Fx, then Fv'; we already committed ourselves to a priori truth (it might be contended) when we rejected Quine's contention that the theory of meaning is an unsalvageable wreck.

One answer to this contention might be Quine's answer, already alluded to in my discussion of Wittgenstein: to derive the individual statements 'If for every x, Fx, then Fv' (where 'v' is a name for some member of the domain the quantifier ranges over) from the principle of universal instantiation (and the fact that implication is validity of the conditional) one needs *logic*; the argument does not show that the 'UI-conditionals' just mentioned (the conditionals corresponding to individual applications of the rule of universal instantiation) are true by meaning theory *alone*. This answer does not affect the argument I gave for rejecting 'Every statement is both true and false'; for that argument did not purport to explain the *origin* of logical truth (whatever that might mean); we were concerned to determine something about the notion of rationality, assuming reasonable constraints and reasoning in a reasonable way (which, of course, means using logic). We were not showing *why* logic is true (whatever that might mean), but rather showing that if there is such a thing as rationality at all, then it seems that it could never be rational to reject one very weak logical principle. That we had to assume logical principles to argue this is not any kind of vicious circle.

Even if the meaning-theoretic argument is advanced in the same spirit as ours, as a defence of the claim that certain statements are unrevisable but not as an explanation of their truth, its conclusion cannot be as strong as the conclusion we reached above. For even if 'for every x, Fx' implies 'Fv' by virtue (in part) of the *meaning* of the quantifier itself, this only shows that the inference $(x)Fx \supset Fv$ must be a good one *in every language that contains the universal quantifier*. Whether an adequate language *must* have or can have quantifiers with such properties as this one is certainly not a question about *meaning*. Just as there are adequate languages that lack the *Euclidean* notion of a straight line, so, it might be claimed, there could be adequate languages that lack the classical quantifiers.

Our argument was that (1) the AIR cannot be accepted by any rational being; (2) it seems reasonable that a fully rational being should see and be able to express the fact that the AIR is incorrect; (3) any clear statement to the effect that the AIR is incorrect can be translated into *our* language here and now by the words 'Not every statement is true'. Only (3) depends at all on meaning theory; (1) and (2) are premisses from the theory of rationality. In particular, I only require that the *whole thought* 'Not every statement is true' should somehow be expressible by a rational being; not that it be expressible in those words. In particular, some rational being might express that thought by a sentence no part of which corresponds to our universal quantifier.

Finally, I am not claiming that it is *analytic* that 'A rational being cannot believe that every statement is true.' Nothing said here commits me to the view that we can develop the theory of rationality by just reflecting on the meaning of the word 'rational'. And this is good, since the whole history of philosophy, methodology, and logic is strong evidence to the contrary.

Revision of Logic

Intuitionists propose to revise classical logic by giving up the *law of the excluded middle*, p v $\sim p$, among others. Such a proposal is instructively different from the proposal to give up p & $\sim p$, which no one has advanced, or to give up the even weaker principles of contradiction discussed above.

I have alluded a number of times to the existence of a family of truth notions: being verified (proved, warrantably assertible, justified, etc.) and being true in the full 'realist' sense (which builds in bivalence and the notion that what is true is *made* true by a mind-independent reality, according to Michael Dummett) being the best-known members of the family. There are other members of the family as well; there are notions of truth like Peirce's which identify truth with some *idealization* of warranted assertibility rather than with (tensed) warranted assertibility itself; and there are notions of truth which I would consider 'realist', but which are not realist in the very strong metaphysical sense Dummett has in mind. I agree with Sellars that the primitive notion of a correct statement does not yet distinguish between these 'realist' and 'non-realist' conceptions of truth; that it represents a generic conception from which the others arise by a process of philosophical reflection.

The law of the excluded middle is not evident on the *generic* notion of truth, however, at least not for *undecidable* statements. If truth is given a 'verificationist' interpretation, and disjunction is given the standard intuitionist semantics (to verify a disjunction one must verify one of the disjuncts, and also verify *that a particular* one of the disjuncts has been verified), then undecidable statements will give rise to instances of $p \vee {\sim}p$ which fail to be true (although their negations are not true either). My argument for the apriority of the law of contradiction (or of a suitably 'hedged' version of the law of contradiction) did not depend on *choosing between* realist and non-realist views of truth; if a decision between these views of truth cannot be made on a priori grounds (or if it can, but it goes *against* the classical view, as Dummett thinks), then not all of classical propositional calculus will be included in the part of logic that is a priori correct. The debate about whether there is a priori truth is somewhat separate from the debate over 'deviant logics', even if some logical principles are a priori (or 'a priori in normal cases': itself a significant weakening of classical claims).

The issues raised by proposals to use modular logic ('quantum logic') in the interpretation of quantum mechanics are still more complex. Quantum logic has been advocated under *both* 'realist' and 'verificationist' construals. The issues posed by the suggestion to adopt quantum logic plus a 'verificationist' semantics are similar to those posed by the suggestion to adopt intuitionist logic; on the other hand, the suggestion to adopt quantum logic plus a 'realist' semantics cannot be properly worked out and evaluated until one has further clarified the notion of 'realism'. If 'realism' is simply the commitment to the empirical model of the cognitive subject as a system which constructs a representation of its environment, for example, then it would seem that realism, in that sense, is compatible with a 'verificationist' account of how the cognitive subject *understands* his representation. Such issues, however, are far beyond the present paper.

Fallibilism

I do not see any reason to believe that the nature of rationality can be figured out a priori. Not only would it be utopian to expect rationality itself to become theoretically transparent to us in the foreseeable future, but even the partial descriptions of rationality we are able to give have had to be revised again and again as our experience with the world, our experience in co-operating with and understanding each other, and our experience with theory construction and explanation have all increased. Even if we restrict ourselves to scientific rationality, the fact is that we construct, test, and evaluate theories today that are of *kinds* undreamed of in earlier centuries. Neither the objects we call 'theories' today (e.g. quantum mechanics and relativity) nor the sorts of considerations involved in the testing and acceptance of these objects are of sorts an ancient Greek could have envisaged.

But is it consistent to say, on the one hand, that some things are a priori, i.e. rational to believe in all epistemically possible worlds, but on the other hand, that the metatheory of rationality on which we base this claim (or the considerations which I have advanced as to what such a theory should say if there really were one worthy of the name) is itself in the process of endless change and revision? In other words, is it consistent to say that any sketch of a theory of rationality or of parts of a theory of rationality that we ever give are to be accepted in the open-minded and tentative spirit that Peirce called 'fallibilism'? The answer is that it *is* consistent; but perhaps it does not seem so, and this may be the deep reason that Quine's appeal to fallibilism tends to convince some scientifically minded philosophers that there are no a priori truths at all.

Of course, if fallibilism requires us to be *sure* that for every statement *s* we accept *there is* an epistemically possible world in which it is rational to deny *s*, then fallibilism is *identical* with the rejection of a priori truth; but surely this is an unreasonable conception of fallibilism. If what fallibilism requires, on the other hand, is that we never be totally sure that *s* is true (even if we believe *s* is a priori), or, even more weakly, that we never be totally sure that the *reasons* we give for holding *s* true are final and contain no element of error or conceptual vagueness or confusion (even when *s* is 'Not every statement is true'), then there is nothing in such a modest and sane fallibilism to prejudge the question we have been discussing.

Quine and Wittgenstein

The present discussion of Quine's view may not seem to connect directly with the problems discussed by Wittgenstein, but the relevance is, in fact, immediate. If there were *nothing* to the idea that logic and mathematics are a priori, then we would resolve the difficulties with Wittgenstein's view by concluding that all of mathematics and logic is empirical. To Kripke's (unpublished) objection that this is incoherent, because the notion of *testing* a statement makes no sense unless *something* is fixed ('*Why should we accept the view that quantum mechanics requires us to change our logic?*' Kripke asks. '*If nothing is a priori, why do we not instead conclude that we should revise the statement that quantum mechanics requires us to change our logic?*'), we could answer, with Quine, that we are not denying the existence of an a priori factor in *all* judgement: we are simply denying that it is as *simple* as a rule that some statements are never to be revised. Answering Wittgenstein in this way would in no way require us to reject the insight contained in 'use' accounts of meaning, or Wittgenstein's insights about the way our practice unfolds the very meaning of our terms. But if, in fact, some logical and/or mathematical truths (the principle of contradiction, 'every number has a successor') *are* a priori, then this is blocked.

On the other hand, if large parts of logic and mathematics are revisable (and many of the parts that are not, as far as we know, revisable for *empirical* reasons are a posteriori in the way that I argued the statement that a proof exists of a certain theorem or that a particular Turing machine halts may be known a posteriori), then any philosophy that takes the *problem* to be: '*given* that logic and mathematics consist of a priori knowledge, how do we account for it?' is also blocked.

Actually, things are even worse. Even with respect to the part of logic and mathematics that is a priori, it seems to me that the apriority tells us something about the nature of *rationality*, not something about the nature of *logic*. There is a temptation to say, 'the truth of the minimal principle of contradiction (*Not every statement is true*) is explained by the fact that (in so far as we are rational) we hold it immune from revision'. But I find this unintelligible.

The analogy people use is to a game such as chess: if we assume 'chess' is a rigid designator for a game with certain rules, 'in chess the rook moves in straight lines' is a necessary truth. Moreover, it was known a priori by the people who invented the game of chess. (Compare Kripke's famous discussion of 'the metre stick in Paris is one metre long'.) In the same way it is suggested, 'Not every statement is true' can be known a priori because it is *we* who have made up the 'language game' to which 'statement', 'not', and 'true' belong.

The trouble is that if we are puzzled about whether there is a *possible* (consistent) game with certain rules, we appeal *not* to our stipulations but to an appropriate theorem of mathematics (which may be quite elementary if the game is simple). But if we are puzzled about why it is *possible* to have a language in which not every statement is true, this is (on the view I am criticizing) supposed to be answered *just* by an appeal to our stipulations or, alternatively, our 'forms of life'. I frankly do not see the analogy. I do not see any explanation. If one gets *comfort* by saying 'the principles of logic (some of them) are true *because* we hold them immune from revision', that is fine (some people enjoy chanting 'Hare Krishna', too), but the 'because' escapes me. Why should one not just as well say, 'We are *able* to stipulate that *some* but not *all* statements should be true (or assertible) *because* the minimal principle of contradiction is true'? My own guess is that the truths of logic we are speaking of are *so* basic that the notion of *explanation* collapses when we try to 'explain' why they are true. I do not mean that there is something 'unexplainable' here; there is simply no room for an explanation of what is presupposed by every explanatory activity, and that goes for philosophical as well as scientific explanations, including explanations that purport to be therapy.

So where does all of this leave us? Let us return for a moment to our earlier example: the statement that Peano arithmetic is consistent (or 10^{20}-consistent). This is hardly a priori in the strong sense: conceivable mathematical findings would lead us to change our minds. (It may, of course, be 'a priori' in weaker senses than I have considered.) There is clearly a *factual* element—an element of *objective combinatorial fact*—in the consistency of Peano arithmetic. But nothing argued here goes against the view that *if* Peano arithmetic *is* consistent as far as human beings can tell (and has no *mathematical* consequences that would lead us to modify it, e.g. provable ω inconsistency), *then* it counts as *true* partly by convention, or something analogous to convention (though not, of course, in the sense of *arbitrary* convention). Quine's view that there may be an *element* of convention, or apriority, or whatever, in mathematical knowledge, as in all knowledge, even where there is some revisability, is unshaken. On the other hand, our notion of rationality cannot be quite as flexible as Quine suggests.

BIBLIOGRAPHY

Ayer, A. J. (1936) *Language, Truth and Logic*, London. [Ch. 4 'The A Priori' reprinted above as selection II.]

Canfield, J. (1975) 'Anthropological Science Fiction and Logical Necessity', *Canadian Journal of Philosophy*, 5, 467–79.

Dummett, M. (1959) 'Wittgenstein's Philosophy of Mathematics', reprinted in his *Truth and Other Enigmas*, London, 1978, 166–85.

Quine, W. V. (1951) 'Two Dogmas of Empiricism', reprinted in his *From a Logical Point of View*, Cambridge, Mass., 1953, 20–46. [Reprinted above as selection III.]

—— (1960) *Word and Object*, Cambridge, Mass.

—— (1966) *The Ways of Paradox*, New York.

Stroud, B. (1965) 'Wittgenstein and Logical Necessity', *Philosophical Review*, 74, 504–18. [Reprinted above as selection IV.]

Wittgenstein, L. (1953) *Philosophical Investigations*, Oxford.

VI

THE TRUTHS OF REASON

RODERICK M. CHISHOLM

> There are also two kinds of truths: those of reasoning and those of
> fact. The truths of reasoning are necessary, and their opposite is
> impossible. Those of fact, however, are contingent, and their
> opposite is possible. When a truth is necessary, we can find the
> reason by analysis, resolving the truth into simpler ideas and
> simpler truths until we reach those that are primary.
>
> LEIBNIZ, Monadology, 33

I. A TRADITIONAL METAPHYSICAL VIEW

REASON, according to one traditional view, functions as a source of
knowledge. This view, when it is clearly articulated, may be seen to
involve a number of metaphysical presuppositions and it is, therefore, unacceptable to many contemporary philosophers. But the
alternatives to this view, once *they* are clearly articulated, may be
seen to be at least problematic and to imply an extreme form of
scepticism.

According to this traditional view, there are certain *truths of
reason* and some of these truths of reason can be known a priori.
These truths pertain to certain abstract or eternal objects—things
such as properties, numbers, and propositions or states of affairs,
things that would exist even if there weren't any contingent things
such as persons and physical objects. To present the traditional
view, we will first illustrate such truths and then we will try to
explain what is meant by saying that we know some of these truths a
priori.

Some of the truths of reason concern what we might call relations
of 'inclusion' and 'exclusion' that obtain among various properties.

Roderick M. Chisholm, 'The Truths of Reason', from *Theory of Knowledge*, 2/e,
© 1977, pp. 34–61. Reprinted by permission of Prentice–Hall, Inc., Englewood
Cliffs, New Jersey.

The relation of *inclusion* among properties is illustrated by these facts: The property of being square includes that of being rectangular, and that of being red includes that of being coloured. The relation of *exclusion* is exemplified by these facts: The property of being square excludes that of being circular, and that of being red excludes that of being blue. To say that one property excludes another, therefore, is to say more than that the one fails to include the other. Being red fails to include being heavy, but it does not exclude being heavy; if it excluded being heavy, as it excludes being blue, then nothing could be both red and heavy.[1]

Other examples of such inclusion and exclusion are these: Being both red and square includes being red and excludes being circular; Being both red and warm-if-red includes being warm; being both non-warm and warm-if-red excludes being red.

These relations are all such that they hold *necessarily*. And they would hold, therefore, even if there weren't any contingent things.

One can formulate more general truths about the relations of inclusion and exclusion. For example, every property F and every property G is such that F's excluding G includes G's excluding F; F's excluding G includes F's including not-G; F excludes non-F, and includes F-or-G. And such truths as these are necessary.

States of affairs or propositions are analogous to properties.[2] Like properties, they are related by inclusion and exclusion; for example, 'some men being Greeks' includes, and is included by, 'some Greeks being men', and excludes 'no Greeks being men'. States of affairs, like properties, may be compound; for example, 'some men being Greek and Plato being Roman'; 'Socrates being wise or Xantippe being wise'. The conjunctive state of affairs, 'Socrates being a man and all men being mortal', includes 'Socrates being mortal' and excludes 'no men being mortal'. Such truths about states of affairs are examples of truths of logic. And such

---

[1] 'Being red excludes being blue' should not be taken to rule out the possibility of a thing being red in one part and blue in another; it tells us only that being red in one part at one time excludes being blue in exactly that same part at exactly that same time. The point might be put even more exactly by saying that it is necessarily true that anything that is red has a part that is not blue.

[2] For the present, I will use 'state of affairs' and 'proposition' more or less interchangeably. Whenever we say of a state of affairs that it 'occurs' or 'obtains', we could say, instead, of a proposition that it is 'true'; and conversely.

truths, according to the traditional doctrine, are all necessary. They would hold even if there had been no Socrates or Greeks or men.

Other truths of reason are those of mathematics; for example, the truths expressed by '2 and 3 are 5' and '7 and 5 are 12'.

2. NOT ALL KNOWLEDGE OF NECESSITY IS A POSTERIORI

When it is said that these truths of reason are known (or are capable of being known) 'a priori', what is meant may be suggested by contrasting them with what is known 'a posteriori'. A single example may suggest what is intended when it is said that these truths may be known without being known a posteriori.

Corresponding to 'Being red excludes being blue', which is a truth about properties, the following general statement is a truth about individual things: 'Necessarily, every individual thing, past, present, or future, is such that if it is red then it is not blue'. If the latter truth were known a posteriori, then it would be justified by some induction or inductions; our evidence presumably would consist in the fact that a great variety of red things and a great variety of non-blue things have been observed in the past, and that up to now, no red things have been blue. We might thus inductively confirm 'Every individual thing, past, present, or future, is such that if it is red then it is not blue'. Reflecting upon this conclusion, we may then go on to make still another step. We will proceed to the further conclusion, 'Being red excludes being blue', and then deduce, 'Necessarily, every individual thing, past, present, or future, is such that if it is red then it is not blue'.

Thus, there might be said to be three steps involved in an inductive justification of 'Necessarily, being red excludes being blue': (1) the accumulation of instances—'This red thing is not blue', 'That blue thing is not red', and so on—along with the summary statement, 'No red thing observed up to now has been blue'; (2) the inductive inference from these data to 'Every individual thing, past, present, and future, is such that if it is red then it is not blue'; (3) the step from this inductive conclusion to 'Being red excludes being blue', or 'Necessarily, every individual thing, past, present, or future, is such that if it is red then it is not blue.'

Why *not* say that such 'truths of reason' are thus known a posteriori?

For one thing, some of these truths pertain to properties that have never been exemplified. If we take 'square', 'rectangular', and 'circular' in the precise way in which these words are usually interpreted in geometry, we must say that nothing is square, rectangular, or circular; things in nature, as Plato said, 'fall short' of having such properties.[3] Hence, to justify 'Necessarily, being square includes being rectangular and excludes being circular', we cannot even take the first of the three steps illustrated above; there being no squares, we cannot collect instances of squares that are rectangles and squares that are not circles.

For another thing, application of induction would seem to presuppose a knowledge of the 'truths of reason'. In setting out to confirm an inductive hypothesis, we must be able to recognize what its consequences would be. Ordinarily, to recognize these we must apply deduction; we take the hypothesis along with other things that we know and we see what is then implied. All of this, it would seem, involves apprehension of truths of reason—such truths as may be suggested by 'For all states of affairs, p and q, the conjunctive state of affairs, composed of p and of either not-p or q, includes q', and 'All As being B excludes some As not being B'. Hence, even if we are able to justify some of the 'truths of reason' by inductive procedures, any such justification will presuppose others, and we will be left with some 'truths of reason' which we have not justified by means of induction.[4]

And finally, the last of the three steps described above—the step from the inductive generalization 'Every individual thing, past, present, and future, is such that if it is red then it is not blue' to 'Being red excludes being blue', or 'Necessarily, every individual thing, past, present, and future, is such that if it is red then it is not blue'—remains obscure.

How do we reach this final step? What justifies us in saying that *necessarily*, every individual thing, past, present, and future, is such that if it is red then it is not blue? The English philosopher, William

---

[3] *Phaedo*, 75 A.
[4] Cf. Gottlob Frege, *The Foundations of Arithmetic* (Oxford: Basil Blackwell, 1950), pp. 16–17; first published in 1884.

Whewell, wrote that the mere accumulation of instances cannot afford the slightest ground for the necessity of a generalization upon those instances. 'Experience,' he said,

can observe and record what has happened; but she cannot find, in any case, or in any accumulation of cases, any reason for what *must* happen. She may see objects side by side, but she cannot see a reason why they must ever be side by side. She finds certain events to occur in succession; but the succession supplies, in its occurrence, no reasons for its recurrence; she contemplates external objects; but she cannot detect any internal bond, which indissolubly connects the future with the past, the possible with the real. To learn a proposition by experience, and to see it to be necessarily true, are two altogether different processes of thought. . . . If anyone does not clearly comprehend this distinction of necessary and contingent truths, he will not be able to go along with us in our researches into the foundations of human knowledge; nor indeed, to pursue with success any speculation on the subject.[5]

3. INTUITIVE INDUCTION

Plato suggested that in order to acquire a knowledge of necessity, we should turn away from 'the twilight of becoming and perishing' and contemplate the world of 'the absolute and eternal and immutable'.[6] According to Aristotle, however, and to subsequent philosophers in the tradition with which we are here concerned, one way of obtaining the requisite intuition is to consider the particular things of this world.

As a result of perceiving a particular blue thing, or a number of particular blue things, we may come to know what it is for a thing to be blue, and thus, we may be said to know what the property of being blue is. And as a result of perceiving a particular red thing, or a number of particular red things, we may come to know what it is for a thing to be red, and thus, to know what the property of being red is. Then, having this knowledge of what it is to be red and of what it is to be blue, we are able to see that being red excludes being blue, and that this is necessarily so.

[5] William Whewell, *Philosophy of the Inductive Sciences Founded upon Their History* (London: J. W. Parker & Son, 1840), pp. 59–61.
[6] *Republic*, 479, 508.

Thus, Aristotle tells us that as a result of perceiving Callias and a number of other particular men, we come to see what it is for a thing to have the property of being human. And then, by considering the property of being human, we come to see that being human includes being animal, and that this is necessarily so.[7]

Looking to these examples, we may distinguish four stages:

1. There is the perception of the individual things—in the one case, the perception of the particular red things and blue things, and in the other, the perception of Callias and the other particular men.

2. There is a process of abstraction—we come to see what it is for a thing to be red and for a thing to be blue, and we come to see what it is for a thing to be a man.

3. There is the intuitive apprehension of certain relations holding between properties—in the one case, apprehension of the fact that being red excludes being blue, and in the other, apprehension of the fact that being rational and animal includes being animal.

4. Once we have acquired this intuitive knowledge, then, *ipso facto*, we also know the truth of reason expressed by 'Necessarily, everything is such that if it is red then it is not blue' and 'Necessarily, everything is such that if it is human then it is animal'.

Aristotle called this process 'induction'. But since it differs in essential respects from what subsequently came to be known as 'induction', some other term, say, 'intuitive induction', may be less misleading.[8]

If we have performed an 'intuitive induction' in the manner described, then we may say that by contemplating the relation between properties we are able to know that being red excludes being blue and thus to know that *necessarily*, everything is such that if it is red then it is not blue. And we can say, therefore, that the universal generalization, as well as the proposition about properties, is known a priori. The order of justification thus differs from that of the enumerative induction considered earlier, where one

---

[7] *Posterior Analytics*, 100ᵃ–100ᵇ.

[8] This term was proposed by W. E. Johnson, *Logic* (London: Cambridge University Press, 1921), Pt. II, pp. 19 ff. Aristotle uses the term 'induction' in the passages cited in the *Posterior Analytics*; cf. *The Nicomachean Ethics*, Bk. VI, ch. 3, 1139ᵇ. Compare Franz Brentano, *The Origin of Our Knowledge of Right and Wrong* (London: Routledge and Kegan Paul, 1969), pp. 111–13.

attempts to justify the statement about properties by reference to a generalization about particular things.

There is a superficial resemblance between 'intuitive induction' and 'induction by simple enumeration', since in each case, we start with particular instances and then proceed beyond them. Thus, when we make an induction by enumeration, we may proceed from 'This *A* is *B*', 'That *A* is *B*', and so on, to 'In all probability, all *A*s are *B*s', or to 'In all probability, the next *A* is *B*'. But in an induction by enumeration, the function of the particular instances is to *justify* the conclusion. If we find subsequently that our perceptions of the particular instances were unveridical, say, that the things we took to be *A*s were not *A*s at all, then the inductive argument would lose whatever force it may have had. In an 'intuitive induction', however, the particular perceptions are only incidental to the conclusion. This may be seen in the following way.

Let us suppose that the knowledge expressed by the two sentences 'Necessarily, being red excludes being blue' and 'Necessarily, being human includes being animal' is arrived at by intuitive induction; and let us suppose further that in each case, the process began with the perception of certain particular things. Neither conclusion depends for its *justification* upon the particular perceptions which led to the knowledge concerned. As Duns Scotus put it, the perception of the particular things is only the 'occasion' of acquiring the knowledge. If we happen to find our perception was unveridical, this finding will have no bearing upon the result. 'If the senses from which these terms were received were all false, or what is more deceptive, if some were false and others true, I still maintain that the intellect would not be deceived about such principles. . . .'[9] If what we take to be Callias is not a man at all, but only a clever imitation of a man, then, if the imitation is clever enough, our deceptive experience will still be an occasion for contemplating the property of being human—the property of being both rational and animal—and thus, for coming to know that being human includes being animal.

Leibniz thus observes: '. . . if I should discover any demonstrative truth, mathematical or other, while dreaming (as might in fact

---

[9] *Philosophical Writings*, ed. and trans. Alan Wolter (New York: Thomas Nelson & Sons, 1962), p. 109; cf. p. 103.

be), it would be just as certain as if I had been awake. This shows us how intelligible truth is independent of the truth of the existence outside of us of sensible and material things.'[10]

It may be, indeed, that to perform an intuitive induction—i.e. to 'abstract' a certain property, contemplate it, and then see what it includes and excludes—we need only to *think* of some individual thing as having that property. By thinking about a blue thing and a red thing, for example, we may come to see that being blue excludes being red. Thus, Ernst Mach spoke of 'experiments in the imagination'.[11] And E. Husserl, whose language may have been needlessly Platonic, said, 'The Eidos, the *pure essence*, can be exemplified intuitively in the data of experience, data of perception, memory, and so forth, but just as readily *also in the mere data of fancy. . .*'[12]

According to this traditional account, then, once we have acquired some concepts (once we know, with respect to certain attributes, just *what* it is for something to have those attributes), we will also be in a position to know just *what* it is for a proposition or state of affairs to be necessary—to be necessarily such that it is true or necessarily such that it obtains. Then, by contemplating or reflecting upon certain propositions or states of affairs, we will be able to see that *they* are necessary.

This kind of knowledge has traditionally been called a priori.

4. AXIOMS

Speaking very roughly, we might say that one mark of an a priori proposition is this: once you understand it, you see that it is true. We might call this the traditional conception of the a priori. Thus Leibniz remarks: 'You will find in a hundred places that the Scholastics have said that these propositions are evident, *ex terminis*, as soon as the terms are understood. . . .'[13]

---

[10] *The Philosophical Works of Leibniz*, ed. G. M. Duncan (New Haven: The Tuttle, Morehouse & Taylor Co., 1908), p. 161.

[11] *Erkenntnis und Irrtum* (Leipzig: Felix Meiner, 1905), pp. 180 ff.

[12] E. Husserl, *Ideas: General Introduction to Phenomenology* (New York: Macmillan, 1931), p. 57.

[13] G. W. Leibniz, *New Essays Concerning Human Understanding*, Bk. IV, ch. 7 (Open Court edition), p. 462. Compare Alice Ambrose and Morris Lazerowitz, *Fundamentals of Symbolic Logic* (New York: Holt, Rinehart and Winston, 1962):

If we say an a priori proposition is one such that 'once you understand it then you see that it is true', we must take the term 'understand' in a somewhat rigid sense. You couldn't be said to 'understand' a proposition, in the sense intended, unless you can grasp *what* it is for that proposition to be true. The properties or attributes that the proposition implies—those that would be instantiated if the proposition were true—must be properties or attributes that you can grasp in the sense that we have tried to explicate. To 'understand' a proposition, in the sense intended, then, it is not enough merely to be able to say what *sentence* in your language happens to express that proposition. The proposition must be one that you have contemplated and reflected upon.

One cannot *accept* a proposition, in the sense in which we have been using the word 'accept', unless one also *understands* that proposition. We might say, therefore, that an a priori proposition is one such that, if you accept it, then it becomes certain for you. (For if you accept it, then you understand it, and as soon as you understand it, it becomes certain for you.) This account of the a priori, however, would be somewhat broad. We know some a priori propositions on the basis of others and these propositions are not themselves such that, once they are understood, then they are certain.

But let us begin by trying to characterize more precisely those a priori propositions which are not known on the basis of any *other* propositions.

Leibniz said that these propositions are the 'first lights'. He wrote: 'The immediate apperception of our existence and of our thoughts furnishes us with the first truths a posteriori, or of fact, i.e. the *first experiences*, as the identical propositions contain the first truths a priori, or of reason, i.e. *the first lights*. Both are incapable of proof, and may be called *immediate*. . . .'[14]

The traditional term for those a priori propositions which are 'incapable of proof' is *axiom*. Thus Frege wrote: 'Since the time of

'A proposition is said to be true a priori if its truth can be ascertained by examination of the proposition alone or if it is deducible from propositions whose truth is so ascertained, and by examination of nothing else. . . . Understanding the words used in expressing these propositions is sufficient for determining that they are true.' p. 17.

[14] *New Essays Concerning Human Understanding*, Bk. IV, ch. 9, p. 499.

antiquity an axiom has been taken to be a thought whose truth is known without being susceptible to demonstration by a logical chain of reasoning.'[15] In *one* sense, of course, every true proposition *h* is capable of proof, for there will always be other true propositions from which we can derive *h* by means of some principle of logic. What did Leibniz and Frege mean, then, when they said that an axiom is 'incapable of proof'?

The answer is suggested by Aristotle. An axiom, or 'basic truth', he said, is a proposition 'which has no other proposition prior to it'; there is no proposition which is 'better known' than it is.[16] We could say that if one proposition is 'better known' than another, then accepting the one proposition is more reasonable than accepting the other. Hence, if an axiomatic proposition is one such that no other proposition is better known than it is, then it is one that is certain. (Let us say that a proposition *h* is *certain* for a person *S*, provided that *h* is evident for *S* and provided that there is no other proposition *i* which is such that it is *more* reasonable for *S* to accept *i* than it is for him to accept *h*.) Hence Aristotle said that an axiom is a 'primary premiss'. Its ground does not lie in the fact that it is seen to follow from *other* propositions. Therefore we cannot prove such a proposition by making use of any premisses that are 'better known' than it is. (By 'a proof', then, Aristotle, Leibniz, and Frege meant more than 'a valid derivation from premisses that are true'.)

Let us now try to say what it is for a proposition or state of affairs to be an *axiom*:

D3.1 *h* is an *axiom* = Df *h* is necessarily such that (i) it is true and (ii) for every *S*, if *S* accepts *h*, then *h* is certain for *S*.

The following propositions among countless others may be said to be axioms in our present sense of the term:

If some men are Greeks, then some Greeks are men.
If Jones is ill and Smith is away, then Jones is ill.
The sum of 5 and 3 is 8.
The product of 4 and 2 is 8.

For most of us, i.e. for those of us who really *do* consider them, they may be said to be *axiomatic* in the following sense:

[15] Gottlob Frege, *Kleine Schriften* (Hildesheim: Georg Olms, 1967), p. 262.
[16] *Posterior Analytics*, Bk. I, ch. 2.

D3.2 *h* is *axiomatic* for *S* =Df (i) *h* is an axiom and (ii) *S* accepts *h*.

We may assume that any conjunction of axioms is itself an axiom. But it does not follow from this assumption that any conjunction of propositions which are axiomatic for a subject *S* is itself axiomatic for *S*. If two propositions are axiomatic for *S* and if *S* does not accept their conjunction, then the conjunction is not axiomatic for *S*. (Failure to accept their conjunction need not be a sign that *S* is unreasonable. It may be a sign merely that the conjunction is too complex an object for *S* to grasp.)

We have suggested that our knowledge of what is axiomatic is a subspecies of our a priori knowledge, that is to say, some of the things we know a priori are *not* axiomatic in the present sense. They are a priori but they are not what Aristotle called 'primary premisses'.

What would be an example of a proposition that is a priori for *S* but not axiomatic for *S*? Consider the last two axioms on our list above; i.e.

The sum of 5 and 3 is 8.
The product of 4 and 2 is 8.

Let us suppose that their conjunction is also an axiom and that *S* accepts this conjunction; therefore the conjunction is axiomatic for *S*. Let us suppose further that the following proposition is axiomatic for *S*.

If the sum of 5 and 3 is 8 and the product of 4 and 2 is 8, then the sum of 5 and 3 is the product of 4 and 2.

We will say that, if, in such a case, *S* accepts the proposition

The sum of 5 and 3 is the product of 4 and 2

then that proposition is a priori for *S*. Yet the proposition may not be one which is such that it is certain for anyone who accepts it. It may be that one can consider *that* proposition without thereby seeing that it is true.

There are various ways in which we might now attempt to characterize this broader concept of the a priori. Thus we might say: 'You know a proposition a priori provided you accept it and it is implied by propositions that are axiomatic for you.' But this would imply that *any* necessary proposition that you happen to accept is one that you know a priori to be true. (Any necessary proposition *h* is implied by any axiomatic proposition *e*. Indeed any necessary proposition *h* is implied by *any* proposition *e*—whether or not *e* is axiomatic and whether or not *e* is true or false. For if *h* is necessary, then, it is necessarily true that, for any proposition *e*, either *e* is false or *h* is true. And to say '*e* implies *h*' is to say it is necessarily true that either *e* is false or *h* is true.) *Some* of the necessary propositions that we accept may *not* be propositions that we know a priori. They may be such that, if we know them, we know them a posteriori—on the basis of authority. Or they may be such that we cannot be said to know them at all.

To capture the broader concept of the a priori, we might say that a proposition is known a priori provided it is axiomatic that the proposition follows from something that is axiomatic. But let us say, more carefully:

D3.3 *h* is known a priori by *S* =Df There is an *e* such that (i) *e* is axiomatic for *S*, (ii) the proposition, *e* implies *h*, is axiomatic for *S*, and (iii) *S* accepts *h*.

We may add that a person knows a proposition a posteriori if he knows the proposition but doesn't know it a priori.[17]

We may assume that what is thus known a priori is evident. But the a priori, unlike the axiomatic, need not be certain. This accords with St Thomas's observation that 'those who have knowledge of the principles [i.e. the axioms] have a more certain knowledge than the knowledge which is through demonstration'.[18]

But is this account too restrictive? What if *S* derives a proposition from a set of axioms, not by means of one or two simple steps, but as a result of a complex proof, involving a series of interrelated steps? If the proof is formally valid, then shouldn't we say that *S* knows the proposition a priori?

I think that the answer is no. Complex proofs or demonstrations,

---

[17] It should be noted that philosophers have used 'a priori' and 'a posteriori' in several different ways; it is not to be assumed that the present definitions are compatible with every such use. Compare David Benfield, 'The A Priori-A Posteriori Distinction', *Philosophy and Phenomenological Research*, 35 (1974), 151–66.

[18] Thomas Aquinas, *Exposition of the Posterior Analytics of Aristotle*, trans. Pierre Conway, Pt. II., Lecture 20, No. 4 (Quebec: M. Doyon, 1952).

as John Locke pointed out, have a certain limitation. They take time. The result is that the 'evident lustre' of the early steps may be lost by the time we reach the conclusion: 'In long deductions, and the use of many proofs, the memory does not always so readily retain.' Therefore, he said, demonstrative knowledge 'is more imperfect than intuitive knowledge'.[19] Descartes also noted that memory is essential to demonstrative knowledge. He remarks in *Rules for the Direction of the Mind* that, if we can *remember* having deduced a certain conclusion step by step from a set of premisses that are 'known by intuition', then even though we may not now recall each of the particular steps, we are justified in saying that the conclusion is 'known by deduction'.[20] But if, in the course of a demonstration, we must rely upon memory at various stages, thus using as premisses contingent propositions about what we happen to remember, then, although we might be said to have 'demonstrative knowledge' of our conclusion, in a somewhat broad sense of the expression 'demonstrative knowledge', we cannot be said to have an a priori demonstration of the conclusion.

Of course, we may make mistakes in attempting to carry out a proof, just as we may make mistakes in doing simple arithmetic. And one might well ask: How can this be, if the propositions we are concerned with are known a priori? Sometimes, as the quotation from Locke suggests, there has been a slip of memory. Perhaps we are mistaken about just *what* the propositions are that we proved at an earlier step—just as, in doing arithmetic, we may mistakenly think we have carried the 2, or we may pass over some figure having thought that we included it, or we may inadvertently include something twice. And there are also occasions when we may just seem to get the a priori proposition wrong. In my haste I say to myself, '9 and 6 are 13', and then the result will come out wrong. But when I do this, I am not really considering the proposition that 9

---

[19] *Essay Concerning Human Understanding*, Bk. IV, ch. 2, sect. 7.
[20] See *The Philosophical Works of Descartes*, ed. E. S. Haldane and G. R. T. Ross (London: Cambridge University Press, 1934), p. 8. Some version of Descartes' principle should be an essential part of any theory of evidence. Compare Norman Malcolm's suggestion: 'If a man previously had grounds for being sure that *p*, and now remembers that *p*, but does not remember what his grounds were', then he '*has* the same grounds he previously had'. *Knowledge and Certainty* (Englewood Cliffs, NJ: Prentice-Hall, 1963), p. 230.

and 6 are 13. I may just be considering the formula, '9 and 6 are 13', which sounds right at the time, and not considering at all the proposition that that formula is used to express.

We have said what it is for a proposition to be known a priori by a given subject. But we should note, finally, that propositions are sometimes said to be a priori even though they may not be known by anyone at all. Thus Kant held that 'mathematical propositions, strictly so called, are always judgements a priori'.[21] In saying this, he did not mean to be saying merely that mathematical propositions are necessarily true; he was saying something about their epistemic status and something about the way in which they could be known. Yet he could not have been saying that all mathematical propositions are known or even believed, by someone or other, to be true; for there are propositions of mathematics that no one knows to be true; and there are propositions of mathematics that no one has ever considered. What would it be, then, to say that a proposition might be a priori even though it has not been considered by anyone? I think the answer can only be that the proposition is one that *could* be known a priori. In other words:

D3.4 *h* is a priori =Df It is possible that there is someone for whom *h* is a priori.

This definition allows us to say that a proposition may be 'objectively a priori'—'objectively' in that it is a priori whether or not anyone knows it a priori.

Our definitions are in the spirit of several familiar dicta concerning the a priori. Thus, we may say, as Kant did, that necessity is a mark of the a priori—provided we mean by this that if a proposition is a priori then it is necessary.[22] For our definitions assure us that whatever is a priori is necessarily true.

The definitions also enable us to say, as St Thomas did, that these propositions are 'manifest through themselves'.[23] For an axiomatic proposition is one such that, once it is reflected upon or considered,

---

[21] I. Kant, *Critique of Pure Reason*, trans. Norman Kemp Smith (London: Macmillan, 1933), p. 52.

[22] Compare *Critique of Pure Reason*, B4 (Kemp Smith edition), p. 44. But we should not assume that if a proposition is necessary and known to be true, then it is a priori.

[23] St Thomas Aquinas, *Exposition of the Posterior Analytics of Aristotle*, Pt. I, Lecture 4, No. 10, p. 26.

then it is certain. What a given person knows a priori may not *itself* be such that, once it is considered, it is certain. But our definition enables us to say that, if a proposition is one that is a priori for you, then you can see that it follows from a proposition that is axiomatic.

Kant said that our a priori knowledge, like all other knowledge, 'begins with experience' but that, unlike our a posteriori knowledge, it does not 'arise out of experience'.[24] A priori knowledge may be said to 'begin with experience' in the following sense. There is no a priori knowledge until some proposition is in fact contemplated and understood. Moreover, the acceptance of a proposition that is axiomatic is sufficient to make that proposition an axiom for whoever accepts it. But a priori knowledge does not 'arise out of experience'. For, if a proposition is axiomatic or a priori for us, then we have all the evidence we need to see that it is true. Understanding is enough; it is not necessary to make any further enquiry.

What Leibniz called 'first truths a posteriori' coincide with what we have called the *directly evident*. And his 'first truths a priori' coincide with what we have called the *axiomatic*. If we chose, we might say that both sets of truths are directly evident—in which case, our account of the directly evident in Chapter 2 of *Theory of Knowledge* could be said to be an account of what is *directly evident* a posteriori, and our account of what is axiomatic could be said to be an account of what is *directly evident* a priori.[25]

5. A PRIORI AND A POSTERIORI

Kant had said, as we have noted, that 'necessity is a mark of the a priori'. We may accept Kant's dictum, if we take it to mean that what is known a priori is necessary.

But is it possible to know a necessary proposition to be true and not to know this a priori? In other words, can we know some necessary propositions a posteriori?

A possible example of a proposition that is known a posteriori and is yet necessary might be a logical theorem which one accepts on the ground that reputable logicians assert it to be true. Whether

---

[24] *Critique of Pure Reason*, B1 (Kemp Smith edition), p. 41.

[25] This terminology is close to that of Franz Brentano. Compare his *The True and the Evident* (London: Routledge & Kegan Paul, 1966), pp. 130 ff.

there are in fact any such propositions depends upon two things, each of them somewhat problematic.

The first is that such a proposition cannot be said to be *known* to be true unless such testimonial evidence is sufficient for knowledge. And this is a question we cannot discuss in the present essay.[26]

The second is that such a proposition cannot be said to be known to be true unless it is one that the man *accepts*. But when a man, as we say, accepts a theorem on the basis of authority and not on the basis of demonstration, is it the theorem *itself* that he accepts or is it what Brentano calls a 'surrogate' for the theorem?[27] If a man reads a logical text, finds there a formula which expresses a certain logical principle, and then, knowing that the author is reputable, concludes that the formula is true, it may well be that the man does *not* accept the logical principle. What he accepts is, rather, the contingent proposition to the effect that a certain formula in a book expresses a logical principle that is true.

But if we waive these difficulties, then perhaps we may say that there is an analytic a posteriori—or at least that some of the logical truths that we know are such that we know them only a posteriori.[28]

But even if some of the things we know a posteriori are logically true, there is at least this additional epistemic relation holding between the necessary and the a priori:

If a man knows—or someone once knew—a posteriori that a certain necessary proposition is true, then *someone* knows a priori that some necessary proposition is true. If the first man bases his knowledge on the testimony of authority, and if this authority in turn bases his knowledge upon the testimony of some other authority, then sooner or later there will be an 'ultimate authority' who knows some proposition a priori.

---

[26] On the importance of testimony for the theory of evidence, compare: James F. Ross, 'Testimonial Evidence', in *Analysis and Metaphysics*, ed. Keith Lehrer (Dordrecht: D. Reidel, 1975), pp. 35–55; and I. M. Bochenski, *Was ist Autorität?* (Freiburg im Breisgau: Herder, 1974).

[27] Cf. Franz Brentano, *Grundzuge der Ästhetik* (Bern: A. Franke, 1959), p. 167.

[28] And so, given Definition D3.4 above, the definition of the 'objective' sense of a priori, we may seriously consider the possibility discussed by Bernard Bolzano: that a proposition 'can be objectively a priori although it is subjectively only a posteriori'. Bernard Bolzano, *Theory of Science*, trans. Rolf George (Oxford: Basil Blackwell, 1972), p. 184.

6. SCEPTICISM WITH RESPECT TO THE A PRIORI

Let us now consider a sceptical objection to what we have been saying.

'You have said what it is for a proposition to be axiomatic for a person and you have given examples of propositions which, you say, are axiomatic for you and presumably for others. But how do you know that those propositions are axiomatic? How do you know that they satisfy the terms of your definitions?

'If you really do know that they are axiomatic, then you must have some *general principle* by means of which you can apply your definitions. There must be something about your experience that guarantees these propositions for you and you must *know* that it guarantees them. But what could the principle be?

'The most you can say, surely, is that such propositions just *seem* to be true, or that when you reflect on them you find you cannot doubt them and that you cannot help but accept them. But, as the history of science makes clear, such facts as these provide no guarantee that the propositions in question are true. Notoriously, there have been ever so many false propositions which reasonable people have found they couldn't doubt. And some of these may well have been taken as axiomatic. Consider the logical paradoxes, for example. People found they couldn't help but believe certain propositions, and as a result they became entangled in contradictions.'

The objection may be summarized as follows:

(1) You cannot know that a given proposition is axiomatic for you unless the proposition is one such that, when you contemplate it, you have a kind of experience—say, a strong feeling of conviction—that provides you with a guarantee that the proposition is true. But

(2) there is no experience which will provide such a guarantee. Therefore

(3) you cannot really know, with respect to any proposition that it is one that is axiomatic.

Is this a valid argument? The conclusion certainly follows from the premises. And, knowing the history of human error, we can hardly question the second of the two premises. But what of the first premiss? If we cannot find any reason to accept the first premiss, then we do not need to accept the conclusion. How, then, would the sceptic defend his first premiss?

There is a certain more general principle to which the sceptic might appeal in the attempt to defend the first premiss. I will call this principle the *generalizability thesis* and formulate it as follows. 'You cannot *know* that any given proposition *p* is true unless you also know two other things. The first of these things will be a certain more *general* proposition *q*; *q* will not imply *p* but it will specify the conditions under which propositions of a certain type are true. And the second thing will be a proposition *r*, which enables you to *apply* this general proposition to *p*. In other words, *r* will be a proposition to the effect that the first proposition *p* satisfies the conditions specified in the second proposition *q*.'

But if the generalizability thesis is true, no one knows anything. Consider the application of the thesis to a single proposition *p*. According to the thesis, if we know *p*, then we know two further propositions—a general proposition *q* and a proposition *r* that applies *q* to *p*. Applying the generalizability thesis to each of the two propositions, *q* and *r*, we obtain four more propositions; applying it to each of them, we obtain eight more propositions; . . . and so on *ad indefinitum*. The generalizability thesis implies, therefore, that we cannot know any proposition to be true unless we know all the members of such an infinite hierarchy of propositions. And therefore it implies that we cannot know any proposition to be true.

The sceptic may reply: 'But in *objecting* to my general principle, you are presupposing that we *do* know something. And this begs the question.' The proper rejoinder is: 'But in *affirming* your general principle, you are presupposing that we *don't* know anything. And *that* begs the question.'

The general reply to a scepticism that addresses itself to an entire area of knowledge can only be this: we do have the knowledge in question, and therefore, any philosophical theory implying that we do not is false. This way of looking at the matter may seem especially plausible in the present instance. It is tempting to say of scepticism, with respect to the truths of reason, what Leonard Nelson said of scepticism, with respect to the truths of mathematics. The advocate of such a scepticism, Nelson said, has invited us to 'sacrifice the clearest and most lucid knowledge that we possess—indeed, the *only* knowledge that is clear and lucid *per se*. I prefer to strike the opposite course. If a philosophy, no matter how attractive or plausible or ingenious it may be, brings me into conflict with mathematics, I conclude that not mathematics but my philosophy is on the wrong track.'[29] There is certainly no *better* ground for scepticism with respect to our knowledge of the truths of reason than there is for scepticism with respect to our knowledge of physical things.[30]

And so what of the sceptic's question, 'How do you know that the proposition that 2 and 4 are 6 is one that is axiomatic?' Let us recall what we said in connection with his question about self-presenting states.[31] The question was: 'How do you know that seeming to have a headache is a self-presenting state?' In dealing with that question, we avoided falling into the sceptic's trap. We said that the only possible answer to such a question is that we *do* know that seeming to have a headache is a self-presenting state. We should follow a similar course in the present case.

The sceptic may not be satisfied with this move and the result will be an impasse that is typical of philosophy and, in particular, of the theory of knowledge.

7. 'PSYCHOLOGISM'

When the sceptic and the dogmatist thus fail to reach an agreement with respect to a given area of knowledge, it is well to ask whether there may not be a misunderstanding with respect to the propositions constituting the area of knowledge. I have said that the propositions in question are concerned with certain abstract entities or eternal objects, such as properties, numbers, and propositions or states of affairs. Is it possible to interpret them in another way?

[29] Leonard Nelson, *Socratic Method and Critical Philosophy* (New Haven: Yale University Press, 1949), p. 184.

[30] 'The preference of (say) seeing over understanding as a method of observation seems to me capricious. For just as an opaque body may be seen, so a concept may be understood or grasped.' Alonzo Church, 'Abstract Entities in Semantic Analysis', *Proceedings of the American Academy of Arts and Sciences*, 80 (1951), 100–12; the quotation is on p. 104.

[31] See Chisholm, *Theory of Knowledge*, 2nd edn. (Englewood Cliffs, NJ, 1977), ch. 2, sect. 8.

Many attempts have been made to provide such a subject-matter.

Of the attempts that have been made to provide such an interpretation, the only ones worthy of consideration are, first, the view that came to be known in the nineteenth century as 'psychologism', and second, its contemporary counterpart, which we might call 'linguisticism'. Much of what can be said in criticism of the one can also be said, *mutatis mutandis*, in criticism of the other.

Theodore Lipps wrote in 1880 that 'logic is either a physics of thinking or it is nothing at all' and he tried to show that the truths of logic are, in fact, truths about the ways in which people think.[32] This is the view that was called 'psychologism' and it was applied generally to the subject-matter of the truths of reason.

A psychologistic interpretation of 'Necessarily, being red excludes being blue' might be: 'Everyone is so constituted psychologically that if he thinks of a thing as being red, then he cannot also then think of it as being blue.' And a psychologistic interpretation of the logical truth 'For any propositions p and q, if p is true and p implies q, then q is true' might be: 'Everyone is so constituted psychologically that if he believes that p is true, and if he believes that p implies q, then he cannot help but believe that q is true.'

But obviously, these psychological sentences do not at all convey what is intended by the sentences they are supposed to translate. The psychological sentences are empirical generalizations about the ways in which people think, and as such, they can be supported only by extensive psychological investigation. Thus, Gottlob Frege said, in connection with the psychologistic interpretation of mathematics: 'It would be strange if the most exact of all the sciences had to seek support from psychology, which is still feeling its way none too surely.'[33] And being empirical generalizations, the psychological sentences are probable at best and are at the mercy of contrary

---

[32] 'Die Aufgabe der Erkenntnistheori', *Philosophische Monatshefte*, Vol. XVI (1880); quoted by Husserl, in *Logical Investigations* (London: Routledge & Kegan Paul, 1970). Vol. I, p. 93. In his *Philosophie der Arithmetik* (Leipzig: C. E. M. Pfeffer, 1891), Husserl defended a version of 'psychologism', but he criticizes that view in *Logical Investigations*.

[33] *The Foundations of Arithmetic*, p. 38; Frege's work was first published in 1884. Cf. Philip E. B. Jourdain, *The Philosophy of Mr. B*rtr*nd R*ss*ll* (London: George Allen & Unwin, 1918). p. 88: 'The psychological founding of logic appears to be not without analogy with the surprising method of advocates of evolutionary ethics, who

instances. The existence somewhere of one unreasonable individual—one man who believed that some things are both red and blue, or one man who believed that a certain proposition *p* is true and also that *p* implies *q*, and who yet refused to believe that *q* is true—would be sufficient to ensure that the psychological sentence is false. And we know, all too well, that there are such men. Their existence, however, has no bearing upon the truths expressed by 'Necessarily, being red excludes being blue' and 'Necessarily, for any propositions *p* and *q*, if *p* is true and if *p* implies *q*, then *q* is true.'

In the face of such difficulties, the proponent of psychologism is likely to modify his view. He will say of sentences expressing the laws of logic and the other truths of reason, that they really express *rules of thought*, and that they are not descriptive sentences telling us how people actually do think. But to see the hopelessness of this approach, we have only to consider the possible ways of interpreting the sentence, 'The laws of logic are rules of thought.'

1. One interpretation would be: 'The laws of logic are ethical truths pertaining to our duties and obligations with respect to thinking.' In this case, the problem of our knowledge of the laws of logic is transferred to the (more difficult) problem of our knowledge of the truths (if any) of ethics.

2. 'The laws of logic are imperatives commanding us to think in certain ways—and imperatives are neither true nor false.' This way of looking at the matter leaves us with the problem of distinguishing between valid and invalid imperatives. For there is a distinction between 'Do not believe, with respect to any particular thing, both that it is red and that it is blue', and 'Do not believe, with respect to any particular thing, that that thing is either red or not red.' The former imperative, surely, is correct or valid, and the latter, incorrect or invalid. If we are not to fall back into scepticism, we must also say that the former is known to be valid and the latter is

expect to discover what *is* good by inquiring what cannibals have *thought* good. I sometimes feel inclined to apply the historical method to the multiplication table. I should make a statistical inquiry among school-children, before their pristine wisdom has been biased by teachers. I should put down their answers to what 6 times 9 amounts to, I should work out the average of their answers to six places of decimals, and should then decide that, at the present stage of human development, this average is the value of 6 times 9.'

known to be invalid. Moreover, it is not possible to construe all of the statements of logic as imperatives. For the logician can also tell us non-imperatively such things as: If you believe that p, and if you believe that p implies q, and if you conform to the imperative, *modus ponens*, then you will also believe that q. This statement is a necessary truth. (A manual of chess, similarly, may give us certain rules in the form of imperatives: 'Move the king only one square at a time.' And possibly these imperatives are neither valid nor invalid. But whether or not they are valid, the chess manual will also contain true indicative sentences—sentences which are not themselves imperatives but which tell us what will happen when, in accordance with the imperatives that the manual lays down, we move the pieces into various positions. 'It is impossible, if white is in such and such a position, for black to win in less than seven moves.' And these statements are also necessary truths.)

3. 'The laws of logic tell us which ways of believing will lead to truth and which will lead to falsehood.' According to this interpretation, our two examples might be thought of as telling us respectively: 'A necessary condition of avoiding false beliefs is to refrain from believing, with respect to any particular thing, both that that thing is red and also that it is blue', and 'A necessary condition of avoiding false beliefs is to refrain from believing, at one and the same time, with respect to any proposition p and q, that p is true, that p implies q, and that q is false.' To see that this way of formulating psychologism leaves us with our problem, let us compare it with a similar psychologistic interpretation of some other subject-matter, say, astronomy. We may say, if we like, that what the statement 'There are nine planets' really tells us is that if we wish to avoid error with respect to the number of planets, it is essential to refrain from believing that there are not nine planets; it also tells us that if we wish to arrive at the truth about the number of planets, it is essential to believe that there *are* nine planets. It is not likely that in so spinning out what is conveyed by 'There are nine planets', we can throw any light upon what the astronomer thinks he knows. In any case, our problem reappears when we compare our new versions of the statements of logic with those of the statements of astronomy. The former, but not the latter, can be prefixed by, 'It is necessary that', and unless we give in to scepticism (which it was the point of

psychologism to avoid), we must say that the result of such a prefixing is also a statement we can know to be true.[34]

8. 'LINGUISTICISM'

A popular conception of the truths of reason at the present time is the linguistic analogue of psychologism. Versions of 'linguisticism' may be obtained merely by altering our exposition of psychologism. We may replace the references to ways in which people *think* by references to ways in which they *use language*, replace the references to what people *believe* by references to what they *write* or *say*, replace 'avoiding false belief' by 'avoiding absurdity', and replace 'rules of thought' by 'rules of language'. The result could then be criticized substantially, *mutatis mutandis*, as before.

Some of the versions of linguisticism, however, are less straight-forward. It is often said, for example, that the sentences formulating the truths of logic are 'true in virtue of the rules of language' and hence, that they are 'true in virtue of the way in which we use words'.[35] What could this possibly mean?

The two English sentences, 'Being red excludes being blue' and 'Being rational and animal includes being animal', could plausibly be said to 'owe their truth', in part, to the way in which we use words. If we used 'being blue' to refer to the property of being heavy, and not to that of being blue, then the first sentence (provided the other words in it had their present use) would be false instead of true. And if we used the word 'and' to express the relation of disjunction instead of conjunction, then the second sentence (again, provided that the other words in it had their present use) would also be false instead of true. But as W. V. Quine has reminded us, 'even so factual a sentence as "Brutus killed Caesar" owes its truth not only to the killing but equally to our using the component words as we do.'[36] Had 'killed', for example, been

---

[34] Cf. the criticism of psychologism in Husserl's *Logical Investigations*, Vol. i, pp. 90 ff. and Rudolf Carnap, *The Logical Foundations of Probability* (Chicago: University of Chicago Press, 1950), pp. 37–42.

[35] See Anthony Quinton, 'The A Priori and the Analytic', in *Necessary Truth*, ed. Robert Sleigh (Englewood Cliffs, NJ: Prentice-Hall, 1972), pp. 89–109.

[36] W. V. Quine 'Carnap and Logical Truth', *The Philosophy of Rudolf Carnap*, ed. P. A. Schilpp (La Salle, Ill.: Open Court, 1963), p. 386.

given the use that 'was survived by' happens to have, then, other things being the same, 'Brutus killed Caesar' would be false instead of true.

It might be suggested, therefore, that the truths of logic and other truths of reason stand in this peculiar relationship to language: they are true 'solely in virtue of the rules of our language', or 'solely in virtue of the ways in which we use words'. But if we take the phrase 'solely in virtue of' in the way in which it would naturally be taken, then the suggestion is obviously false.

To say of a sentence that it is true *solely* in virtue of the ways in which we use words, or that it is true *solely* in virtue of the rules of our language, would be to say that the only condition that needs to obtain in order for the sentence to be true is that we use words in certain ways or that there be certain rules pertaining to the way in which words are to be used. But let us consider what conditions must obtain if the English sentence 'Being red excludes being blue' is to be true. One such condition is indicated by the following sentence which we may call *T*:

> The English sentence 'Being blue excludes being red' is true if, and only if, being blue excludes being red.

Clearly, the final part of *T*, the part following the second 'if', formulates a necessary condition for the truth of the English sentence 'Being red excludes being blue'; but it refers to a relationship among properties and not to rules of language or ways in which we use words (to suppose otherwise would be to make the mistake, once again, of confusing use and mention in language). Hence, we cannot say that the only conditions that need to obtain in order for 'Being red excludes being blue' to be true is that we use words in certain ways or that there be certain rules pertaining to the ways in which words are to be used; and therefore, the sentence cannot be said to be true solely in virtue of the ways in which we use words.

9. ANALYSING THE PREDICATE OUT OF THE SUBJECT

The terms 'analytic' and 'synthetic' were introduced by Kant in order to contrast two types of categorical judgement. It will not be

inaccurate to interpret 'judgement', in Kant's sense, to mean the
same as what we mean by 'proposition'. The terms 'analytic' and
'synthetic' are used in much of contemporary philosophy to refer
instead to the types of *sentence* that express the types of judgement
to which Kant referred. And perhaps Kant's view is best expressed
by reference to sentences: an analytic *judgement* or *proposition* is
one that is expressible in a certain type of *sentence*. But what type of
sentence?

An analytic judgement, according to Kant, is a judgement in
which 'the predicate adds nothing to the concept of the subject'. If I
judge that all squares are rectangles, then, in Kant's terminology,
the concept of the subject of my judgement is the property of being
square, and the concept of the predicate is the property of being
rectangular. Kant uses the term 'analytic', since, he says, the
concept of the predicate helps to 'break up the concept of the
subject into those constituent concepts that have all along been
thought in it'.[37] Since being square is the conjunctive property of
being equilateral and rectangular, the predicate of the judgement
expressed by 'All squares are rectangular' may be said to 'analyse
out' what is contained in the subject. An analytic judgement, then,
may be expressed in the form of an explicit redundancy: e.g.
'Everything is such that if it is both equilateral and rectangular then
it is rectangular.' To deny such an explicit redundancy would be to
affirm a *contradictio in adjecto*, for it would be to judge that there
are things which both have and do not have a certain property—in
the present instance, that there is something that both is and is not
rectangular. Hence, Kant said that 'the common principle of all
analytic judgements is the law of contradiction'.[38]

What might it mean to say, with respect to a sentence of the form
'Everything that is an *S* is a *P*' that the predicate-term can be
analysed out of the subject-term?

One thing that might be meant is this: that what the sentence
expresses can *also* be expressed in a sentence in which the predicate-
term is the same as the subject-term. Thus the predicate of
'Everything that is a man is a rational animal' could be said to be
analysed out of the subject, since what the sentence expresses can

---

[37] *Critique of Pure Reason*, A7 (Kemp Smith edition), p. 48.
[38] *Prolegomena to Any Future Metaphysics*, sect. 2.

also be expressed by saying 'Everything that is a rational animal is a rational animal'. But not all of the traditional examples of propositions that are analytic may be expressed in sentences wherein the subject-term and the predicate-term are the same.

Consider the sentence:

(1) All squares are rectangles.

What this sentence expresses may also be put as:

(2) Everything that is an equilateral thing and a rectangle is a rectangle.

Sentence (2) provides us with a paradigm case of a sentence in which the predicate-term ('a rectangle') may be said to be analysed out of the subject-term ('an equilateral thing and a rectangle').

We may note that, in sentence (2), the predicate-term is *also* part of the subject-term. Shall we say, then, that the predicate of a sentence is *analysed out* of the subject if the predicate is the same as the subject or if the subject is a conjunction of two terms one of which is the predicate? This definition would be somewhat broad, for it would require us to say that in the following sentence the predicate is analysed out of the subject:

(3) Everything that is a square and a rectangle is a rectangle.

But (3) does not exhibit the type of analysis that is to be found in (2). Thus in (3) the subject-term ('a square and a rectangle') is redundant (given 'a square' in the subject we don't *need* to add 'a rectangle'), but in (2) the subject-term ('an equilateral thing and a rectangle') is not redundant.

We could say, somewhat more exactly, that a predicate-term is *analysed out* of a subject-term provided the subject-term is such that either it is itself the predicate-term or it is a conjunction of independent terms one of which is the predicate-term. But what is it for two terms to be 'independent'?

We may say, of certain pairs of terms in a given language, that one of the terms *logically implies* the other in that language. Thus in English 'square' logically implies 'rectangle', and 'red thing' logically implies 'coloured thing'. These terms may be said to be such that in English they are *true of*, or *apply to*, certain things. And the English language is necessarily such that 'rectangle' applies to everything that 'square' applies to, and it is also necessarily such that 'coloured thing' applies to everything that 'red' applies to.[39] To say, then, '*T logically implies R* in language *L*' is to say this: *L* is necessarily such that *R* applies in *L* to all those things to which *T* applies in *L*.

Now we may say what it is for two terms to be *independent*—what it is for two terms to be logically independent of each other in a given language.

Two terms are *logically independent* of each other in a given language provided only that the terms and their negations are such that no one of them logically implies the other in that language.[40] Thus 'red thing' and 'square' are logically independent in English, for the four terms, 'red thing', 'square', 'non-red thing', and 'non-square' are such that no one of them implies the other in English.

We can now say, somewhat more exactly, what it is for the predicate-term *P*, of a sentence in a given language *L*, to be *analysed out* of the subject-term *S*. First of all, the sentence will be an '*all S is P*' sentence; that is to say, the sentence will be necessarily such that it is true in *L*, if and only if, for every *x*, if *S* applies to *x* in *L*, then *P* applies to *x* in *L*. And second, either the subject-term *S* is itself the same as *P* or it is a conjunction of logically independent terms one of which is *P*.

Finally, we may define the Kantian sense of 'analytic proposition' as follows: A proposition is analytic provided only it may be expressed in a sentence in which the predicate-term is analysed out of the subject-term.

To see how the definitions may be applied, consider the following

---

[39] And so we do not define 'English language' in terms of the people who speak it or the lands wherein it is spoken. In our use of the word 'English', we may say 'English is necessarily such that in it "red" applies to things that are red.' But if we defined 'English' as the language spoken, say, by Englishmen or in England, we could not say 'English is *necessarily* such that in it "red" applies to things that are red.' Englishmen *could* have used 'blue', or any other word, in the way in which, in fact, they use 'red'.

[40] A term *T* may be said to be *a negation* of a term *S* in a given language *L* provided this condition holds: either *T* is part of *S*, or *S* is part of *T*; and *L* is necessarily such that, for every *x*, *T* is true of *x* in *L*, if and only if *S* is not true of *x* in *L*. Thus 'non-square' is a negation of 'square' in English (and 'square' a negation of 'non-square') since one is part of the other and since English is necessarily such that 'square' is true of any given thing if and only if 'non-square' is not true of that thing.

sentences, each of which may be said to express an analytic proposition, in the traditional sense of the term 'analytic':

All fathers are parents.
No bachelors are married.
All dogs are dogs or cats.

What these three sentences express in English may also be put as follows:

Everything that is a male and a parent is a parent.
Everything that is a male human and a thing that is unmarried is a thing that is unmarried.
Everything that is (i) a dog or a cat and (ii) a dog or a non-cat is a dog or a cat.

The last three sentences are sentences in which the predicate is analysed out of the subject. And therefore the propositions expressed by the first sentences are all analytic.[41]

10. THE SYNTHETIC A PRIORI

Kant raised the question: Is there a synthetic a priori? Are there synthetic propositions that we know a priori to be true?

If we construe 'analytic proposition' in the way in which we have tried to spell out (by reference to the predicate of a sentence being 'analysed out of' the subject), and if, as many philosophers do, we take 'synthetic proposition' to mean the same as 'proposition which is not analytic', then Kant's question may not be particularly interesting. For, it would seem, there are many propositions which we know a priori and which are not analytic, in this restricted sense of the term 'analytic'. Among them are such propositions as:

If there are more than 7 dogs, then there are more than 5 dogs.
If there are either dogs or cows but no cows, then there are dogs.
If all men are mortal and Socrates is a man, then Socrates is mortal.

---

[41] If we define 'father' as 'male parent', and 'mother' as 'female parent', then we would have to say of a father who changes his sex that he becomes a mother. And analogously for a mother. Perhaps to accommodate our language to the possibility of sex-change, we should define 'father', not merely as 'male parent', but as 'parent who was male at the time of procreation'. And analogously for 'mother'.

But when philosophers ask whether there are synthetic propositions that we know a priori to be true, they are not usually thinking of such propositions as these. They are thinking rather of propositions which can be expressed naturally in English in the form 'All *S* are *P*'. Given what we have said about the nature of analytic propositions, we may put the question, 'Is there a synthetic a priori?', somewhat more exactly as follows:

Are there any propositions which are such that: (i) they are known by us a priori; (ii) they can be expressed in English in the form 'Everything which is *S* is *P*'; and yet (iii) they are *not* such that in English their predicate-terms can be analysed out of their subject-terms?

Let us consider, then, certain possible examples of 'the synthetic a priori', so conceived.

1. One important candidate for the synthetic a priori is the knowledge that might be expressed by saying either 'Being square includes being a shape' or 'Necessarily, everything that is square is a thing that has a shape'. The sentence 'Everything that is square is a thing that has a shape' recalls our paradigmatic 'Everything that is square is a rectangle'. In the case of the latter sentence, we were able to 'analyse the predicate out of the subject': We replaced the subject-term 'square' with a conjunctive term, 'equilateral thing and a rectangle', and were thus able to express our proposition in the form:

Everything that is an *S* and a *P* is a *P*

where the terms replacing '*S*' and '*P*' are such that neither is implied by the other or by the negation of the other. But can we do this with 'Everything that is square has a shape'?

The problem is to fill in the blank in the following sentence:

Everything that is a ____ and a thing that has a shape is a thing that has a shape

in the appropriate way. This means we should find a term such that: (i) the resulting sentence will express what is expressed by 'Everything that is square has a shape'; (ii) the term will neither imply nor be implied by 'thing that has a shape'; and (iii) the negation of our term will neither imply nor be implied by 'thing that has a shape'. With what term, then, can we fill the blank?

We might try 'either a square or a thing that does not have a shape', thus obtaining 'Everything that is (i) either a square or a thing that does not have a shape and (ii) a thing that has a shape is a thing that has a shape.' But the sentence thus obtained is not one in which the predicate is analysed out of the subject. The two terms making up the subject, namely (i) 'either a square or a thing that does not have a shape' and (ii) 'a thing that has a shape', are such that, in our language, any negation of the second logically implies the first (i.e. 'not such as to be a thing that has a shape' logically implies 'either a square or a thing that does not have a shape'). We do not have a sentence, therefore, in which the predicate can be said to be analysed out of the subject; for the two terms making up the subject are not logically independent in our language.

What if we fill in the blank by 'square', thus obtaining 'Everything that is a square and a thing that has a shape is a thing that has a shape'? This will not help us, for the two terms making up the subject—'square' and 'a thing that has a shape'—are such that, in our language, the first logically implies the second; hence they are not logically independent of each other; and therefore the sentence is not one in which the predicate is analysed out of the subject. And if we drop the second term from the subject, as we can without any loss, we will be back where we started.

And so we have not found a way of showing that 'Everything that is square has a shape' is analytic. But the sentence expresses what we know a priori to be true. And therefore, it would seem, there is at last some presumption in favour of the proposition that there is a synthetic a priori.

There are indefinitely many other propositions presenting essentially the same difficulties as 'Everything that is square has a shape'. Examples are: 'Everything red is coloured'; 'Everyone who hears something in C-sharp minor hears a sound'. The sentences express what is known a priori, but no one has been able to show that they are analytic.[42]

It has been suggested that the sentences giving rise to the problem of the synthetic a priori are really 'postulates about the meanings of words', and therefore, that they do not express what is synthetic a

[42] Cf. C. H. Langford, 'A Proof that Synthetic A Priori Propositions Exist', *Journal of Philosophy*, 46 (1949), 20–4.

priori. But if the suggestion is intended literally, then it would seem to betray the confusion between use and mention that we encountered earlier. A postulate about the meaning of the word 'red', for example, or a sentence expressing such a postulate, would presumably mention the word 'red'. It might read, 'The word "red" may be taken to refer to a certain colour', or perhaps, 'Let the word "red" be taken to refer to a certain colour'. But 'Everything that is red is coloured', although it uses the words 'red' and 'coloured', doesn't mention them at all. Thus, there would seem to be no clear sense in which it could be said really to be a 'meaning postulate' or to refer in any way to words and how they are used.

2. What Leibniz called the 'disparates' furnish us with a second candidate for the synthetic a priori. These are closely related to the type of sentence just considered, but involve problems that are essentially different. An example of a sentence concerned with disparates would be our earlier 'Being red excludes being blue' or (alternatively put) 'Nothing that is red is blue.'[43] Philosophers have devoted considerable ingenuity to trying to show that 'Nothing that is red is blue' can be expressed as a sentence that is analytic, but so far as I have been able to determine, all of these attempts have been unsuccessful. Again, it is recommended that the reader try to re-express 'Nothing that is red is blue' in such a way that the predicate may be 'analysed out' of the subject in the sense we have described above.

3. It has also been held, not without plausibility, that certain ethical sentences express what is synthetic a priori. Thus, Leibniz, writing on what he called the 'supersensible element' in knowledge, said: '. . . but to return to *necessary truths*, it is generally true that we know them only by this natural light, and not at all by the experience of the senses. For the senses can very well make known, in some sort, what is, but they cannot make known what *ought to be* or what could not be otherwise.'[44] Or consider the sentence, 'All pleasures, as such, are intrinsically good, or good in themselves, whenever and wherever they may occur.' If this sentence expresses

---

[43] Cf. John Locke, *Essay Concerning Human Understanding*, Bk. IV, ch. 1, sect. 7; Franz Brentano, *Versuch über die Erkenntnis* (Leipzig: Felix Meiner, 1925), pp. 9–10.
[44] Quoted from *The Philosophical Works of Leibniz*, p. 162.

something that is known to be true, then what it expresses must be synthetic a priori. To avoid this conclusion, some philosophers deny that sentences about what is intrinsically good, or good in itself, *can* be known to be true.[45]

11. AN UNTENABLE DUALISM?

But many philosophers now believe that the distinction between the analytic and the synthetic has been shown to be untenable; we should consider what reasons there might be for such a belief. Ordinarily, it is defended by reference to the following facts. (1) In drawing a distinction between analytic and synthetic sentences, one must speak of *necessity*, as we have done, or employ concepts, e.g. that of *synonymy*, that can be explicated only by reference to necessity. Thus we have spoken of a language being *necessarily* such that, if a given term applies to a thing in that language, then a certain other term also applies to that thing in that language. (2) There is no reliable way of telling, merely by observing a man's behaviour, whether the language he then happens to be using is one which is *necessarily* such that if a given term applies to something in that language then a certain other term applies to that thing in that language. And (3) it is not possible, by reference merely to linguistic behaviour, to say what it is for a language to be *necessarily* such that, for two given terms, if the one applies to something in that language then the other also applies to that thing in that language.[46]

But these three propositions, even if they are true, are not sufficient to yield the conclusion (4) that the distinction between the analytic and the synthetic is untenable. If we attempt to formulate the additional premiss that would be needed to make the argument valid, we will see that it must involve a philosophical generalization—a generalization concerning what conditions must obtain if the distinction between the analytic and the synthetic is to be tenable. And how would the generalization be defended? This

---

[45] Cf. the discussion of this question in chs. 5 and 6 in William Frankena. *Ethics*, 2nd edn., (Englewood Cliffs, NJ: Prentice-Hall, 1973).

[46] Cf. W. V. Quine, 'Two Dogmas of Empiricism', in *From a Logical Point of View*, esp. pp. 20–37, and Morton White, 'The Analytic and the Synthetic: An Untenable Dualism', in *Semantics and the Philosophy of Language*, ed. Leonard Linsky, (Urbana: University of Illinois Press, 1952), pp. 272–86.

question should be considered in the light of what we have said about scepticism and the problem of the criterion. Of the philosophical generalizations that would make the above argument valid, none of them, so far as I know, has ever been defended. It is not accurate, therefore, to say that the distinction between the analytic and the synthetic has been *shown* to be untenable.

VII

A PRIORI KNOWLEDGE, NECESSITY, AND CONTINGENCY

SAUL A. KRIPKE

PHILOSOPHERS have talked (and, of course, there has been considerable controversy in recent years over the meaningfulness of these notions) about various categories of truth, which are called 'a priori', 'analytic', 'necessary'—and sometimes even 'certain' is thrown into this batch. The terms are often used as if *whether* there are things answering to these concepts is an interesting question, but we might as well regard them all as meaning the same thing. Now, everyone remembers Kant (a bit) as making a distinction between 'a priori' and 'analytic'. So maybe this distinction is still made. In contemporary discussion very few people, if any, distinguish between the concepts of statements being a priori and their being necessary. At any rate I shall *not* use the terms 'a priori' and 'necessary' interchangeably here.

Consider what the traditional characterizations of such terms as 'a priori' and 'necessary' are. First the notion of a prioricity is a concept of epistemology. I guess the traditional characterization from Kant goes something like: a priori truths are those which can be known independently of any experience. This introduces another problem before we get off the ground, because there's another modality in the characterization of 'a priori', namely, it is supposed to be something which *can* be known independently of any experience. That means that in some sense it's *possible* (whether we do or do not in fact know it independently of any experience) to know this independently of any experience. And possible for whom? For God? For the Martians? Or just for people with minds like ours? To make this all clear might involve a host of problems all of its own about what sort of possibility is in question here. It might be best therefore, instead of using the phrase 'a priori truth', to the extent that one uses it at all, to stick to the question of whether a particular person or knower knows something a priori or believes it true on the basis of a priori evidence.

I won't go further too much into the problems that might arise with the notion of a prioricity here. I will say that some philosophers somehow change the modality in this characterization from *can* to *must*. They think that if something belongs to the realm of a priori knowledge, it couldn't possibly be known empirically. This is just a mistake. Something may belong in the realm of such statements that *can* be known a priori but still may be known by particular people on the basis of experience. To give a really common-sense example: anyone who has worked with a computing machine knows that the computing machine may give an answer to whether such and such a number is prime. No one has calculated or proved that the number is prime; but the machine has given the answer: this number is prime. We, then, if we believe that the number is prime, believe it on the basis of our knowledge of the laws of physics, the construction of the machine, and so on. We therefore do not believe this on the basis of purely a priori evidence. We believe it (if anything is a posteriori at all) on the basis of a posteriori evidence. Nevertheless, maybe this could be known a priori by someone who made the requisite calculations. So '*can* be known a priori' doesn't mean '*must* be known a priori'.

The second concept which is in question is that of necessity. Sometimes this is used in an epistemological way and might then just mean a priori. And of course, sometimes it is used in a physical way when people distinguish between physical and logical necessity. But what I am concerned with here is a notion which is not a notion of epistemology but of metaphysics, in some (I hope) non-pejorative sense. We ask whether something might have been true, or might have been false. Well, if something is false, it's obviously not necessarily true. If it is true, might it have been otherwise? Is it possible that, in this respect, the world should have been different from the way it is? If the answer is 'no', then this fact about the world is a necessary one. If the answer is 'yes', then this fact about the world is a contingent one. This in and of itself has nothing to do with anyone's knowledge of anything. It's certainly a philosophical thesis, and not a matter of obvious definitional equivalence, either that everything a priori is necessary or that everything necessary is a priori. Both concepts may be vague. That may be another problem. But at any rate they are dealing with two different domains, two different areas, the epistemological and the metaphysical. Consider, say, Fermat's last theorem—or the Goldbach conjecture. The Goldbach conjecture says that an even number greater than 2 must be the sum of two prime numbers. If this is true, it is presumably necessary, and, if it is false, presumably necessarily false. We are taking the classical view of mathematics here and assume that in mathematical reality it is either true or false.

If the Goldbach conjecture is false, then there is an even number, n, greater than 2, such that for no primes p_1 and p_2, both $< n$, does $n = p_1 + p_2$. This fact about n, if true, is verifiable by direct computation, and thus is necessary if the results of arithmetical computations are necessary. On the other hand, if the conjecture is true, then every even number exceeding 2 is the sum of two primes. Could it then be the case that, although in fact every such even number is the sum of two primes, there might have been such an even number which was not the sum of two primes? What would that mean? Such a number would have to be one of 4, 6, 8, 10, . . .; and, by hypothesis, since we are assuming Goldbach's conjecture to be true, each of these can be shown, again by direct computation, to be the sum of two primes. Goldbach's conjecture, then, cannot be contingently true or false; whatever truth-value it has belongs to it by necessity.

But what we can say, of course, is that right now, as far as we know, the question can come out either way. So, in the absence of a mathematical proof deciding this question, none of us has any a priori knowledge about this question in either direction. We don't know whether Goldbach's conjecture is true or false. So right now we certainly don't know anything a priori about it.

Perhaps it will be alleged that we *can* in principle know a priori whether it is true. Well, maybe we can. Of course an infinite mind which can search through all the numbers can or could. But I don't know whether a finite mind can or could. Maybe there just is no mathematical proof whatsoever which decides the conjecture. At any rate this might or might not be the case. Maybe there is a mathematical proof deciding this question; maybe every mathematical question is decidable by an intuitive proof or disproof. Hilbert thought so; others have thought not; still others have thought the question unintelligible unless the notion of intuitive proof is replaced by that of formal proof in a single system. Certainly no one formal system decides all mathematical questions, as we know from Gödel. At any rate, and this is the important thing, the question is not trivial; even though someone said that it's necessary, if true at all, that every even number is the sum of two primes, it doesn't follow that anyone knows anything a priori about it. It doesn't even seem to me to follow without some further philosophical argument (it is an interesting philosophical question) that anyone *could* know anything a priori about it. The 'could', as I said, involves some other modality. We mean that even if no one, perhaps even in the future, knows or will know a priori whether Goldbach's conjecture is right, in principle there is a way, which *could* have been used, of answering the question a priori. This assertion is not trivial.

The terms 'necessary' and 'a priori', then, as applied to statements, are *not* obvious synonyms. There may be a philosophical argument connecting them, perhaps even identifying them; but an argument is required, not simply the observation that the two terms are clearly interchangeable. (I will argue below that in fact they are not even coextensive—that necessary a posteriori truths, and probably contingent a priori truths, both exist.)

I think people have thought that these two things must mean the same for these reasons:

First, if something not only happens to be true in the actual world but is also true in all possible worlds, then, of course, just by running through all the possible worlds in our heads, we ought to be able with enough effort to see, if a statement is necessary, that it is necessary, and thus know it a priori. But really this is not so obviously feasible at all.

Second, I guess it's thought that, conversely, if something is known a priori it must be necessary, because it was known without looking at the world. If it depended on some contingent feature of the actual world, how could you know it without looking? Maybe the actual world is one of the possible worlds in which it would have been false. This depends on the thesis that there can't be a way of knowing about the actual world without looking that wouldn't be a way of knowing the same thing about every possible world. This involves problems of epistemology and the nature of knowledge; and of course it is very vague as stated. But it is not really *trivial* either. More important than any particular example of something which is alleged to be necessary and not a priori or a priori and not necessary, is to see that the notions are different, that it's not trivial to argue on the basis of something's being something which maybe we can only know a posteriori, that it's not a necessary truth. It's not trivial, just because something is known in some sense a priori, that what is known is a necessary truth.

Another term used in philosophy is 'analytic'. Here it won't be too important to get any clearer about this in this talk. The common examples of analytic statements, nowadays, are like 'bachelors are unmarried'. Kant (someone just pointed out to me) gives as an example 'gold is a yellow metal', which seems to me an extraordinary one, because it's something I think that can turn out to be false. At any rate, let's just make it a matter of stipulation that an analytic statement is, in some sense, true by virtue of its meaning and true in all possible worlds by virtue of its meaning. Then something which is analytically true will be both necessary and a priori. (That's sort of stipulative.)

Another category I mentioned was that of certainty. Whatever certainty is, it's clearly not obviously the case that everything which is necessary is certain. Certainty is another epistemological notion. Something can be known, or at least rationally believed, a priori, without being quite certain. You've read a proof in the math book; and, though you think it's correct, maybe you've made a mistake. You often do make mistakes of this kind. You've made a computation, perhaps with an error.

. . . . .

Let's use some terms quasi-technically. Let's call something a *rigid designator* if in every possible world it designates the same object, a *non-rigid* or *accidental designator* if that is not the case. Of course we don't require that the objects exist in all possible worlds. Certainly Nixon might not have existed if his parents had not gotten married, in the normal course of things. When we think of a property as essential to an object we usually mean that it is true of that object in any case where it would have existed. A rigid designator of a necessary existent can be called *strongly rigid*.

One of the intuitive theses I will maintain in these talks is that *names* are rigid designators. Certainly they seem to satisfy the intuitive test: although someone other than the US President in 1970 might have been the US President in 1970 (e.g. Humphrey might have), no one other than Nixon might have been Nixon. In the same way, a designator rigidly designates a certain object if it designates that object wherever the object exists; if, in addition, the object is a necessary existent, the designator can be called *strongly rigid*. For example, 'the President of the US in 1970' designates a certain man, Nixon; but someone else (e.g. Humphrey) might have been the President in 1970, and Nixon might not have; so this designator is not rigid.

In these lectures I will argue, intuitively, that proper names are rigid designators, for although the man (Nixon) might not have been the President, it is not the case that he might not have been Nixon (though he might not have been *called* 'Nixon'). Those who have argued that to make sense of the notion of rigid designator, we must antecedently make sense of 'criteria of transworld identity' have precisely reversed the cart and the horse; it is *because* we can refer (rigidly) to Nixon, and stipulate that we are speaking of what might have happened to *him* (under certain circumstances), that 'transworld identifications' are unproblematic in such cases.[1]

The tendency to demand purely qualitative descriptions of counterfactual situations has many sources. One, perhaps, is the confusion of the epistemological and the metaphysical, between a prioricity and necessity. If someone identifies necessity with a prioricity, and thinks that objects are named by means of uniquely identifying properties, he may think that it is the properties used to identify the object which, being known about it a priori, must be used to identify it in all possible worlds, to find out which object is

[1] Of course I don't imply that language contains a name for every object. Demonstratives can be used as rigid designators, and free variables can be used as rigid designators of unspecified objects. Of course when we specify a counterfactual situation, we do not describe the whole possible world, but only the portion which interests us.

Nixon. As against this, I repeat: (1) Generally, things aren't 'found out' about a counterfactual situation, they are stipulated; (2) possible worlds need not be given purely qualitatively, as if we were looking at them through a telescope. And we will see shortly that the properties an object has in every counterfactual world have nothing to do with properties used to identify it in the actual world.

.   .   .   .   .   .

Above I said that the Frege–Russell view that names are introduced by description could be taken either as a theory of the meaning of names (Frege and Russell seemed to take it this way) or merely as a theory of their reference. Let me give an example, not involving what would usually be called a 'proper name', to illustrate this. Suppose someone stipulates that 100 degrees centigrade is to be the temperature at which water boils at sea level. This isn't completely precise because the pressure may vary at sea level. Of course, historically, a more precise definition was given later. But let's suppose that this were the definition. Another sort of example in the literature is that one metre is to be the length of S where S is a certain stick or bar in Paris. (Usually people who like to talk about these definitions then try to make 'the length of' into an 'operational' concept. But it's not important.)

Wittgenstein says something very puzzling about this. He says: 'There is one thing of which one can say neither that it is one metre long nor that it is not one metre long, and that is the standard metre in Paris. But this is, of course, not to ascribe any extraordinary property to it, but only to mark its peculiar role in the language game of measuring with a metre rule.'[2] This seems to be a very 'extraordinary property', actually, for any stick to have. I think he must be wrong. If the stick is a stick, for example, 39.37 inches long (I assume we have some different standard for inches), why isn't it one metre long? Anyway, let's suppose that he is wrong and that the stick is one metre long. Part of the problem which is bothering Wittgenstein is, of course, that this stick serves as a standard of length and so we can't attribute length to it. Be this as it may (well, it may not be), is the statement 'Stick S is one metre long', a necessary truth? Of course its length might vary in time. We could make the

[2] *Philosophical Investigations*, §50.

definition more precise by stipulating that one metre is to be the length of S at a fixed time t_0. Is it then a necessary truth that stick S is one metre long at time t_0? Someone who thinks that everything one knows a priori is necessary might think: 'This is the *definition* of a metre. By definition, stick S is one metre long at t_0. That's a necessary truth.' But there seems to me to be no reason so to conclude, even for a man who uses the stated definition of 'one metre'. For he's using this definition not to *give the meaning* of what he called the 'metre', but to *fix the reference*. (For such an abstract thing as a unit of length, the notion of reference may be unclear. But let's suppose it's clear enough for the present purposes.) He uses it to fix a reference. There is a certain length which he wants to mark out. He marks it out by an accidental property, namely that there is a stick of that length. Someone else might mark out the same reference by another accidental property. But in any case, even though he uses this to fix the reference of his standard of length, a metre, he can still say, 'if heat had been applied to this stick S at t_0, then at t_0 stick S would not have been one metre long'.

Well, why can he do this? Part of the reason may lie in some people's minds in the philosophy of science, which I don't want to go into here. But a simple answer to the question is this: Even if this is the *only* standard of length that he uses,[3] there is an intuitive difference between the phrase 'one metre' and the phrase 'the length of S at t_0'. The first phrase is meant to designate rigidly a certain length in all possible worlds, which in the actual world happens to be the length of the stick S at t_0. On the other hand 'the length of S at t_0' does not designate anything rigidly. In some counterfactual situations the stick might have been longer and in some shorter, if various stresses and strains had been applied to it. So we can say of this stick, the same way as we would of any other of the same substance and length, that if heat of a given quantity had been applied to it, it would have expanded to such and such a length. Such a counterfactual statement, being true of other sticks with identical physical properties, will also be true of this stick.

---

[3] Philosophers of science may see the key to the problem in a view that 'one metre' is a 'cluster concept'. I am asking the reader hypothetically to suppose that the 'definition' given is the *only* standard used to determine the metric system. I think the problem would still arise.

There is no conflict between that counterfactual statement and the definition of 'one metre' as 'the length of S at t_0', because the 'definition', properly interpreted, does *not* say that the phrase 'one metre' is to be *synonymous* (even when talking about counterfactual situations) with the phrase 'the length of S at t_0', but rather that we have *determined the reference* of the phrase 'one metre' by stipulating that 'one metre' is to be a *rigid* designator of the length which is in fact the length of S at t_0. So this does *not* make it a necessary truth that S is one metre long at t_0. In fact, under certain circumstances, S would not have been one metre long. The reason is that one designator ('one metre') is rigid and the other designator ('the length of S at t_0') is not.

What then, is the *epistemological* status of the statement 'Stick S is one metre long at t_0', for someone who has fixed the metric system by reference to stick S? It would seem that he knows it a priori. For if he used stick S to fix the reference of the term 'one metre', then as a result of this kind of 'definition' (which is not an abbreviative or synonymous definition), he knows automatically, without further investigation, that S is one metre long.[4] On the other hand, even if S is used as the standard of a metre, the *metaphysical* status of 'S is one metre long' will be that of a contingent statement, provided that 'one metre' is regarded as a rigid designator: under appropriate stresses and strains, heatings or coolings, S would have had a length other than one metre even at t_0. (Such statements as 'Water boils at 100 degrees centigrade, at sea level' can have a similar status.) So in this sense, there are contingent a priori truths. More important for present purposes, though, than accepting this example as an instance of the contingent a priori, is its illustration of the distinction between 'definitions' which fix a reference and those which give a synonym.

In the case of names one might make this distinction too. Suppose the reference of a name is given by a description or a cluster of descriptions. If the name *means the same* as that description or cluster of descriptions, it will not be a rigid designator. It will not necessarily designate the same object in all possible worlds, since other objects might have had the given properties in other possible worlds, unless (of course) we happened to use essential properties

---

[4] Since the truth he knows is contingent, I choose *not* to call it 'analytic', stipulatively requiring analytic truths to be both necessary and a priori.

in our description. So suppose we say, 'Aristotle is the greatest man who studied with Plato'. If we used that as a *definition*, the name 'Aristotle' is to mean 'the greatest man who studied with Plato'. Then of course in some other possible world that man might not have studied with Plato and some other man would have been Aristotle. If, on the other hand, we merely use the description to *fix the referent* then that man will be the referent of 'Aristotle' in all possible worlds. The only use of the description will have been to pick out to which man we mean to refer. But then, when we say counterfactually 'suppose Aristotle had never gone into philosophy at all', we need not mean 'suppose a man who studied with Plato, and taught Alexander the Great, and wrote this and that, and so on, had never gone into philosophy at all', which might seem like a contradiction. We need only mean, 'suppose that *that man* had never gone into philosophy at all'.

It seems plausible to suppose that, in some cases, the reference of a name is indeed fixed *via* a description in the same way that the metric system was fixed. When the mythical agent first saw Hesperus, he may well have fixed his reference by saying, 'I shall use "Hesperus" as a name of the heavenly body appearing in yonder position in the sky.' He then fixed the reference of 'Hesperus' by its apparent celestial position. Does it follow that it is part of the *meaning* of the name that Hesperus has such and such position at the time in question? Surely not: if Hesperus had been hit earlier by a comet, it might have been visible at a different position at that time. In such a counterfactual situation we would say that Hesperus would not have occupied that position, but not that Hesperus would not have been Hesperus. The reason is that 'Hesperus' rigidly designates a certain heavenly body and 'the body in yonder position' does not—a different body, or no body might have been in that position, but no other body might have been Hesperus (though another body, not Hesperus, might have been *called* 'Hesperus'). Indeed, as I have said, I will hold that names are always rigid designators.

．　　．　　．　　　．　　　．

I guess the main thing I'll talk about now is identity statements between names. But I hold the following about the general case.

First, that characteristic theoretical identifications like 'Heat is the motion of molecules', are not contingent truths but necessary truths, and here of course I don't mean just physically necessary, but necessary in the highest degree—whatever that means. (Physical necessity *might* turn out to be necessity in the highest degree. But that's a question which I don't wish to prejudge. At least for this sort of example, it might be that when something's physically necessary, it always is necessary *tout court*.) Second, that the way in which these have turned out to be necessary truths does not seem to me to be a way in which the mind–brain identities could turn out to be either necessary or contingently true. So this analogy has to go. It's hard to see what to put in its place. It's hard to see therefore how to avoid concluding that the two are actually different.

Let me go back to the more mundane case about proper names. This is already mysterious enough. There's a dispute about this between Quine and Ruth Barcan Marcus.[5] Marcus says that identities between names are necessary. If someone thinks that Cicero is Tully, and really uses 'Cicero' and 'Tully' as names, he is thereby committed to holding that his belief is a necessary truth. She uses the term 'mere tag'. Quine replies as follows, 'We may tag the planet Venus, some fine evening, with the proper name "Hesperus". We may tag the same planet again, some day before sunrise, with the proper name "Phosphorus". When we discover that we have tagged the same planet twice our discovery is empirical. And not because the proper names were descriptions.'[6] First, as Quine says when we discovered that we tagged the same planet twice, our discovery was empirical. Another example I think Quine gives in another book is that the same mountain seen from Nepal and from Tibet, or something like that, is from one angle called 'Mt. Everest' (you've heard of that); from another it's supposed to be called 'Gaurisanker'. It can actually be an empirical discovery that Gaurisanker is Everest. (Quine says that the example is actually false. He got the example from Erwin Schrödinger. You wouldn't think the inventor of wave mechanics got things that wrong. I don't

---

[5] Ruth Barcan Marcus, 'Modalities and Intensional Languages' (comments by W. V. Quine, plus discussion), *Boston Studies in the Philosophy of Science* (Dordrecht: Reidel, 1963), pp. 77–116.   [6] p. 101.

know where the mistake is supposed to come from. One could certainly imagine this situation as having been the case; and it's another good illustration of the sort of thing that Quine has in mind.)

What about it? I wanted to find a good quote on the other side from Marcus in this book but I am having trouble locating one. Being present at that discussion, I remember[7] that she advocated the view that if you really have names, a good dictionary should be able to tell you whether they have the same reference. So someone should be able, by looking in the dictionary, to say that Hesperus and Phosphorus are the same. Now this does not seem to be true. It does seem, to many people, to be a consequence of the view that identities between names are necessary. Therefore the view that identity statements between names are necessary has usually been rejected. Russell's conclusion was somewhat different. He did think there should never be any empirical question whether two names have the same reference. This isn't satisfied for ordinary names, but it is satisfied when you're naming your own sense datum, or something like that. You say, 'Here, this, and that (designating the same sense datum by both demonstratives).' So you can tell without empirical investigation that you're naming the same thing twice; the conditions are satisfied. Since this won't apply to ordinary cases of naming, ordinary 'names' cannot be genuine names.

What should we think about this? First, it's true that someone can use the name 'Cicero' to refer to Cicero and the name 'Tully' to refer to Cicero also, and not know that Cicero is Tully. So it seems that we do not necessarily know a priori that an identity statement between names is true. It doesn't follow from this that the statement so expressed is a contingent one if true. This is what I've emphasized in my first lecture. There is a very strong feeling that leads one to think that, if you can't know something by a priori ratiocination, then it's got to be contingent: it might have turned out otherwise; but nevertheless I think this feeling is wrong.

Let's suppose we refer to the same heavenly body twice, as 'Hesperus' and 'Phosphorus'. We say: Hesperus is that star over there in the evening; Phosphorus is that star over there in the

[7] p. 115.

morning. Actually, Hesperus is Phosphorus. Are there really circumstances under which Hesperus wouldn't have been Phosphorus? Supposing that Hesperus is Phosphorus, let's try to describe a possible situation in which it would not have been. Well, it's easy. Someone goes by and he calls two *different* stars 'Hesperus' and 'Phosphorus'. It may even be under the same conditions as prevailed when we introduced the names 'Hesperus' and 'Phosphorus'. But are those circumstances in which Hesperus is not Phosphorus or would not have been Phosphorus? It seems to me that they are not.

Now, of course I'm committed to saying that they're not, by saying that such terms as 'Hesperus' and 'Phosphorus', when used as names, are rigid designators. They refer in every possible world to the planet Venus. Therefore, in that possible world too, the planet Venus is the planet Venus and it doesn't matter what any other person has said in this other possible world. How should *we* describe this situation? He can't have pointed to Venus twice, and in the one case called it 'Hesperus' and in the other 'Phosphorus', as we did. If he did so, then 'Hesperus is Phosphorus' would have been true in that situation too. He pointed maybe neither time to the planet Venus—at least one time he didn't point to the planet Venus, let's say when he pointed to the body he called 'Phosphorus'. Then in that case we can certainly say that the name 'Phosphorus' might not have referred to Phosphorus. We can even say that in the very position when viewed in the morning that we found Phosphorus, it might have been the case that Phosphorus was not there—that something else was there, and that even, under certain circumstances it would have been *called* 'Phosphorus'. But that still is not a case in which Phosphorus was not Hesperus. There might be a possible world in which, a possible counterfactual situation in which, 'Hesperus' and 'Phosphorus' weren't names of the things they in fact are names of. Someone, if he did determine their reference by identifying descriptions, might even have used the very identifying descriptions we used. But still that's not a case in which Hesperus wasn't Phosphorus. For there couldn't have been such a case, given that Hesperus is Phosphorus.

Now this seems very strange because in advance, we are inclined to say, the answer to the question whether Hesperus is Phosphorus might have turned out either way. So aren't there really two possible worlds—one in which Hesperus was Phosphorus, the other in which Hesperus wasn't Phosphorus—in advance of our discovering that these were the same? First, there's one sense in which things might turn out either way, in which it's clear that that doesn't imply that the way it finally turns out isn't necessary. For example, the four-colour theorem might turn out to be true and might turn out to be false. It might turn out either way. It still doesn't mean that the way it turns out is not necessary. Obviously, the 'might' here is purely 'epistemic'—it merely expresses our present state of ignorance, or uncertainty.

But it seems that in the Hesperus–Phosphorus case, something even stronger is true. The evidence I have before I know that Hesperus is Phosphorus is that I see a certain star or a certain heavenly body in the evening and call it 'Hesperus', and in the morning and call it 'Phosphorus'. I know these things. There certainly is a possible world in which a man should have seen a certain star at a certain position in the evening and called it 'Hesperus' and a certain star in the morning and called it 'Phosphorus'; and should have concluded—should have found out by empirical investigations—that he names two different stars, or two different heavenly bodies. At least one of these stars or heavenly bodies was not Phosphorus, otherwise it couldn't have come out that way. But that's true. And so it's true that given the evidence that someone has antecedent to his empirical investigation, he can be placed in a sense in exactly the same situation, that is a qualitatively identical epistemic situation, and call two heavenly bodies 'Hesperus' and 'Phosphorus', without their being identical. So in that sense we can say that it might have turned out either way. Not that it might have turned out either way as to Hesperus's being Phosphorus. Though for all we knew in advance, Hesperus wasn't Phosphorus, that couldn't have turned out any other way, in a sense. But being put in a situation where we have exactly the same evidence, qualitatively speaking, it could have turned out that Hesperus was not Phosphorus; that is, in a counterfactual world in which 'Hesperus' and 'Phosphorus' were not used in the way that we use them, as names of this planet, but as names of some other objects, one could have had qualitatively identical evidence and concluded that 'Hesperus' and 'Phosphorus' named two different objects.[8] But we, using the names as we do right now, can say in advance, that if Hesperus and Phosphorus are one and the same, then in no other possible world can they be different. We use 'Hesperus' as the name of a certain body and 'Phosphorus' as the name of a certain body. We use them as names of those bodies in all possible worlds. If, in fact, they are the *same* body, then in any other possible world we have to use them as a name of that object. And so in any other possible world it will be true that Hesperus is Phosphorus. So two things are true: first, that we do not know a priori that Hesperus is Phosphorus, and are in no position to find out the answer except empirically. Second, this is so because we could have evidence qualitatively indistinguishable from the evidence we have and determine the reference of the two names by the positions of two planets in the sky, without the planets being the same.

Of course, it is only a contingent truth (not true in every other possible world) that the star seen over there in the evening is the star seen over there in the morning, because there are possible worlds in which Phosphorus was not visible in the morning. But that contingent truth shouldn't be identified with the statement that Hesperus is Phosphorus. It could only be so identified if you thought that it was a necessary truth that Hesperus is visible over there in the evening or that Phosphorus is visible over there in the morning. But neither of those are necessary truths even if that's the way we pick out the planet. These are the contingent marks by which we identify a certain planet and give it a name.

· · · · ·

We have concluded that an identity statement between names, when true at all, is necessarily true, even though one may not know it a priori. Suppose we identify Hesperus as a certain star seen in the evening and Phosphorus as a certain star, or a certain heavenly body, seen in the morning; then there may be possible worlds in which two different planets would have been seen in just those positions in the evening and morning. However, at least one of

[8] There is a more elaborate discussion of this point in the third lecture, in *Naming and Necessity*, where its relation to a certain sort of counterpart theory is also mentioned.

them, and maybe both, would not have been Hesperus, and then that would not have been a situation in which Hesperus was not Phosphorus. It might have been a situation in which the planet seen in this position in the evening was not the planet seen in this position in the morning; but that is not a situation in which Hesperus was not Phosphorus. It might also, if people gave the names 'Hesperus' and 'Phosphorus' to these planets, be a situation in which some planet other than Hesperus was called 'Hesperus'. But even so, it would not be a situation in which Hesperus itself was not Phosphorus.[9]

Some of the problems which bother people in these situations, as I have said, come from an identification, or as I would put it, a confusion, between what we can know a priori in advance and what is necessary. Certain statements—and the identity statement is a paradigm of such a statement on my view—if true at all must be necessarily true. One does know a priori, by philosophical analysis, that if such an identity statement is true it is necessarily true.

[9] Recall that we describe the situation in our language, not the language that the people in that situation would have used. Hence we must use the terms 'Hesperus' and 'Phosphorus' with the same reference as in the actual world. The fact that people in that situation might or might not have used these names for different planets is irrelevant. So is the fact that they might have done so using the very same descriptions as we did to fix their references.

VIII

KRIPKE ON THE A PRIORI AND THE NECESSARY

ALBERT CASULLO

PHILOSOPHERS have traditionally believed that there is a close connection between the categories of a priori propositions and necessary propositions. One widely held thesis about the nature of this connection is that all a priori knowledge is of necessary propositions and that all necessary propositions are knowable a priori.[1] Saul Kripke has recently argued that this traditional account is mistaken. In 'Identity and Necessity'[2] he argues that there are necessary a posteriori propositions, while in 'Naming and Necessity'[3] he argues, in addition to this, that there are contingent a priori propositions. The primary concern of this paper is to examine Kripke's arguments in order to determine whether he has succeeded in calling the traditional account into question.

I

Kripke's claim that there are necessary a posteriori propositions

Albert Casullo, 'Kripke on the A Priori and the Necessary', from *Analysis*, 37 (1977), 152–59. Copyright 1977 Albert Casullo.

[1] For example, Kant states in the *Critique of Pure Reason*, trans. Norman Kemp Smith (New York: St Martin's Press, 1965), p. 11, that 'Any knowledge that professes to hold a priori lays claim to be regarded as absolutely necessary.' Leibniz claims in *The Monadology* that 'There are also two kinds of *truths*, those of *reasoning* and those of *fact*. Truths of reasoning are necessary and their opposite is impossible, and those of *fact* are contingent and their opposite is possible. When a truth is necessary its reason can be found by analysis, resolving it into more simple ideas and truths until we reach those which are primitive.' See *Leibniz: Selections*, ed. P. P. Wiener (New York: Charles Scribner's Sons, 1951), p. 539.

[2] Saul A. Kripke, 'Identity and Necessity', in *Identity and Individuation*, ed. M. K. Munitz (New York: New York University Press, 1971).

[3] Saul A. Kripke, 'Naming and Necessity', in *Semantics of Natural Language*, eds. D. Davidson and G. Harman (Dordrecht: D. Reidel, 1972).

arises in the context of a discussion of essential properties. He begins with the following consideration:

Supposing this lectern is in fact made of wood, could this very lectern have been made from the very beginning from ice, say frozen from water in the Thames? One has a considerable feeling that it could *not*, though in fact one certainly could have made a lectern of water from the Thames, frozen it into ice by some process, and put it right there in place of this thing. If one had done so, one would have made, of course, a *different* object.[4]

Therefore, in any counterfactual situation in which this lectern existed, it would not have been made from water from the Thames frozen into ice. Kripke goes on to argue that if the essentialist view is correct, then there are necessary propositions knowable only a posteriori. He summarizes his argument in the following manner:

In other words, if *P* is the statement that the lectern is not made of ice, one knows by a priori philosophical analysis, some conditional of the form 'if *P*, then necessarily *P*'. If the table is not made of ice, it is necessarily not made of ice. On the other hand, then, we know by empirical investigation that *P*, the antecedent of the conditional, is true—that this table is not made of ice. We can conclude by *modus ponens*:

$$P \supset \Box P$$
$$P$$
$$\overline{}$$
$$\Box P$$

The conclusion—'$\Box P$'—is that it is necessary that the table not be made of ice, and this conclusion is known a posteriori, since one of the premises on which it is based is a posteriori.[5]

Therefore, since presumably what a certain lectern is made of can be known *only* a posteriori, the essentialist view can be accommodated only if one rejects the thesis that all necessary propositions are knowable a priori.

The claim that if there are essential properties then there are necessary propositions which are knowable only a posteriori is ambiguous, and two different interpretations of it must be distinguished. In order to see this ambiguity, one must distinguish between knowledge of the truth value of a proposition and knowledge of its general modal status. One has *knowledge of the truth*

---

[4] *Identity and Individuation*, p. 152.   [5] Ibid., p. 153.

value of a proposition when one knows whether it is true or false. One has *knowledge of the general modal status* of a proposition when one knows whether it is a necessary proposition or a contingent one. Letting '*Fa*' stand for the proposition '*a* has the property *F*' where *F* is an essential property of *a*, one can now see that the claim that there is only a posteriori knowledge of necessary propositions such as '*Fa*' can be interpreted in either of the following two ways: (1) '*Fa*' is knowable only a posteriori, and '*Fa*' is a necessary proposition, or (2) that '*Fa*' is a necessary proposition is knowable only a posteriori. If there are essential properties, then it would follow that one could have only a posteriori knowledge of the *truth value* of necessary propositions such as '*Fa*'. But, even if there are essential properties, it would not follow that there can be, let alone can only be, a posteriori knowledge of the *general modal status* (or necessity) of propositions such as '*Fa*'.

The claim that even if there are essential properties, it would not follow that there can be only a posteriori knowledge of the *general modal status* of some necessary propositions, might seem to be in conflict with Kripke's conclusion. For he maintains that if there are such properties, then '$\Box P$' is knowable only a posteriori. Therefore, we seem to have a case of a posteriori knowledge of the necessity (or general modal status) of a proposition. This is not so, however. One must distinguish between the general modal status and the specific modal status of a proposition. By the *general modal status* of a proposition I mean its being necessary or its being contingent, regardless of whether it is necessarily true or necessarily false, or contingently true or contingently false. By the *specific modal status* of a proposition I mean its being necessarily true, necessarily false, contingently true, or contingently false. One must also recognize that knowledge of the specific modal status of a proposition consists of knowledge of its general modal status together with knowledge of its truth value. Hence, in cases where one's knowledge of *both* the general modal status of a proposition and its truth value is a priori, knowledge of its specific modal status would also be a priori. But in cases where one's knowledge of the truth value of a proposition is a posteriori, knowledge of its specific modal status would be a posteriori, even if knowledge of its general modal status is a priori.

Kripke's claim that '$\Box P$' is knowable only a posteriori is a claim about knowledge of the specific modal status of a proposition and is based on the fact that where 'P' is a proposition about a physical object possessing a property, its truth value is knowable only a posteriori. But Kripke clearly does not deny that knowledge of the general modal status of propositions about essential properties is a priori. (He says that 'if P is the statement that the lectern is not made of ice, *one knows by a priori philosophical analysis*, some conditional of the form "if P, then necessarily P" '.)[6] Therefore, the existence of essential properties would entail that there are necessary propositions whose truth value and specific modal status are knowable only a posteriori, but it would not entail that there are necessary propositions whose general modal status is knowable only a posteriori.

The question whether Kripke's claims about knowledge of propositions such as 'Fa' conflict with the traditional account of the relationship between a priori and necessary propositions is a difficult one to answer, since its proponents did not distinguish between the truth value, specific modal status, and general modal status of a proposition. We can conclude that if there are essential properties like those suggested by Kripke, then it would be incorrect to maintain that the truth value of all necessary propositions can be known a priori. From this it follows that it would also be incorrect to maintain that the *specific* modal status of all necessary propositions can be known a priori. But the existence of such properties would not call into question the claim that the *general* modal status of all necessary propositions can be known a priori.

II

In 'Naming and Necessity' Kripke attempts to strengthen his claim that the traditional account of the relationship between a priori and necessary propositions is mistaken by providing an example of a proposition which is contingent but knowable a priori. His discussion begins with a consideration of Wittgenstein's comments about the standard metre. Wittgenstein claimed, 'There is *one* thing of which one can say neither that it is one metre long, nor that it is not

---

[6] Ibid. The emphasis is mine.

one metre long, and that is the standard metre in Paris.'[7] Kripke disagrees: 'If the stick is a stick, for example, 39.37 inches long (I assume we have some different standard for inches), why isn't it one metre long?'[8] He then goes on to raise the question whether the proposition that the standard metre is one metre long at time t_0 is a necessary truth. He argues that the proposition is not necessary even if one grants that by definition the standard metre is one metre long at time t_0 because

the 'definition', properly interpreted, does *not* say that the phrase 'one metre' is to be *synonymous* (even when talking about counterfactual situations) with the phrase 'the length of S at t_0' but rather we have *determined the reference* of the phrase 'one metre' by stipulating that 'one metre' is to be a *rigid* designator of the length which is in fact the length of S at t_0. So this does *not* make it a necessary truth that S is one metre long at t_0.[9]

Kripke goes on to claim that for a person who fixes the metric system by reference to stick S at t_0, the proposition 'Stick S is one metre long at t_0' is known a priori:

For if he used stick S to fix the reference of the term 'one metre', then as a result of this kind of 'definition' (which is not an abbreviative or synonymous definition), he knows automatically, without further investigation, that S is one metre long.[10]

Therefore, the proposition that stick S is one metre long at t_0 is both contingent and knowable a priori.

In order to evaluate this argument we must distinguish the following two sentences: (1) S is one metre long at t_0; (2) The length of S at t_0 is one metre. A further distinction must also be made between two possible interpretations of the second sentence. We may follow Donnellan by pointing out that the definite description 'the length of S at t_0' can be used either attributively or referentially.[11] (I shall not attempt to defend the distinction here.) When a

[7] Ludwig Wittgenstein, *Philosophical Investigations*, trans. G. E. M. Anscombe (Oxford: Basil Blackwell, 1968), p. 25.

[8] *Semantics of Natural Language*, p. 274. [Also this volume, selection VII, p. 151.]

[9] Ibid., p. 275. [Also this vol., p. 153.]

[10] Ibid.

[11] See Keith S. Donnellan, 'Reference and Definite Descriptions', *The Philosophical Review*, 75 (1966): 281–304. On page 25 he states, 'A person who uses a definite description attributively in an assertion states something about whoever or

speaker uses the sentence, 'The length of S at t_0 is one metre', to introduce the term 'one metre', he might be making either of the two following claims: (*a*) he wishes to introduce 'one metre' as the name of the length of S at t_0 *whatever* that length might be; (*b*) there is a particular length which he has in mind and which he can identify independently of the truth of the proposition that it is the length of S at t_0, and it is *this* length which he wishes to call 'one metre'. Depending on how the definite description is used to introduce the term 'one metre', what is asserted by (2) and, consequently, also what is asserted by (1) will change.

If one uses the definite description attributively in introducing 'one metre' by means of sentence (2), then one is using 'one metre' as the name of the length of S at t_0 whatever it may be. The term is not being introduced as the name of a particular length which the speaker has singled out but as the name of whatever length happens to satisfy the definite description. This method of introducing the term results in what Kripke calls an 'abbreviative definition', for the speaker is using the term 'one metre' as an abbreviation for the phrase 'the length of S at t_0'. As a result of this definition, the proposition expressed by the sentence 'The length of S at t_0 is one metre' is a necessary one, true solely in virtue of the terms used in expressing it. Since it is true solely in virtue of the meanings of its terms, it is also knowable a priori. If the term 'one metre' is introduced in this manner, the proposition expressed by the sentence 'S is one metre long' is also a necessary one. Since 'one metre' is an abbreviation for 'the length of S at t_0', the proposition expressed by the sentence 'S is one metre long' is identical to the one expressed by the sentence 'S has at t_0 whatever length it does have at t_0' which is trivially true. Hence, if the term 'one metre' is introduced by means of a sentence which uses the definite description attributively, both propositions—that expressed by the sentence 'The length of S at t_0 is one metre' and that expressed by the sentence 'S is one metre long at t_0—are necessary and a priori.

The situation is not the same, however, if one uses the definite

whatever is the so-and-so. A speaker who uses a definite description referentially in an assertion, on the other hand, uses the description to enable his audience to pick out whom or what he is talking about and states something about that person or thing'.

description referentially in introducing the term 'one metre' by means of sentence (2), for the speaker is not introducing 'one metre' as the name of whatever length happens to satisfy the definite description 'the length of S at t_0'. Instead, he is introducing it as the name of a *particular* length to which he tries to call attention by using the definite description. He uses this particular definite description because he believes that S in fact has the length he wishes to name. But if it should happen that due to some peculiar environmental conditions S does not have the length he thought it had, then the speaker would have introduced 'one metre' as the name of the length which he thought S had, rather than the one which it in fact had. Therefore, the term 'one metre' is not being used as a synonym for 'the length of S at t_0' but as the name of a particular length, whether or not it is in fact the length of S at t_0.

Since this point might not be clear in the case of lengths, let us consider the case of colours. Suppose someone were to introduce the term 'red' using the definite description 'the colour of S at t_0' referentially. Also, suppose that he is using the definite description to refer to the colour red; but, because of some peculiar lighting conditions unknown to the speaker and everyone else in the immediate vicinity of S, although S appears red, it is in fact white. Since the speaker was using the definite description to draw attention to a particular colour, and it was that particular colour he wished to name 'red', he would have introduced 'red' as the name of the colour red despite the fact that the colour satisfying the definite description 'the colour of S at t_0' was white. In such a case, a necessary proposition does result in virtue of the definition of 'red'. This necessary proposition, however, is not satisfactorily expressed by the sentence 'the colour of S at t_0 is red'. It is more accurately captured by the sentence, '*This* colour is red', where 'this colour' refers to the colour the speaker singled out using the definite description. This proposition is also knowable a priori, since it can be known solely on the basis of the definition of 'red'.

Returning to our original example, introducing 'one metre' as the name of a particular length to which one calls attention with the definite description 'the length of S at t_0' also yields a necessary proposition, which can be best expressed by the sentence '*This* length is one metre', where 'this length' refers to the length to which

the speaker was calling attention. This proposition is also knowable
a priori. But this is not true of the proposition expressed by the
sentence 'S is one metre long'. Since 'one metre' has been introduced as the name of a particular length, the proposition expressed
by the sentence 'S is one metre long' is no longer identical to the one
expressed by the sentence 'S has whatever length it does have'.
Instead, what it asserts is more accurately expressed by the compound sentence 'S has this length (rather than another), and this
length is one metre'. As was stated above, the second conjunct is
both necessary and knowable a priori. But this is not true of the first
conjunct. For, as Kripke correctly points out, it is a contingent fact
about S that it has any particular length; had the environmental
conditions been different at t_0, S would have had a different length
at t_0. We must notice, however, that this conjunct is also knowable
only a posteriori. For although one knows a priori that the length
one singled out with the definite description 'the length of S at t_0' is
one metre, one does not know a priori that S *in fact* has that length.
One can know this only on the basis of a posteriori considerations,
such as the manner in which the object appears and the conditions
under which it appears in that way. Therefore, the sentence 'S is one
metre long at t_0' expresses a contingent and a posteriori proposition
when 'one metre' is introduced by means of a sentence which uses
the definite description 'the length of S at t_0' referentially.

Let us consider again our example of the speaker who introduces
the term 'red' using the definite description 'the colour of S at t_0'
referentially. Although he knows a priori that *this* colour is red, he
does not know a priori that S is red, for he does not know a priori
that S has the colour he named 'red'. If he were to infer that S was
red on the basis of the manner in which he introduced the term
'red', not only would he be unjustified, but he would also be
mistaken in this case, since, by hypothesis, S is in fact white at t_0. He
would be justified in believing that S is red at t_0 only if he knew that S
appears red and that only red objects appear red under the conditions in which S appears red. But both of these facts can be known
only a posteriori. Therefore, his knowledge that S is red is a
posteriori. It is based on his knowledge that S has this particular
colour (rather than another), which is a posteriori, and his knowledge that this colour is red, which is a priori.

It might be argued that there is a third way of introducing the term 'one metre' which has not been considered.[12] When a speaker uses the definite description 'the length of S at t_0' attributively in introducing 'one metre', there are two possibilities: (1) the speaker might be using the definite description to give the meaning of the term, in which case 'one metre' is an abbreviation for 'the length of S at t_0'; or (2) the speaker might be using the definite description to fix the reference of the term, in which case 'one metre' is the name (or rigid designator) of whatever length S happens to have at t_0. Although we have considered the first case, we have neglected the second. The primary reason for neglecting this case is that it does not constitute a genuine possibility. Since, by hypothesis, the description is not used referentially, how can one generate a genuine name from it? How can one, relying solely on the description, provide the term with reference? The appeal to the vague and unexplained notion of 'fixing reference' does not by itself provide answers to these questions. If the term is to be a genuine name, rather than merely an abbreviation of the description, there must be criteria for its use which are not simply the criteria for the use of the description. It must be possible, at least in principle, for someone to determine whether the term is used correctly on future occasions without relying on the description. (This, of course, would be possible if the description had been used referentially.) If this is not possible, then it is no longer clear in what sense the term is *not* a mere abbreviation of the description and the distinction between the term's being a name and its being such an abbreviation appears to be of little consequence. Therefore, at the very least, Kripke owes us much further explanation.

The failure to provide a convincing example of a contingent a priori proposition removes the basis of Kripke's second argument against the traditional account of the relationship between the a priori and the necessary. He has not given us any reason to suppose that the traditional philosophers were mistaken in claiming that all a priori knowledge is of necessary propositions.[13]

---

[12] This point is due to the editor of *Analysis*.

[13] I am indebted to Professor Panayot Butchvarov for a number of illuminating discussions on several aspects of this paper.

IX

ANALYTICITY, NECESSITY, AND APRIORITY[1]

R. G. SWINBURNE

THIS paper seeks to investigate the extent of overlap between the analytic, the necessary, and the a priori.

'Analytic' is a philosopher's term, and different philosophers have given different definitions of it. For Kant, who introduced the term, an 'analytic judgement' is one in which 'the predicate B belongs to the subject A, as something which is (covertly) contained in this concept A'.[2] The judgement adds 'nothing through the predicate to the concept of the subject, but merely (breaks) it up into these constituent concepts that have all along been thought in it, although confusedly'. A synthetic judgement, in contrast, was one in which 'B lies outside the concept A'. Kant's classification of judgements, or, as we should say, statements or propositions, was only meant to apply to 'judgements in which a relation of a subject to the predicate is thought'. For this reason later philosophers have considered Kant's definition too narrow.[3] They have felt intuitively that the kind of distinction which Kant made had application not merely within the class of subject–predicate propositions but within the wider class of all propositions. They therefore sought to define such a distinction. A large number of definitions have been provided, but I would claim that basically they fall into three

R. G. Swinburne, 'Analyticity, Necessity, and Apriority', from *Mind* 84 (1975), 225–43. Reprinted by permission of Oxford University Press.

[1] I am grateful to colleagues at Keele for their helpful criticisms of an earlier version of this paper.

[2] I. Kant, *Critique of Pure Reason*, A6–7, B10 (translated by N. Kemp Smith, London, 1929).

[3] There are difficulties too in Kant's talk of one concept 'containing' another. See F. Waismann, 'Analytic–Synthetic', republished (from *Analysis*) in his *How I See Philosophy* (London, 1968), pp. 122–207. See pp. 122 ff.

groups.[4] Of these, I argue, definitions of the first type seem inherently unsatisfactory; definitions of the second and third types can both be made satisfactory, and when tidied up, some definitions of the two types prove to be equivalent.

A definition of the first type defines an analytic proposition by reference to the notions of logical truth and synonymy. For example, Quine considers the suggestion that an analytic proposition is one which 'can be turned into a logical truth by putting synonyms for synonyms', a logical truth being 'a statement which is true and remains true under all reinterpretations of its components other than the logical particles'.[5] Against this, there stands, first, Quine's objection that no satisfactory definition of synonymity has ever been given. I do not find this a compelling objection. Two expressions are 'synonymous' if and only if they 'mean the same', a phrase common enough in non-philosophical talk. So long as we can say often enough whether or not two expressions mean the same, a failure to provide a definition in other terms would not seem a drawback. It seems to me that we can often enough say just this. Synonymity may be context-relative; if it is, then the definition should permit only substitution of expressions synonymous in the context in question.[6]

There are, however, two substantial connected difficulties with a definition of this type. The first concerns the notion of logical truth. This is defined by reference to 'logical particles', and these are

---

[4] In 'The Analytic–Synthetic Controversy' (*Australasian Journal of Philosophy*, 50 (1972), 107–23) D. A. T. Gasking distinguishes (p. 108) 'nine traditional definitions of analyticity'. Of these the ninth is of my first type, the first two are of my second type, and the others of my third type. In 'The A Priori and the Analytic' (*Proceedings of the Aristotelian Society*, 64 (1963–4), 31–54) Anthony Quinton distinguishes (pp. 32 ff.) four main interpretations of 'analytic'. His second interpretation is Kant's, his fourth is of my first type, and his first and third are of my second type.

[5] W. V. O. Quine, 'Two Dogmas of Empiricism' in his *From a Logical Point of View*, 2nd edn., (New York, 1963), p. 22 f. A definition of this type is suggested by Frege. See G. Frege, *The Foundations of Arithmetic*, trans. J. L. Austin (Oxford, 1953), p. 4.

[6] As Waismann pointed out (op. cit., pp. 133 ff.) you need to substitute not merely synonymous words but synonymous sentences in order to reduce many propositions to truths of logic. Even if 'planet' is synonymous with 'body which moves round the sun', 'planets move round the sun' can only be reduced to a truth of logic if we can substitute for it the synonymous sentence 'everything which is a planet is a body which moves round the sun'.

either enumerated, or defined (roughly) as words which have application in any context, i.e. 'topic-neutral' words. If they are enumerated, the resulting definition of the analytic seems intolerably *ad hoc*—why to be analytic does a proposition have to be reduced to one in which just *those* particles alone are invariant? But the definition of 'logical particle' is incredibly woolly. No word at all has application in literally *any* context—'if' only has application if we are talking about possibilities, and 'all' only if we are talking about all the members of some class. And if 'if' and 'all' are classified as logical particles, why not 'when', 'after', 'on top of', 'material body', 'thought', 'feeling' . . . where do you stop? Quinton has attempted to meet this difficulty by explaining topic-neutrality in terms of implicit definability. He defines 'a logical term as one whose meaning is wholly specified by implicit definitions'.[7] To understand 'later than', or 'on top of', he would claim, ostensive definition of some sort is necessary; hence, these expressions are not purely logical terms. 'Not', 'and', 'if', and perhaps 'more ϕ than'[8] are, however, introduceable by mere implicit definition. Unfortunately, however, Quinton gives no definition of 'implicit definition'. However, a natural definition (which, I suggest, brings out what Robinson wants to say about it in his book on definition[9]) is the following. An implicit definition of a term 'ϕ' is a process which conveys the meaning of 'ϕ' by producing sentences (? sentences expressing analytic propositions) in which 'ϕ' is correctly used. (If we write 'sentences expressing analytic propositions' instead of 'sentences' the definition of course becomes viciously circular.) But on this very natural definition of 'implicit definition', surely any word whatever can have its 'meaning wholly specified by

---

[7] Op. cit., p. 49.

[8] Quinton's attempt (p. 50) to show that 'more ϕ than' is a logical term runs into a difficulty. He admits that 'the principles of asymmetry and transitivity do not wholly fix the sense of "more ϕ than" since they remain necessarily true if "less ϕ than" is substituted and "more" and "less" do not mean the same'. He then goes on to claim that 'however this objection is to be dealt with it does not show "more ϕ than" to be a non-logical term. For the difference between "more" and "less" must be as topic-neutral as they are.' But that will not do at all. For Quinton has expounded topic-neutrality in terms of implicit definability, and unless further principles of implicit definition beyond the principles of asymmetry and transitivity can be found which distinguish between 'more' and 'less', then 'more ϕ than' is not a logical term on Quinton's account of logical terms.

[9] R. Robinson, *Definition* (Oxford, 1950), pp. 106 ff.

implicit definition'. Given a rich enough vocabulary, you can convey the meaning of 'red' or 'constant' or 'leather', etc., etc., by producing sentences which use those words correctly. And if your vocabulary is too poor, not even 'not', 'and', and 'if' can have their meaning conveyed in this way. I conclude that Quinton's attempt to distinguish logical truths in terms of logical particles is a failure.

Besides this objection, there is a further objection to the proposed definition of an 'analytic proposition'. This is that, although this is a wider definition than Kant's, there are many propositions which, many would feel intuitively, are true for much the same reasons as propositions classified by this definition as analytic, and which yet do not on it fall into the analytic category—typically, for example, 'nothing is red and green all over'.[10]

A definition of the second type defines an analytic proposition by reference to its deriving its truth solely from the meanings of words (or semantic rules). Some definitions of this type have been expressed very unhappily in the past. Thus Ayer: 'a proposition is analytic when its validity depends solely on the definitions of the symbols it contains.'[11] Since arguments rather than propositions are normally said to be valid, let us substitute 'truth' for 'validity' in the definition. The more substantial difficulty is that it is not clear which symbols a proposition contains since sentences containing different symbols may express the same proposition. So let us try the following amendment: 'a proposition is analytic if and only if any sentence which expresses it expresses a true proposition and does so solely because the words in the sentence mean what they do'. The fact that the words mean what they do, that is, is by itself sufficient to make the statement true—how rocks are arranged on Mars or the Romans behaved in Gaul, etc., etc., does not affect the truth value. This seems to me a perfectly satisfactory definition. A Quinean might say that we need a satisfactory definition of 'meaning' before we can use this definition, but that is false. The notion of words having this or that meaning has a natural home in non-philosophical

---

[10] Quinton seems to suggest (op. cit., p. 51) that 'nothing can be red and green all over' is reducible to 'nothing can be a member of two species of a genus' which is a truth which implicitly defines its terms. But even if the latter suggestion were in some sense true (and it seems to me highly implausible) it seems clear that no mere substitution of synonymous expressions will effect the 'reduction'.

[11] A. J. Ayer, *Language, Truth and Logic*, 2nd edn., (London, 1946), p. 78.

talk and needs no elucidation from the philosopher in order to enable us to recognize cases of sentences which express true propositions solely because the words in them mean what they do. Recognizing such cases is, I suggest, something which we can often do.

A definition of the third type defines an analytic proposition in terms of the self-contradictoriness or incoherence of its negation. One such definition is that an analytic proposition is one whose 'negation is self-contradictory'. If it is meant by this that the negation has to be explicitly of the form 'p and not-p', then this definition is obviously far too narrow—even 'all bachelors are unmarried' fails to come out as analytic. But if the self-contradictoriness of the negation needs only be implicit we need to be told how it is to be recognized. This point suggests the following amended definition: 'a proposition is analytic if and only if its negation entails an explicitly self-contradictory proposition' (i.e. a proposition which says that something is the case and that it is not the case, that is a statement of the form 'p and not-p' such as 'it is blue and it is not blue').[12] By this test 'all bachelors are unmarried' comes out as analytic. Assuming the existential commitment of 'all' the entailment can be demonstrated as follows. 'It is not the case that all bachelors are unmarried', entails 'some unmarried men are not unmarried' which entails that there are certain persons, call them xs such that 'xs are unmarried and it is not the case that xs are unmarried'. (If the existential commitment of 'all' is not assumed, a different deduction will make the point.) To apply this definition you need to have explained to you the meaning of 'entails' and 'negation' as well as the meaning of 'self-contradictory proposition'. I have already explained the meaning of 'self-contradictory proposition'. The task is easy enough for the other two terms. The negation of a proposition is a proposition which says that things are not as the former proposition says. A proposition p entails a proposition q if and only if p is not consistent with the negation of q, i.e. the claim that q is buried within the claim that p. This can be

---

[12] This account of analytic propositions has its origin in the account which Leibniz gives of truths of reason. These are those propositions which, by analysis, can be resolved into 'identical propositions, whose opposite contains an express contradiction', *Monadology*, pp. 33–5 (Leibniz's *Philosophical Writings*, trans. Mary Morris, London, 1934).

spelt by many obvious examples which should make clear the senses of 'consistent' and 'buried' involved. There is every reason to suppose that in consequence of this learning process men will agree in the vast majority of cases, though no doubt not in all, as to when a statement is analytic on the definition being discussed.

An alternative definition in the same tradition is: 'a proposition is analytic if and only if its negation is not coherent'. I understand by a coherent proposition one which it makes sense to suppose is true; one such that we can conceive of, that is imagine or suppose, it and any other proposition which is entailed by the original proposition, being true. The latter clause is important for bringing out the sense of coherence involved. We want to say that it is analytic that $\sqrt{4} = 2$. But it is conceivable that $\sqrt{4} = 2$ and also conceivable that $\sqrt{4} \neq 2$. For what can be believed is conceivable and schoolboys sometimes believe that $\sqrt{4} = 2$ and sometimes believe that $\sqrt{4} \neq 2$. But $\sqrt{4} \neq 2$ entails that $2 \times 2 \neq 4$ and so that $2 + 2 \neq 4$ and so that $1 + 1 + 1 + 1 \neq 4$ and so that $3 + 1 \neq 4$—which is not conceivable. A man could not suppose that '$3 + 1 \neq 4$' expressed a true proposition if he understood by the terms used what we understand by them, e.g. understood by '4' the number next after 3, and so he cannot conceive of the proposition which we express by '$3 + 1 \neq 4$' being true. (Of course in order to derive from '$\sqrt{4} \neq 2$' what is entailed by it, we need to know the language of mathematics, the rules for operating with mathematical symbols— and schoolboys often do not know those very well.)

I believe that the two definitions of the third type given above are equivalent, in the sense that any proposition which satisfies the one will satisfy the other. Clearly if a proposition p entails a self-contradictory proposition then p is incoherent for it has buried in it a claim that something is so and that it is not so—and it is not conceivable that things should be thus. The converse needs a longer proof. There are a limited number of propositional forms which logicians have codified. A proposition will state that an object has a certain property or that a certain relation holds between two certain objects, or that there exists an object with such-and-such properties. Now take a proposition of one of these forms, for example a proposition ascribing a property to an object. Such a proposition will have the form 'ϕ is ψ'. If such a proposition is incoherent, then being ϕ must be being an object of a certain sort being which is incompatible with having the property of being ψ. For if there were no incompatibility between being the sort of thing which is ϕ, and the sort of thing which can be ψ, how could there be any incoherence in a thing being both? So there is an incompatibility between being ϕ and being ψ, and so there will be buried within 'ϕ is ψ' a contradiction which can be brought to the surface by deriving from it what is entailed by the proposition. Examples bear out this point. Take a typically incoherent proposition of the above form, e.g. 'Honesty weighs 10 pounds'. 'a is honesty' entails 'a is not a physical object'. (Physical objects and honesty, one may say loosely, are different kinds of thing.) 'a has weight' entails 'a is a physical object'. (Only a physical object, something with spatial location, is the kind of thing that can have weight.) Hence 'honesty weighs ten pounds' entails 'there is something which both is and is not a physical object', that is a self-contradictory proposition. This type of argument can clearly be generalized for propositions of other forms to show generally that if a proposition is incoherent it entails a self-contradictory proposition. Hence the two definitions of the third type are equivalent.

I now proceed to argue further that the two definitions of the third type are equivalent to the definition which I proposed of the second type. I will take the definition in terms of coherence in order to show this. On this definition a proposition p is analytic if and only if its negation is incoherent. Now whether a proposition is coherent or incoherent is solely a matter of what it says—the fact that it says what it does, is alone sufficient to make it coherent, or incoherent, as the case may be. So the fact that the negation of an analytic proposition p says what it does, that not-p, is alone sufficient to make it false. That being so, the fact that p says what it does is alone sufficient to make it true. That a sentence expresses the proposition it does is a consequence solely of what the words in the sentence mean. If p is true just because of what it says, then any sentence which expresses it will express a true proposition solely because the words in the sentence mean what they do. Hence if a proposition is analytic on the definition of the third type, it will be analytic on the definition of the second type. Conversely, if a proposition is analytic on the later definition, any sentence which expresses p will express a true proposition and do so solely because the words in it mean what they do. In that case the fact that p is true is a consequence merely of what it says. Hence that the negation of p, that is not-p, is false, is also a consequence merely of what it says. So the assertion of the negation will be in words which have such a meaning that the falsity of the negation lies buried in them. Hence the assertion of the negation contains its own falsity buried within it and so is incoherent. Hence any proposition analytic on the definition of the second type will be analytic on the definition of the third type also.

I conclude that there is at least one useful definition of 'analytic' of the second type and two of the third, and that these are equivalent. I suspect that any usable definition of 'analytic' which was not evidently too narrow, and which was moderately faithful to the original intuition behind the delimitation of the class, would prove to be equivalent to the definitions which I have favoured. I shall henceforward operate with these definitions. A synthetic proposition is then naturally defined as any proposition other than an analytic proposition or the negation of an analytic proposition. I emphasize again that in order to apply these definitions we have to understand the terms which occur in them. I claim that these terms are either terms which have a perfectly regular use in non-philosophical discourse or terms which can be defined by terms of the former type, at any rate with the help of examples.

What next of necessity? In ordinary talk whether a proposition is rightly termed 'necessary' depends very much on the context. We may naturally and truly say 'In order to get from London to Paris in less than four hours it is necessary to go by air' or 'to obtain social security benefits it is necessary to fill in a form'. The necessity is relative to a set of assumptions which form the context of utterance. In the first case these are that the only ways of getting to Paris are the normal commercial alternatives (air, or combinations of boat/hovercraft with rail/bus). In the second case these are that social security benefits are allocated in accordance with law and administrative directive. The same considerations apply to the use of cognate terms such as 'must', 'got to', 'have to', 'cannot but', etc. Such propositions as 'I have to go to London next week' or 'he must have called while I was out' may be true—yet the truth of such propositions derives in part from the contextual assumptions which are naturally made. Now of many things which we would ordinarily wish to say are necessary, philosophers who use 'necessary' in their technical discussions would wish to deny the necessity. It therefore becomes them to state what are the assumptions against the background of which they are asserting necessity or the sense in which they are using the term 'necessary'. Unlike 'analytic' and 'a priori', 'necessary' is not a term coined by philosophers. If philosophers give it a special use they have to say what it is.

Kant gives us no help. He uses the term 'necessary' without explanation. Philosophers often say that their interest in necessity is in logical necessity and they then define 'logically necessary' either as equivalent in meaning to 'analytic' or in such a way that the logically necessary becomes a proper subclass of the analytic. We saw earlier that Quine suggested a definition of the latter kind, according to which a proposition was 'logically true'—which I take as equivalent to 'logically necessary'—if and only if it is true and remains true under all reinterpretations of the components other than logical particles. Propositions such as 'if it is raining, it is raining' and 'either it is raining or it is not raining' are often supposed to come out as logically necessary under this definition, while propositions such as 'all bachelors are unmarried', although analytic, are not logically necessary under this definition. You need to substitute synonymous expressions in order to turn the latter into a logical truth. We saw earlier the unsatisfactoriness of a definition of a logical truth of the type which Quine considers. I know of no other type of definition according to which the logically necessary comes out as a proper subclass of the analytic. The alternative which is taken by many philosophers is to use 'logically necessary' as a synonym for 'analytic'. Some philosophers go further and state or take for granted the equivalence of analyticity with necessity *simpliciter*, which gives us a first usable defining criterion of 'necessary proposition':

(A) A proposition is necessary if and only if it is analytic.

Such an account however reduces to triviality a philosopher's claim that the only necessity which there is is that of analytic propositions. It seems to beg the interesting questions. A number of writers of recent and not so recent years have suggested as examples of necessary propositions propositions which are almost certainly not analytic. Their suggestions that the propositions which they cite are necessary seem to have a certain plausibility. I shall attempt to delineate alternative defining criteria for 'necessary propositions', which yield alternative ways of understanding necessity, according to one or more of which the propositions which the various writers cite could be classed as necessary.

My second defining criterion for a 'necessary proposition' is the following:

> (B) A proposition is necessary if and only if it is incoherent to suppose that the individuals in fact picked out by the referring expressions in the sentence which expresses it do not have the properties and/or relations claimed by the proposition.

I understand by a referring expression either any proper name, or a definite description which picks out the individual or individuals which the proposition is 'about'. In either case the proposition will presuppose rather than state the existence of the individuals referred to. Propositions are often 'about' individuals, attributing to them properties or actions. 'The President will be away next week' is about the President, and 'his boss is very irritable' is about the boss. It is of course sometimes unclear which constituents of sentences pick out the individuals which they are about. Is 'among those who called last week was the representative from the trade union' about the representative or not? Sometimes only the context can reveal, and sometimes not even that can reveal. But the undoubted fact that it is sometimes not clear which, if any, expressions are referring expressions does not call into question the equally undoubted fact that it is often clear enough which expressions are referring expressions.

As an example of a proposition necessary on criterion (B) but not on criterion (A) we may take:

> (1) The number which is the number of the planets is greater than six.

The negation of (1) is the proposition that states that the number which is the number of the planets is not greater than six. This seems to be a coherent proposition, given the understanding of coherence outlined earlier. Yet the referring expression 'the number which is the number of the planets' in fact picks out the number nine and it is not coherent to suppose that nine is no greater than six. So (1), though not analytic, seems necessary on criterion (B). The converse situation is illustrated by:

(2) The author of Hamlet wrote Hamlet.

The negation of (2) is the proposition which states that the author of Hamlet did not write Hamlet and that is incoherent. On the other hand, it is clearly coherent to suppose that the person in fact picked out by 'the author of Hamlet', i.e. Shakespeare, in fact did not write Hamlet. Although it is necessary that whoever wrote Hamlet wrote Hamlet, it is by no means necessary that the man who actually did should have done so. So (2), although analytic, is not necessary on criterion (B). It is easy to construct other examples of the same pattern as (2). Although 'the Prime Minister is Prime Minister' cannot but be true, the Prime Minister might never have become Prime Minister—he might have become a professional musician instead.

It is Kripke[13] more than anyone else[14] who in the last year or two has drawn our attention to the complexity of examples such as (1) and (2)—although his concern has been somewhat more with the possibility of propositions being necessary without being a priori (and conversely) than with the possibility of propositions being necessary without being analytic (and conversely). But Kripke does not in his discussion provide precise definitions of the terms involved—'necessary', 'analytic', and 'a priori'.[15] I have attempted to provide a criterion of necessity—criterion (B)—which will, I suggest, classify as necessary many of those propositions which Kripke wishes to call necessary. Apart from (1) above, (3), (4), and (5) below are examples of propositions of different kinds which, Kripke suggests, we might wish to classify as necessary.

[13] See his 'Identity and Necessity' in *Identity and Individuation*, ed. M. K. Munitz, New York, 1971, and 'Naming and Necessity' in *Semantics of Natural Language*, ed. D. Davidson and G. Harman, Dordrecht, 1972.

[14] But see also A. Plantinga, 'World and Essence', *Philosophical Review*, 79 (1970), 461–92; and Baruch A. Brody, 'Why Settle For Anything Less Than Good Old-Fashioned Aristotelian Essentialism?', *Noûs*, 7 (1973), 351–65, for work along similar lines to Kripke's.

[15] See the discussion on pp. 260–4 of 'Naming and Necessity'. [See also selection VII above.]

(3) Nixon is a person.[16]

(4) The lectern in front of Kripke was not from the very beginning of its existence made of ice.[17]

(5) Tully is Cicero.[18]

On the assumption that (3), (4), and (5) are true, Kripke wishes to claim that they are necessary. (3) is necessary, Kripke suggests, because nothing would be Nixon unless that thing were a person. Nixon only exists as long as he is a person. (4) is necessary because a lectern would not be *that* lectern if it had always been made of ice. (5) is necessary because 'Tully' and 'Cicero' in fact pick out the same person and that person must be identical with himself.

If we adopt criterion (B) of necessity, it seems highly plausible to suppose that at any rate (4) and (5) are necessary propositions. (5) is necessary because it is not coherent to suppose that the individual picked out by both 'Cicero' and 'Tully' is not self-identical. As regards the lectern in front of Kripke we can imagine different things having happened to it from the things that actually happened; but this is imagining things happening to the lectern which was in fact continuous with the lectern in front of Kripke. So one can imagine that lectern having been turned into ice at some earlier time. But it is not coherent to suppose that *that* lectern has always been made of ice, for given that that lectern never has been made of ice, that would not be a supposition about the lectern in fact continuous with Kripke's lectern. (3) is a more dubious case—could not Nixon turn into a chimpanzee and remain Nixon?—but if we do regard it as necessary, it is surely because we do not find it coherent to suppose that the individual who is Nixon be anything other than a person.

Necessity of type (B) seems to be the necessity to which Kripke is drawing our attention. If that is so there is no need to read anything too deeply metaphysical into Kripke's necessity. Like necessity of type (A), necessity of type (B) arises because there are limits to what can be coherently thought. If a referring expression is to pick out an individual, there have to be criteria which distinguish that individual from others. Hence it will not be coherent to imagine that

[16] 'Naming and Necessity', pp. 268 ff.
[17] 'Identity and Necessity', p. 152. [See also selection VIII above.]
[18] 'Identity and Necessity', pp. 156 ff.

individual not satisfying those criteria. It is from that incoherence that type (B) necessity arises.

A further sense of 'necessary' is suggested by the writings of some recent writers on the philosophy of religion. They have interpreted the claim that God is a necessary being as the claim that he is not dependent for his existence on anything else.[19] This suggests the following defining criterion of a necessary proposition:

> (C)   A proposition *p* is necessary if and only if it is true, but its being true is not (was not, or will not be) brought about by anything the description of which neither entails nor is entailed by *p*.

By (C) of course all analytic propositions such as 'all bachelors are unmarried' come out again as necessary. They do not depend for their truth on anything the description of which neither entails nor is entailed by them. 'All bachelors are unmarried' does not depend for its truth on the genetic characteristics or social habits of bachelors. You may want to say that it depends for its truth on all unmarried men being unmarried. But then the description of that fact, the proposition 'all unmarried men are unmarried' entails 'all bachelors are unmarried'. If traditional theism is true, 'there is a God' is also necessary by criterion (C). This is because, given traditional theism, God's existence does not depend on anything else—unless you count such things as the existence of an omnipotent being as something else. But the description of such things constitutes a proposition which entails or is entailed by 'there is a God'. If theistic views are false, 'the Universe exists' is no doubt a necessary proposition. If atoms were indestructible and there were exactly ten billion billion of them, then 'there are ten billion billion atoms' would be a necessary proposition by criterion (C).

Another way in which 'necessary' has been understood in the past—although it may seem to us an unnatural one—is this. A being is said to be a necessary being if he is by nature eternal and unperishable. The scholastics called the angels and the stars necessary beings for this reason. A being is 'by nature' eternal and unperishable if it will continue to exist for ever, and never decay—

[19] See, for example, John H. Hick, 'Necessary Being', *Scottish Journal of Theology*, 14 (1961), 353–69, and R. L. Franklin, 'Some Sorts of Necessity', *Sophia*, 3 (1964), 15–24, both of whom have written along these lines.

but for divine action. For the scholastics God differed from other necessary beings in being an 'unconditioned' necessary being—i.e. unlike them, he did not owe his necessary existence to anything else. The scholastics did not so naturally apply the term 'necessary' to propositions, but their use of 'necessary' can easily be given application to propositions. We can say that:

(D) A proposition is necessary if and only if it is a tensed proposition, describing truly how things are now which always will be true and always has been true since the first moment at which it was true.[20] (If we wish to provide an account as close as possible to the scholastic, we can add 'but for the supernatural action of God', but I ignore this complication.)

The word 'tensed' is important. All true tenseless propositions such as 'In 49 BC Caesar crosses the Rubicon' or 'In AD 1973 there are nine members of staff of the Keele philosophy department' are eternally true. Most true tensed propositions, such as 'Mary is sitting' or 'John is ill' are not however eternally true. But if the universe will always exist in the future (whether or not God keeps it in existence), and the universe has never ceased to exist, then 'the universe exists' is a necessary proposition in sense (D). So too is 'there are atoms' if there are atoms, there have never ceased to be atoms, and there always will be atoms hereafter. Any tensed analytic proposition comes out as necessary by criterion (D). But on both criteria (C) and (D) of 'necessary' not all necessary propositions are analytic.

I have distinguished four alternative criteria for being a necessary proposition; there are, I suspect, further kinds of proposition which it would not be odd to term 'necessary'. For example, we can have a criterion for being a necessary proposition according to which a (tenseless) proposition is necessary at this or that time, e.g.:

(E) A proposition p is necessary at a time t if and only if p is true and it is not coherent to suppose that any agent by his action at or subsequent to t can make p false.

[20] Anthony Kenny, 'God and Necessity' in *British Analytical Philosophy*, ed. B. Williams and A. Montefiore, has a slight variant in the scholastic tradition on this criterion. He uses a criterion according to which a tensed proposition is a necessary proposition if it does not change its truth-value, i.e. is always true or always false.

Then true propositions about events at some time become necessary on criterion (E) when that time is past—given that it is incoherent to suppose that agents can by their actions affect what is past. All analytic propositions come out as necessary on this criterion also, but of course the converse does not hold.

Necessary propositions are contrasted with 'contingent' ones. A natural definition of a contingent proposition is that a contingent proposition is any proposition which is not necessary and is not the negation of a necessary proposition. Each way of understanding 'necessary' then has a different way of understanding 'contingent' contrasted with it.

What finally of the a priori? An a priori proposition is one which can be known a priori, one of which a priori knowledge can be had. Kant understood by 'a priori knowledge, not knowledge independent of this or that experience but knowledge absolutely independent of all experience'.[21] Modern philosophers who have been so prolific in their definitions of 'analytic' have not in general attempted rival definitions of 'a priori' to Kant's. They have usually used the term in a somewhat Kantian sense without precise definition, or they have simply equated 'a priori' with 'necessary'—an equation which appears to beg interesting questions in this field. Writers who have made this equation have appealed to the text of Kant as justification for doing so. Quinton writes that one meaning of 'a priori' is 'following Kant, necessary'.[22] I do not myself find this equation in the text, at any rate the text of the Introduction to the *Critique of Pure Reason* in the second edition. There are there arguments to show that if we know a necessary truth we know it a priori.[23] The rest of the *Critique* assumes that all a priori truths are necessary. But it does not seem to me that Kant rules out the possibility of necessary truths which are not knowable a priori because they are not knowable at all. (There might be necessary truths about the noumenal world unknowable by any being.)

There seem to me to be at least three senses of 'a priori' which

---

[21] Op. cit., B2.   [22] Op. cit., p. 32.

[23] Jonathan Bennett (*Kant's Analytic*, Cambridge, 1966, p. 9) claims that 'the context [of the Introduction] clearly implies that necessity and universality are entailed by apriority as well as entailing it', but I cannot myself see that the context does imply this.

might be distilled from Kant's discussion and subsequent use of the term. They are:

(a) A proposition is a priori if and only if it can be known to be true by an agent who has had no experience at all.

(b) A proposition is a priori if and only if it can be known by an agent to be true, his claim to knowledge being irrefutable by any (coherently describable) experiences.

(c) A proposition is a priori if and only if it is necessary and can be known to be necessary.

If a proposition satisfies (a) it will satisfy (b), for if it can be known to be true in advance of experience, it can be known that no subsequent experience will upset it. But if a proposition satisfies (b) it need not therefore satisfy (a), for it might be knowable only through having some experience. If a proposition satisfies (c), it will satisfy (b). For if an agent knows that a proposition is necessary (in any of the senses described) he knows that his subsequent experience will not refute it. However, there is no reason to suppose that a proposition which satisfies (c) (in any of the senses of 'necessary') need satisfy (a). For even if a man knows a proposition to be necessary, there is no reason to suppose that he could have come to have that knowledge without any experience at all.

Does satisfaction of (a) or (b) entail satisfaction of (c)? That depends in part on the sense in which 'necessary' is to be understood. However, if it is understood in any of the senses (A), (B), (C), or (D), satisfaction of (b) does not entail satisfaction of (c). For one proposition which can be known by an agent and is irrefutable by any coherently describable experiences is the proposition that there are experiences. Yet this is not necessary in any of senses (A), (B), (C), or (D).

I shall not discuss whether satisfaction of (a) entails satisfaction of (c), or indeed discuss definition (a) further. This is because (a) seems to be not a very useful definition of 'a priori' at all. For in the view of the vast majority of philosophers human beings do not in fact have any knowledge before they have some experience of the world. Kant explicitly affirms this view. He writes that 'there can be no doubt that all our knowledge begins with experience. For how should our faculty of knowledge be awakened into action did not

objects affecting our sense partly of themselves produce representations. . . . In the order of time therefore we have no knowledge
antecedent to experience, and with experience all our knowledge
begins.'[24] One could of course consider whether logically possible
beings could know certain things in advance of experience. Before
we did so, we would need to define 'experience' rather carefully—Is
a being who reflects on the meaning of 'bachelor' having an
experience or not? But I do not think that an elaboration of 'a
priori' along these lines would be of much use in elucidating its
normal use, for most philosophers have used the term profitably
without it occurring to them that they were making claims about the
states of beings who have had no experiences at all. Kant certainly
did not think of 'a priori' in this way.

That leaves us with (b) and (c). What Kant meant by 'knowledge
absolutely independent of all experience' is knowledge which
comes to us through experience but is not contributed by experience. Although our knowledge that all bachelors are unmarried
comes to us through experience (by reading books, hearing people
talk, etc.), it is not contributed by experience. But how are we to
recognize the knowledge that is not contributed by experience?
Kant's answer is that 'necessity and strict universality are . . . sure
criteria of a priori knowledge, and are inseparable from one
another'.[25] In effect he proposes my definition (c), and this seems to
me a definition which will have the consequence of classifying as a
priori the propositions which most philosophers would judge to be a
priori. Most philosophers would not wish to classify 'there are
experiences' as a priori. Nevertheless, if we do adopt definition (c),
we should bear in mind that the adoption of this stipulated definition does not immediately rule out the possibility of agents having
all sorts of knowledge of contingent matters of fact which they do
not in some sense derive from their experience of the world.

So then an a priori proposition is a necessary proposition which
can be known to be such. I do not add 'by man' to the definition
(though Kant might have wished to) in view of complexities to
which that would lead—e.g. the need to settle whether a being of
enormous powers would be a man. In what sense is 'necessary' to be
taken in this definition? Different definitions would result from

---

[24] Op. cit., B1.   [25] Op. cit., B4.

taking 'necessary' in different senses. But the only definition—if the sense of 'necessary' is to be taken from among those which I have delineated[26]—which will yield as members of the class of a priori propositions roughly those and only those propositions which philosophers generally have wished to call a priori is the definition which takes 'necessary' in sense (A) as 'analytic'. Philosophers would be very unhappy about calling 'the number which is the number of the planets is greater than six' or 'there are atoms' a priori propositions, even though they might admit that they were necessary in senses (B)[27] and (C) respectively, and could be known to be so. I therefore suggest that we take 'necessary' in the definition of 'a priori' in sense (A). That definition then becomes:

A proposition is a priori if and only if it is analytic and can be known to be such.

This definition does have the unfortunate disadvantage of making the answer to Kant's big question whether there are any synthetic a priori propositions trivially obvious. I have reached this result, however, only through having an understanding of 'analytic' much wider than Kant's. It will be seen that many of the propositions which Kant or later writers have wished to classify as synthetic a priori come out as analytic on my understanding of 'analytic'.[28] Examples are '$5 + 7 = 12$', 'a straight line is the shortest line joining its end points', and 'nothing can be red and green all over'.

Our definition of 'a priori' suggests various definitions of 'a posteriori'. A natural one is the following: an a posteriori proposition is any contingent proposition which, if true, can be known to be true. ('Contingent' is here understood in the sense of 'synthetic'.)

On our definition of 'a priori', since not all propositions necessary

---

[26] It is of course possible that some defining criterion of necessity, other than those which I have delineated would also yield a class of a priori propositions which contained as members roughly those, and only those, propositions which philosophers have generally wished to call a priori.

[27] Kripke's papers set out to show that there are many propositions necessary in his sense which are not a priori.

[28] Some of Kant's candidates for the status of synthetic a priori propositions are of course more tricky. I have argued elsewhere that 'every event has a cause' and 'there is only one space' are not analytic and hence by the above definition not a priori. For the former see my 'Physical Determinism' in *Knowledge and Necessity*, ed. G. N. A. Vesey, London, 1970, and for the latter see ch. 2 of my *Space and Time*, London, 1968.

in senses (B), (C), (D), and (E) are analytic, not all such propositions are a priori. However, all a priori propositions are analytic. All analytic propositions are necessary in senses (C) and (E) (and tensed analytic propositions are necessary in sense (D)). Hence all a priori propositions are also necessary in senses (C) and (E) (and, if tensed, in sense (D)). Not all a priori propositions are necessary in sense (B), since as we have seen, some propositions which we know to be analytic are not necessary in sense (B). Clearly all a priori propositions are necessary in sense (A), that is analytic. But are all analytic propositions a priori, that is can all analytic propositions be known to be such? Now of course many analytic propositions may be so complex that man cannot recognize them to be analytic. But could there be an analytic proposition in which the analyticity was so deeply buried that no rational being could recognize the analyticity?

A proposition p is analytic if and only if its negation, not-p, entails an explicitly self-contradictory proposition. So a rational being would be able to know of any analytic proposition p that it was analytic if he could deduce from not-p the explicitly self-contradictory proposition entailed by it. But a rational being of sufficient ability could always deduce from a proposition any proposition entailed by it, and so could always come to know of any proposition not-p which entailed an explicitly self-contradictory proposition that it did so. Hence a rational being of sufficient ability could always come to know of any analytic proposition p that it was analytic.

Against this it might be argued that in some cases an infinite number of logical steps might be needed to get from not-p to the self-contradictory proposition; and in such cases, although the entailment existed, it could not be shown to exist by a rational being in a finite time—a rational being could not in a finite time run through the infinite number of logical steps needed to deduce the self-contradictory proposition. 'Every even number is the sum of two primes' (Goldbach's Conjecture) may be an analytic truth, although no one has yet proved it to be so. To show it to be so you would need to be able to show that 'not every even number is the sum of two primes' entailed a self-contradictory proposition. But there might be no general proof that it did so. The self-contradiction might consist in the contradiction involved in the conjunction of 'not every even number is the sum of two primes' with the infinite conjunction of analytic propositions asserting of each even number that it is the sum of two primes and the proposition that the numbers referred to are all the even numbers that there are. (These propositions, if analytic, are entailed by any proposition including 'not every even number is the sum of two primes'.) To prove the infinite conjunction you might need to prove for each of the infinite number of even numbers separately that it was the sum of two primes.

But, although, as in this case, an infinite number of logical steps would need to be traversed to prove that a proposition entailed a self-contradiction, I do not see why a rational being of sufficient ability could not perform the task in a finite time. Contrary to Zeno, agents can often perform an infinite number of actions of certain types in a finite time. They can, for example, perform the infinite number of actions which constitute traversing the infinite number of smaller and smaller intervals involved in running a mile, in a finite time.[29] They can run in a finite time first half a mile, then a quarter of a mile, then an eighth of a mile . . . etc., etc. . . . all in five minutes. In a similar way, to perform an infinite number of proofs in a finite time, you would need to take less and less time on each proof. Each proof would take a finite time, as of course it would need to—for to prove something involves passing from a state of ignorance to one of knowledge and that takes time. If there is some minimum finite time (say $\frac{1}{10}$ second) needed for a certain agent to perform a proof, then that agent cannot perform an infinite number of proofs in a finite time. No doubt there is such a time for man and so he cannot perform an infinite number of proofs in a finite time. But there might be agents who could perform a proof in an interval of time smaller than any interval you like to name and such agents would appear to be able to run through an infinite number of proofs in a finite time.

I conclude that a rational being of sufficient ability could always come to know of any analytic proposition that it was analytic. My original claim withstands the objection discussed in the last two paragraphs. I conclude that all analytic propositions are a priori (though man may well be unable ever to detect the analyticity of some analytic propositions).

---

[29] See Adolf Grünbaum, *Modern Science and Zeno's Paradoxes*, London, 1968. Grünbaum's discussion on pp. 90 ff. of the Peano Machine has special relevance to our topic.

X

APRIORITY AND NECESSITY*

PHILIP KITCHER

AFTER defining the notion of a priori knowledge early in the *Critique of Pure Reason*, Kant claims that 'Necessity and strict universality are thus sure criteria of a priori knowledge, and are inseparable from one another.' Kant's claim sets the stage for his subsequent usage.[1] In the rest of the *Critique* he uses 'necessary' and 'a priori' interchangeably, often at some cost to the clarity of his arguments. Kant's successors have followed suit, taking the equivalence of the notions of necessity and apriority for granted. Recently, however, a paper by Saul Kripke has provoked closer scrutiny of this piece of philosophical lore.[2] I intend to continue the investigation.

I

I shall begin with the notion of apriority. 'A priori' is an epistemological predicate, applying primarily to pieces of knowledge, and only derivatively to propositions. Following Kant's own definition, we may take a priori knowledge to be knowledge which is independent of experience; a priori truths are those truths which we could know a priori. But what exactly does this mean?

Let me summarize an answer which I have given in detail elsewhere.[3] Roughly, a priori knowledge is knowledge obtained in

Philip Kitcher, 'Apriority and Necessity', from *Australasian Journal of Philosophy*, 58 (1980), 89–101. Reprinted by permission of the Editor and the author.

* I am grateful to David Fair, Hilary Kornblith, and George Sher for helpful discussions.

[1] Kant defines apriority at B3. He asserts the equivalence of apriority and necessity at B4.

[2] 'Naming and Necessity' in *Semantics of Natural Language*, ed. D. Davidson and G. Harman (Dordrecht: D. Reidel, 1972), pp. 253–355, 763–9.

[3] In 'A Priori Knowledge', *Philosophical Review*, 89, no. 1 (Jan. 1980). That paper contains motivation for the conditions given in this section, as well as clarification of some of the notions involved. My aim in the present paper is not to repeat my defence of the analysis but to draw out some of its consequences for traditional ideas about necessity and apriority.

such a way that it could have been obtained in the same way if the knower had had different experiences. Think of a human as a cognitive device with a particular type of structure. To say that the device knows a priori that *p* is to say that it knows that *p* and that the belief that *p* was generated in such a way that, given any possible experience which would have enabled the device (with the structure it has) to form the belief that *p*, that mode of belief-generation would have been available to the device and, if exercised, would have produced knowledge that *p*.

The account indicated here presupposes a *psychologistic* view of knowledge: that is, it assumes that cases of belief which are items of knowledge are distinguished from cases of mere true belief by the characteristics of the psychological process which produced the belief state. Let us call these processes which produce knowledge *warrants* for the beliefs that they generate. Then I take a priori knowledge to be knowledge produced by an *a priori warrant*, and I suppose that the conditions on a priori warrants are as follows.

α is an a priori warrant for X's belief that *p* if and only if α is a process such that, given any total sequence of experiences which would have enabled X to form the belief that *p*, then
(*a*) some process of the same type[4] as α could produce in X a belief that *p*
(*b*) if a process of the same type as α were to produce in X a belief that *p* then that process would warrant X's belief that *p*
(*c*) if a process of the same type as α were to produce in X a belief that *p* then *p*.

I want to make two points about this characterization. Firstly, I intend that the modal and conditional notions should implicitly refer to the native structure of the kind of being X is. When we consider, for example, counterfactual situations in which humans have different experiences, we should hold fixed the cognitive capacities which distinguish *Homo sapiens*. Worlds in which extra faculties come into play are irrelevant in assessing the apriority of an item of knowledge. When we ask, for example, whether, given a

---

[4] Roughly, I take types to be determined by principles of functional or physiological taxonomies. For further discussion, see 'A Priori Knowledge'.

particular sequence of experiences, a particular type of process would be available to a person, we restrict our attention to counter-factual situations in which the person has the capacities enjoyed by actual humans.

My second point is a disclaimer. I shall not try to say what the objects of belief and knowledge are. For ease of reference I shall refer to them as 'propositions', but I shall give no account of propositions or their conditions of identity. My reluctance stems from a desire to remain as neutral as possible on this issue: I would like my conclusions to be independent of a particular account of propositional attitudes. Nevertheless, it is clear that questions about the identity of attitudes across possible worlds will arise when the analysis I have given is applied. Most cases will be unprob-lematic. We can identify a person's belief in a different world by noting that she can employ a particular sentence, using the words as we do, to express what she believes. However, as we shall see below, investigation of the equivalence of necessity and apriority will lead to cases in which this easy approach must be scrutinized. So I shall return below to particular instances of the problem of identifying attitudes, but my treatment of them will preserve neutrality on the issue of the objects of the attitudes.

II

The classical equation of necessity and apriority rests on a pair of theses.

> (1) If it is necessary that p then p can be known a priori.
> (2) If p can be known a priori then it is necessary that p.

The use of the passive neatly glosses over the question of who the knower is supposed to be. Is (1) intended to assert that necessary truths are knowable a priori by some people, by all people, by some actual rational beings or by some conceivable rational beings? If we read (1) as declaring that some conceivable rational being can know a priori any necessary truth then the thesis is probably trivial: I suspect that we can conceive of rational beings who know *all* truths a priori! But surely our interest is primarily in ourselves. We are concerned with the possibilities of *human* knowledge. So I shall rewrite both (1) and (2) to make this concern explicit. There will be a stronger and a weaker version of each.

(3) If it is necessary that p then there is a human who can know a priori that p.

(4) If it is necessary that p then any human can know a priori that p.

(5) If there is a human who can know a priori that p then it is necessary that p.

(6) If every human can know a priori that p then it is necessary that p.

My formulations are intended to suggest that the modalities occurring in the traditional theses should be read *de re* rather than *de dicto*. I think it would be wrong, for example, to construe (1) as

(7) If it is necessary that p then it is possible that every human know a priori that p.

My reason is that there are possible worlds in which there are no humans, so that (7) is trivial. The existence of such worlds also makes it true that if p then it is possible that every human know a priori that p. Kant and his successors were not interested in such banalities. They believed that actual people have the capacity for a priori knowledge of necessary truths.

In line with the treatment of modal and conditional notions in the analysis of apriority, I shall assume that the notion of possibility involved in (3)–(6) holds fixed the cognitive capacities of persons. The intent of the traditional doctrine is not to defend (4), say, by pointing out that each of us could be subjected to a miraculous metamorphosis, after which we would be able to know all necessary truths a priori. Rather, the idea is that, as we are, with the kinds of faculties which are standard human equipment, we can know all necessary truths a priori. I take it that is by no means obvious, and that, if true, it is an exciting epistemological point.

One immediate response to (3) and (4), as I have glossed them, might be that, in their present form, they are far too strong, and that they burden the classical view with hopeless excess claims. For, surely, there are some truths which are just too complicated for us to understand, and there are, presumably, necessary truths in this category. Hence, there would be some necessary truths which we can't know because we are incapable of understanding them. The traditional doctrine should concede the point and restrict its claims to necessary truths which we can comprehend. I shall therefore consider versions of (3) and (4) which decrease the scope of the antecedent in the suggested way. In the end, we shall see that this manoeuvre makes little difference.

III

For reasons which will become apparent, I shall begin with (5) and (6). My first task will be to diagnose an error in a popular argument for (5).

The argument runs as follows. 'Suppose that someone knows a priori that p, but that it is not necessary that p. Her knowledge must have been obtained without benefit of information from experience. In that case, information about the world must be irrelevant. But information about the world can't be irrelevant unless it is necessary that p.[5] The reason this fails is not hard to discern. If someone knows a priori that p then her knowledge must be generated by a particular kind of process, one which meets the conditions (a)–(c). This does not imply that p is necessary. The process could supply all the information needed to warrant belief in a contingent truth.

To see this more clearly, consider the *Gedankenexperiment* which underlies the argument. We consider a case of a priori knowledge that p where it is contingent that p. We then imagine the knower behaving as she does when she obtains her a priori knowledge, locating her in one of the worlds in which it is false that p. By hypothesis, her belief in both worlds is generated in the same way, and, since she hasn't looked at the worlds, she can't tell the difference. So either she can't have genuine a priori knowledge that p or it must be necessary that p. But the *Gedankenexperiment* rests on the supposition that there are worlds in which it is false that p *and* in which the knower performs as she does in the actual world, and

---

[5] Kripke (op. cit., p. 263) takes this argument to represent the primary motivation for rejecting the contingent a priori. I discuss the argument from a slightly different perspective in section V of 'A Priori Knowledge'.

this supposition goes beyond the hypothesis that it is contingent that *p*. So there is an illegitimate step in the argument.

Nor is the point merely academic. There are some contingent truths which are such that we could not believe them and be wrong. (More generally, there are some contingent truths such that we could not come to believe them in particular definite ways and be mistaken.) Consider my present token of 'I exist.' Clearly, there are worlds in which I don't exist at this time, and worlds in which I never exist, so my token makes a contingently true statement. But there are no worlds in which, at this time, I believe that I exist and in which my belief is false. So we have a counterexample to the assumption on which the *Gedankenexperiment* used to support (5) depends. Is this also a counterexample to (5)?

I think it is. I don't know much about the way in which my current belief that I exist is produced, but I am confident that it is of the right type to give me knowledge. Moreover, it seems that, so long as I think about the issue and my belief is a product of my reflection upon it, I know that I exist. More exactly, at all times at which I have a belief which I express by tokening 'I exist', my belief is warranted if it is the product of my reflective thought. Now, any experiences I might have, so long as they enable me to formulate to myself the question of my own existence, would enable me to believe that I exist on the basis of reflective thought about the issue; if I come to believe that I exist in this way, then, I suggest, my belief is warranted, no matter what potentially disruptive experiences I may have had; and, trivially, if I come to believe that I exist then my belief is true. Hence I claim that I know a priori that I exist.

My a priori knowledge of my own existence is evanescent. The item of a priori knowledge expressed in my current token of 'I exist' will no longer be available to me in five minutes' time. For though I shall then be able to proceed as I do now, and though my performance will lead me to *an* item of a priori knowledge, I shall not then be able to know a priori what I now know a priori. Suitably disruptive experiences could deprive me of my warrant for believing that I existed at previous times. I can continually know a priori a succession of propositions which I express by successively tokening 'I exist', but each of my items of a priori knowledge vanishes with the passing moment.

Of course, each of these pieces of fleeting a priori knowledge can be used to obtain a piece of a priori knowledge which is available at different times. I can use any of the propositions which I successively know a priori to infer to the truth of the proposition that, at some time, I exist. Given that this elementary inference preserves apriority, then there is a proposition which I can continue to know a priori, despite the fact that my a priori grounds for it are constantly shifting.

The examples adduced so far undermine (5), but they do not yet refute (6). For I have not yet shown that there are contingent propositions which *anyone* can know a priori. There is an obvious way to extend the idea of the last paragraph to argue against (6). On the basis of our knowledge of our own existence, each of us can know a priori that something exists. Moreover, at any time at which a person exists, that person can know a priori that at some time something exists.

Does this discredit (6)? It does if we include among the possible worlds the empty world, for then we shall have an example of a contingent truth which is knowable a priori by anyone. However, some may protest that there is no possible world in which nothing ever exists: any possible world contains abstract objects, sets and numbers, for example. We could answer the protest by strengthening our example, arguing that each of us can know a priori that at some time some non-abstract object exists (perhaps, that some animate object exists), but this would require us to show that we can know a priori that we are not abstract objects (or that we are animate). I shall not pursue this debate further. For there is, I think, a more interesting way of trying to rebut (6).

IV

I shall begin obliquely, by considering an example which is close to that of our knowledge of our own existence, which will be important for our future discussion. I currently believe that I am actual, or, if you like, that I actually exist. My belief is generated in much the same way as my belief that I exist, and, of course, both beliefs are true. Do I know a priori that I am actual?

'Actual' is, I think, an indexical.[6] That is, just as a standard user of English in our world refers to our world using 'actual', so too an inhabitant of another world who uses English in standard fashion refers to that world with 'actual'. The indexicality of 'actual' raises problems in applying the account of apriority which I have given. To test the apriority of my knowledge of my actuality, we have to see if I could have known what I do, given different experiences. But what is the relevant sense of 'knowing what I do'? Here we face an instance of the problem of identifying attitudes. In another possible world, if I utter 'I am actual', I attribute to myself existence in that world. Granted that I use English in the standard way and that my utterance expresses one of my beliefs, have I, in the appropriate sense, expressed the *same* belief that I actually express by uttering 'I am actual'?

It is tempting to think that we should give a negative answer. Just as my tokens of 'I'm hot now' express different beliefs at different times, so, we might say, my tokens of 'I'm actual' express different beliefs at different worlds. To express what I used to say using the temporal indexical 'now', I need a way of locating my previous temporal position. Analogously, we might suggest that, to express in a world w what I actually express by saying 'I'm actual' requires me to be able to locate the actual world from my perspective in w. Now the question of the apriority of my knowledge of my own actuality begins to look very peculiar indeed. What we have to do, apparently, is to consider those possible worlds in which my experiences suffice to enable me to locate the actual world and to ask whether, in them, I can come to know what I actually express by saying 'I'm actual', in the way that I actually come to know this. If there are any such worlds, and I come to believe in them what I actually express by saying 'I'm actual', then I shall, of course, be mistaken. But are there any such worlds?

Something has gone awry. We have been misled by the temporal analogy. Although 'actual' is an indexical, we should not assume that the application of my analysis, with its use of modal idioms, will treat 'actual' like other indexicals. The intuitive idea of apriority

---

[6] See David Lewis, *Counterfactuals* (Oxford: Blackwell, 1973), pp. 85–7; Bas van Fraassen, 'The Only Necessity is Verbal Necessity', *Journal of Philosophy*, 74 (1977), 71–85; Robert Stalnaker, 'Possible Worlds', *Noûs*, 10 (1976), 75–6.

concerns those items of knowledge which could have survived if different possible experiences had made up our actual experience. So, when we consider the impact of other experiences on our knowledge, we must treat the possible worlds in which those experiences occur as if they were actual. To exploit the analogy with 'logical space', it is not as if we are imagining ourselves going somewhere else where the scenery is different and wondering what we could have done there, but rather that we are imagining what we could have done *at home*, given different scenery.[7] When we view matters from this perspective, we see that the line of reasoning of the last paragraph is misguided, and that we do not need to answer the bizarre questions to which it leads. For the purposes of applying my analysis of apriority, the appropriate identification of attitude is to treat tokens of 'I'm actual', uttered in different worlds, as expressing the same belief. For we are interested in knowing whether, if our experiences in other worlds had made up our actual experience, we could have known what we would have expressed by 'I'm actual' in the way that we actually do. To put it another way, although a token of 'I'm actual' produced in another world expresses a different proposition from that expressed by a token of 'I'm actual' produced in the actual world, this difference is irrelevant. For we are interested in what would have been expressed if the conditions obtaining in that other world had been actual.

Once this point is appreciated, then the apriority of our knowledge of our own actuality will follow from a similar argument to that invoked to show that we know a priori that we exist. Hence, I shall conclude that each of us knows a priori that she is actual. The next sections will reveal what we can make of this conclusion.

v

So far, I haven't considered the examples which Kripke had adduced against the thesis that only necessary truths can be known a priori. Kripke's cases begin from the classical idea that we can know a priori some necessary truths on the basis of performance of linguistic stipulations. Traditionalists would be happy with the following story: I introduce a new term, 'snook', declaring that it

[7] Similar points are made by Stalnaker, op. cit., p. 69.

shall apply to exactly those things which are hairless, green, and less than two feet tall; on the basis of my declaration, I know a priori that all snooks are hairless. Kripke's insight is that a description can be employed in two different ways in this type of stipulative act.[8] The new expression can be introduced as an abbreviation for the description (as in my story), or the description can be used to *fix the reference* of the new expression. On the latter usage, the description's function is to pick out the individual (or set) to which the new expression actually refers. The difference can be exposed by considering the reference of the expression in different possible worlds. If the expression abbreviates the description, then, in any possible world, it refers to what satisfies the description in that world. If the description fixes the reference, then, in any possible world, the expression refers to what satisfies the reference in the actual world. (I ignore, for the sake of convenience, the possibility of reference failure.)

Suppose, then, that we use a description to fix the reference of a new expression, say a name. According to Kripke, we know a priori that, if the bearer of the name exists then he/she/it satisfies the description. But there are many cases in which it is possible that the actual object which bears the name should not satisfy the description. Hence, we can have a priori knowledge of contingent truths. Kripke's clearest example is a reconstruction of Leverrier's introduction of the name 'Neptune'.[9] According to Kripke, we can imagine Leverrier fixing the referent of 'Neptune' by using the description 'the body which causes perturbations in the orbit of Uranus'. On this basis, Leverrier could have known a priori that if Neptune exists then Neptune causes perturbations in the orbit of Uranus, but the proposition known is contingent.

In discussing this example, Keith Donnellan notes that what Leverrier did is irrelevant.[10] Kripke's case would be made even if the use of descriptions to fix reference was only a theoretical possibility, never actually employed by speakers. We can simplify the example by omitting the historical trappings. Suppose that I

---

[8] See Kripke, op. cit., pp. 274–7.

[9] Ibid, footnote 33, pp. 347–8.

[10] Keith S. Donnellan, 'The Contingent A Priori and Rigid Designators', *Midwest Studies in Philosophy*, Vol. ii, pp. 12–27. Subsequent references to Donnellan are to this paper.

decide to introduce the name 'Shorty' into my vocabulary, using the description 'the shortest spy' to fix its reference. On Kripke's account, I know a priori that if Shorty exists then Shorty is a spy, even though Shorty might have existed and preferred plumbing to spying.

Donnellan questions this account. He would object that, although I may truly be said to know a priori that the sentence 'If Shorty exists then Shorty is a spy' expresses a truth, I don't know a priori that if Shorty exists then Shorty is a spy. (Parallel remarks can be made about Kripke's reconstructed Leverrier.) My predicament is analogous to that of someone who has heard a sentence in a language she doesn't know uttered by a sincere and reliable speaker of the language. Donnellan candidly admits that this method of analysing the Kripkean cases leads to some peculiar consequences. For example, speakers of English apparently know (a priori?) that 'If Shorty exists then Shorty is a spy' is true if and only if Shorty exists then Shorty is a spy. So it is hard to see why I can't (at least) come to know that if Shorty exists then Shorty is a spy, on the basis of the knowledge obtained through my reference fixing, and this conclusion seems at odds with Donnellan's analogy.

Donnellan thinks that these consequences are forced on him by the following dilemma. If I know that if Shorty exists then Shorty is a spy, then I would have to believe that if Shorty exists then Shorty is a spy. Any such belief would either be *de dicto* or *de re*. If the belief were *de dicto* then the name 'Shorty' would have to have descriptive content. But, since the description 'the shortest spy' was only used to fix the reference of 'Shorty', the name 'Shorty' is not an abbreviation for the description and it lacks descriptive content. So the belief cannot be *de dicto*. But, if the belief were *de re* then I would have to stand in an appropriate causal relationship to the appropriate *res*, and I do not stand in that relationship. This can be seen by imagining that I meet the shortest spy and discover that he is the shortest spy. I would be wrong to say 'I knew a priori that you were the shortest spy'. So my belief can't be *de re* either. Hence I cannot have the belief.

This brief summary does not do justice to the impressive case which Donnellan mounts against the view that the belief in question can be *de re*. But the dilemma can be avoided by looking more closely at the first limb. The fact that 'the shortest spy' was used to fix the reference of 'Shorty' does show that the name 'Shorty' does not have a *particular* descriptive content. However, to use that description to fix the reference of 'Shorty', I must intend to use 'Shorty' as an abbreviation for a closely related description: 'Shorty' must abbreviate 'the shortest actual spy'.[11] So, contrary to the argument of the first limb of the dilemma, I have a *de dicto* belief in the proposition that if there is a shortest actual spy then the shortest actual spy is a spy. Once we have reformulated the case in this way, I think it is obvious how it works. There is a contingent proposition which I know a priori, and I know it a priori in the same way that I know a priori that I am actual. Moreover, any other actual person can perform the same trick, obtaining a priori knowledge of the same proposition, so that we have a counterexample (in fact, a whole family of counterexamples) to (6). When we understand Donnellan's dilemma, we see that Kripke has simply given a new twist to a familiar type of case. Given that we can know a priori that As are As, and given that we can know a priori that we are actual, we can develop a vast corpus of a priori knowledge of contingent truths. For we can always move a priori from knowledge that actual As are actual As to knowledge that actual As are As. Stipulation and reference fixing simply make this move look more exciting.

Towards the end of his paper, Donnellan concludes that 'the contingent a priori is not very scary and not very interesting'. Despite the fact that I reject his analysis of the Kripkean cases, I think that this evaluation of them is correct. Anyone can come to know many contingent truths a priori—if she wants to. But to do so, she must perform linguistic acts which are at odds with the standard functions of language. Our aims are normally to communicate with others—and thus to use words co-referentially with others—and to talk about what there is in a revealing way. These aims do not accord well with private stipulation. Usually, we let our references adjust to those of fellow speakers, and we allow that the descriptions we initially use to characterize an intended referent may be

---

[11] In his discussions of Donnellan's paper ('Naming and Knowing', *Midwest Studies in Philosophy*, Vol. ii, pp. 28–41), Stephen Schiffer makes a similar point (see p. 35). However, Schiffer's formulation of the point depends on a particular view of propositions and it does not offer a general strategy for dealing with Kripke's cases.

either misleading or even incorrect.[12] Hence, while stipulation is always a *possible* activity, it is not clear that it is a *rational* one. By engaging in widespread stipulation, we could vastly increase our a priori knowledge, but I think that it would be unreasonable to do so. This point applies not only to the Kripkean cases but also to the traditional idea of obtaining a priori knowledge of necessary truths by stipulating that a new expression shall abbreviate a description. I believe that the point is important, but a full argument for it would take me too far afield. It is sufficient to note that there are fundamental examples of a priori knowledge of contingent truths, knowledge of our own existence and our own actuality; that, grafting on to these examples the traditional idea of a priori knowledge by linguistic stipulation, we obtain a large class of counterexamples to (5) and (6); and, finally, that if the device of stipulation should prove odd or irrational then this will affect equally the Kripkean cases and those examples which have been the mainstay of much traditional thinking about the a priori.

VI

I now want to turn my attention to (3) and (4), using the considerations developed in the last two sections. I'll begin with Kripke's alleged counterexamples.

On Kripke's account of names the truth expressed by 'if Hesperus exists then Hesperus = Phosphorus' is necessary. 'Hesperus' and 'Phosphorus' are alleged to be *rigid designators*, that is, in any world in which they designate, they designate what they designate in the actual world, namely Venus. As a result, if Venus exists in a particular possible world then 'Hesperus' and 'Phosphorus' both designate Venus in that world, so that 'Hesperus = Phosphorus' is true in that world. On the other hand, if Venus does not exist in the world in question, the 'Hesperus' fails to designate in that world, so that 'Hesperus exists' is false in that world. Either way, 'if Hesperus exists, then Hesperus = Phosphorus' comes out true. So it is necessarily true that if Hesperus

---

[12] See, for example, Hilary Putnam, 'Is semantics Possible?' (in *Naming, Necessity and Natural Kinds,* ed. Stephen P. Schwartz (Ithaca: Cornell University Press, 1977), pp. 102–18), especially pp. 113 ff.

exists then Hesperus = Phosphorus. Apparently, however, we could not have known that if Hesperus exists, then Hesperus = Phosphorus, without the help of experience. So we have an example of a necessary truth which could not have been known a priori.[13]

There is a way to question the example. Imagine a world in which Venus exists and in which someone, simultaneously, baptizes Venus as 'Hesperus' and 'Phosphorus'. Doesn't this person have a way of knowing a priori that, if Hesperus exists, then Hesperus = Phosphorus? The natural response is to say that she doesn't know a priori the proposition which Kripke denies that we can know a priori. She uses the same words we use, and she uses them to express an item of a priori knowledge, but what she knows is not what we know, because she uses the words differently. Once again, we encounter tricky questions about the identification of attitudes across possible worlds. Our imagined speaker uses 'Hesperus' and 'Phosphorus' to refer to the same object (Venus) that we refer to using those expressions, and, since 'Hesperus' and 'Phosphorus' are supposed to be rigid designators, it is not clear what other semantic property of them, apart from their reference, is available to differentiate our usage from that of the imagined speaker. What further conditions on usage must be imposed if her usage is to accord sufficiently with ours for us to attribute to her knowledge of what we know? If we demand that the referents of 'Hesperus' and 'Phosphorus' be fixed for her in exactly the way they are for us, then we shall be able to block the objection, but at the cost of setting the standards for identity of attitude very high. It isn't at all plausible to claim that you and I can only express the same belief, using the same sentence, if the referents of our words are fixed in the same way. I think that there are many cases in which the causal chains which fix the reference of personal proper names vary from speaker to speaker. The referents of the names of those we know well are fixed through chains of direct causal contact (rather than through chains which extend back to some baptismal ceremony) and these chains can easily be different for different people.[14] Hence, to defend

[13] Kripke, op. cit., pp. 306–8. [Also see this volume, selection VII, pp. 154–60.]
[14] This contention fits well with the picture of reference developed in Michael Devitt, 'Singular Terms', *Journal of Philosophy*, 71 (1974), 183–205, and in my 'Theories, Theorists and Theoretical Change', *Philosophical Review*, 87 (1978), 529–47.

Kripke's own case against the objection, we must find a way to allow identity of attitude when modes of reference differ, without permitting *any* mode of reference to count.

I shan't try to settle this thorny issue, because I think that there is another way to show that (3) and (4) are incorrect. The point is intimately related to one made in discussing the contingent a priori. Consider any English sentence of form [The *F* is *G*]. We can *rigidify* this sentence by distributing tokens of 'actual' and 'actually' in it in appropriate ways, thereby obtaining a sentence which is necessary if the original sentence is true. So, for example, if [The *F* is *G*] is true then a rigidification of it, [The actual *F* is actually *G*], is necessarily true. To see this, consider what happens when we evaluate [The actual *F* is actually *G*], as used by us, at any possible world. At any world, [the actual *F*], as we use it, refers to the referent of [the *F*] in the actual world, an object *d*, let us say. At any world, the phrase [actually *G*], as we use it, has as its extension the extension of *G* in the actual world, a set α, let us say. [The actual *F* is actually *G*] is true at a world just in case the referent of [the actual *F*] at that world belongs to the extension of [actually *G*] at the world, that is, just in case $d \varepsilon \alpha$. Clearly $d \varepsilon \alpha$ just in case [The *F* is *G*] is true (at our world, the actual world). So, if [The *F* is *G*] is true then, as we use it, [The actual *F* is actually *G*] is necessarily true. We can generalize the point: appropriate insertions of 'actual' and 'actually' can yield a necessarily true sentence from any true sentence. (One trivial way to perform the trick is to prefix the entire sentence with 'Actually'.)

Suppose now that (4) were true. Let *S* be any true sentence. Any human must be able to know a priori the truths expressed by rigidifications of *S*. I suggested above that any of us can know a priori that he is actual. But if we know a priori that we are actual and we know a priori the truth expressed by some rigidification of *S*, then we can infer a priori to the truth expressed by *S*. Consider, for concreteness, the example used in the last paragraph. If I know a priori that the actual *F* is actually *G* and I know a priori that I am actual, then, by putting my two pieces of knowledge together, I can know a priori that the *F* is *G*. Hence, since any sentence has rigidifications, (4) entails that anyone can know any truth a priori, and this surely achieves a *reductio* of the classical doctrine, which hoped to draw an important division *within* human knowledge. Nor are things much better if we replace (4) with (3). For, by parallel reasoning, (3) entails that, for any truth, someone can know that truth a priori, and this, too, does violence to traditional notions. Finally, if anyone is prepared to bite the bullet and claim that, after all, the set of truths knowable a priori is not just a small élite, then she must provide an explanation of how we could have so much a priori knowledge.

As I noted in section II, (3) and (4) are reasonably restricted to truths which we can understand. But this restriction is of no avail with the present problem. Given that we can understand a sentence we can surely understand some rigidification of it. Hence, even on the restricted version, we would be forced to conclude that we can know a priori the truth expressed by some rigidification of S, whence the argument of the last paragraph would again produce disastrous consequences.

VII

We have seen that the traditional theses (3)–(6) are mistaken. There is one other theme, loosely connected with (3)–(6), which has also been part of traditional doctrine.[15] Many writers are tempted to suppose that our knowledge *that* a proposition is necessary must be a priori knowledge. I want briefly to consider this alleged connection between necessity and apriority.

There are complications which stem from the fact that we can obtain empirical knowledge that a proposition is necessary if we have empirical knowledge that the proposition is true and if we know that propositions of that kind are necessary. Other complications result from our ability to know things on the authority of others. These factors do not touch the central intuition. However our modal knowledge is extended and transmitted, there is a strong temptation to think that it must begin from items of a priori knowledge.

This conclusion results, I think, from one line of reasoning, which

---

[15] This part of the traditional doctrine also is explicit in Kant, who claims that knowledge of necessity cannot be derived from experience (B15). Kant's terminology helps him to conflate knowledge of the truth of a necessary proposition with knowledge of its necessity, and he is thus sometimes led to claim that whenever we know propositions which are necessary we know them a priori.

is rarely explicit but extremely pervasive. We imagine someone who has a piece of *primary modal knowledge*, knowledge that a proposition is necessary, which she has gained for herself and which does not result from the application of more general items of modal knowledge. What could warrant her belief? We are inclined to think that the warrant could not be any kind of perceptual process, and that perception could play no essential part in it. Perceptual processes appear to reflect only the features of the actual world; they seem to give us no access to other possible worlds. Hence, no perceptual process could warrant us in believing that something is true of all possible worlds. Moreover, for the same reason, perceptual processes could not supply us with any essential information. Thus we conclude that primary modal knowledge must be a priori.

Whatever the merits of the picture of possible worlds and our access to them which this line of reasoning presents,[16] I think that there is a problem in the last step of the argument, a problem which my analysis of apriority makes clear. Let us assume that warrants for items of primary modal knowledge do not involve the processing of perceptual information. For concreteness, let us suppose, as I think some champions of the argument would like us to believe, that primary modal knowledge is obtained by some clearly non-perceptual process such as abstract reflection or experimentation in imagination. It does not follow that primary modal knowledge is a priori. Condition (*b*) of my analysis of 'a priori warrant' brings out the important idea that a priori warrants have to be able to discharge their warranting function, no matter what background of disruptive experience we may have. But the fact that a process is non-perceptual does not rule out the possibility that the ability of that process to warrant belief might be undermined by radically disruptive experiences. I can imagine experiences whch would convince me that my own efforts at experimentation in imagination

---

[16] The argument under consideration presupposes a particular view of possible worlds and our access to them: the possible worlds are imagined as laid out like stars in a galaxy; perception gives us access to one of them, and it is thus supposed to be impossible for us to use perception to arrive at features which hold of all of them; reason, however, is able to transcend the interstellar spaces. Champions of possible worlds semantics for modal logic will insist that this picture is not forced on them. See Kripke, op. cit., pp. 267 ff. and Stalnaker, op. cit., pp. 65–70.

(for example) were an extremely unreliable guide to anything at all. Hence, the last step in the popular argument illegitimately conflates non-perceptual sources of knowledge with sources of a priori knowledge.

Since I think that this argument provides the *only* basis for the thesis that primary modal knowledge must be a priori, I conclude that another traditional effort to salvage a connection between necessity and apriority has failed. There is no apparent reason to deny that there are many truths which are known to be necessary but little a priori knowledge.

VIII

Kripke's discussion and his examples call into question the traditional doctrine that necessity and apriority are equivalent. But, if my arguments are correct, the foibles of the doctrine are largely independent of the special machinery which Kripke has introduced. The doctrine has survived, I think, because of the gloom which has enveloped the notion of a priori knowledge. I have tried to dispel the gloom, and to give the traditional doctrine the burial it deserves.

NOTES ON THE CONTRIBUTORS

C. I. LEWIS (1883–1964) taught philosophy at the University of California, Berkeley from 1911 to 1920 and at Harvard University from 1920 until his retirement in 1953. At Harvard he was the Edgar Pierce Professor of Philosophy from 1930 to 1953. His books include: *A Survey of Symbolic Logic* (1918), *Mind and the World Order* (1929), *Symbolic Logic* (written with C. H. Langford) (1932), *An Analysis of Knowledge and Valuation* (1946), and *The Ground and Nature of the Right* (1955).

A. J. AYER was Grote Professor of the Philosophy of Mind and Logic at the University of London from 1946 to 1959 and Wykeham Professor of Logic at the University of Oxford from 1959 to 1978. Among his books are: *Language, Truth, and Logic* (1936), *The Foundations of Empirical Knowledge* (1940), *The Problem of Knowledge* (1956), *Probability and Evidence* (1972), and *Philosophy in the Twentieth Century* (1982).

W. V. QUINE, formerly Edgar Pierce Professor of Philosophy at Harvard University, is now Professor Emeritus at Harvard. His books include: *From a Logical Point of View* (1953), *Word and Object* (1960), *The Ways of Paradox* (1966), *The Roots of Reference* (1974), *Philosophy of Logic* (1970), and *Theories and Things* (1981).

BARRY STROUD is Professor of Philosophy at the University of California at Berkeley. He has written *Hume* (1977) and *The Significance of Philosophical Scepticism* (1984).

HILARY PUTNAM has been Professor of Philosophy at Harvard University since 1965, where he is also the Walter Beverley Pearson Professor of Modern Mathematics and Mathematical Logic. He has published *Mathematics, Matter, and Method* (1975), *Mind, Language, and Reality* (1975), *Meaning and the Moral Sciences* (1978), *Reason, Truth, and History* (1981), and *Realism and Reason* (1983).

RODERICK M. CHISHOLM, formerly Romeo Elton Professor of Philosophy and Natural Theology and Andrew W. Mellon Professor of the Humanities at Brown University, is now Professor Emeritus at Brown. Among his books are: *Perceiving: A Philosophical Study* (1957), *Theory of Knowledge* (1966; 2nd edn., 1977), *Person and Object* (1976), *The First Person* (1981), and *The Foundations of Knowing* (1982).

SAUL A. KRIPKE is McCosh Professor of Philosophy at Princeton University. He has published, in addition to a number of important articles, *Naming and Necessity* (1980) and *Wittgenstein on Rules and Private Language* (1982).

ALBERT CASULLO is Associate Professor of Philosophy at the University of Nebraska at Lincoln. He has published a number of epistemology articles in philosophy journals.

R. G. SWINBURNE, formerly Professor of Philosophy at the University of Keele, is now Nolloth Professor of the Philosophy of the Christian Religion at the University of Oxford (Oriel College). Among his books are: *Space and Time* (1968), *An Introduction to Confirmation Theory* (1973), *The Existence of God* (1979), and *Faith and Reason* (1979). Also, he is the editor of *The Justification of Induction* (1974) in the present series.

PHILIP KITCHER is Professor of Philosophy at the University of California at San Diego. He has published *Abusing Science: The Case Against Creationism* (1982), *The Nature of Mathematical Knowledge* (1983), *Vaulting Ambition: Sociobiology and the Quest for Human Nature* (1986), and a number of epistemology articles in philosophy journals.

BIBLIOGRAPHY

PAUL K. MOSER

I. BOOKS AND ANTHOLOGIES

Benacerraf, Paul, and Hilary Putnam, eds. *Philosophy of Mathematics*. Englewood Cliffs, NJ: Prentice-Hall, 1964.

Bennett, Jonathan. *Kant's Analytic*. Cambridge: Cambridge University Press, 1966.

Blackburn, Simon, ed. *Meaning, Reference, and Necessity*. Cambridge: Cambridge University Press, 1975.

Bunge, Mario. *Intuition and Science*. Englewood Cliffs, NJ: Prentice-Hall, 1962.

Harris, J. F., and R. H. Severens, eds. *Analyticity: Selected Readings*. Chicago: Quadrangle Books, 1970.

Holtzman, S., and C. Leich, eds. *Wittgenstein: To Follow a Rule*. London: Routledge & Kegan Paul, 1981.

Kitcher, Philip. *The Nature of Mathematical Knowledge*. New York: Oxford University Press, 1983.

Kripke, Saul A. *Naming and Necessity*. Cambridge: Harvard University Press, 1980. Excerpted in selection VII, this volume.

Martin, R. M. *The Notion of Analytic Truth*. Philadelphia: University of Pennsylvania Press, 1959.

Pap, Arthur. *The A Priori in Physical Theory*. New York: King's Crown Press, 1946.

———. *Semantics and Necessary Truth*. New Haven: Yale University Press, 1958.

Pasch, Alan. *Experience and the Analytic: A Reconsideration of Empiricism*. Chicago: University of Chicago Press, 1958.

Price, H. H. *Thinking and Experience*, 2nd edn. London: Hutchinson, 1969.

Reichenbach, Hans. *Relativitätstheorie und Erkenntnis A Priori*. Berlin, 1920.

Resnik, M. D. *Frege and the Philosophy of Mathematics*. Ithaca: Cornell University Press, 1980.

Rosenthal, Sandra. *The Pragmatic A Priori: A Study in the Epistemology of C. I. Lewis*. St Louis, Mo: Warren H. Green, 1976.

Sleigh, R. C., ed. *Necessary Truth*. Englewood Cliffs, NJ: Prentice-Hall, 1972.

Steiner, Mark. *Mathematical Knowledge*. Ithaca: Cornell University Press, 1975.

Stich, Stephen, ed. *Innate Ideas*. Berkeley: University of California Press, 1975.

Strawson, P. F. *The Bounds of Sense*. London: Methuen, 1966.

Sumner, L. W., and J. Woods, eds. *Necessary Truth*. New York: Random House, 1969.

Wittgenstein, Ludwig. *Philosophical Investigations*, 3rd edn. Oxford: Basil Blackwell, 1967.

——. *Remarks on the Foundations of Mathematics*, 3rd edn. Cambridge: MIT Press, 1978.

Wright, Crispin. *Wittgenstein on the Foundations of Mathematics*. Cambridge: Harvard University Press, 1980.

2. ARTICLES AND CHAPTERS

Austin, J. L. 'Are There A Priori Concepts?' Chapter 2 in Austin, *Philosophical Papers*, 2nd edn. Edited by J. O. Urmson and G. J. Warnock. Oxford: Oxford University Press, 1970.

Ayer, A. J. 'The A Priori'. Chapter 4 of Ayer, *Language, Truth, and Logic*, 2nd edn. London: Victor Gollancz, Ltd., 1946. Also selection II, this volume.

Barker, S. F. 'Are Some Analytic Propositions Contingent?' *Journal of Philosophy*, 63 (1966), 637–9.

Beck, Lewis White. 'Can Kant's Synthetic Judgments Be Made Analytic?' *Kant-Studien* 47 (1955), 168–81. Reprinted in *Kant: A Collection of Critical Essays*, pp. 3–22. Edited by Robert Paul Wolff. Garden City, NY: Doubleday, 1967.

——. 'Kant's Theory of Definition'. *The Philosophical Review* 65 (1956), 179–91. Reprinted in *Kant: A Collection of Critical Essays*, pp. 23–36. Edited by Robert Paul Wolff. Garden City, NY: Doubleday, 1967.

Ben Zeev, Aaron. 'The Analytic, Synthetic, and "A Priori" '. *Scientia* 114 (1979), 481–93.

Benacerraf, Paul. 'Mathematical Truth'. *Journal of Philosophy* 70 (1973), 661–79.

Benfield, David. 'The A Priori–A Posteriori Distinction'. *Philosophy and Phenomenological Research* 35 (1974), 151–66.

Bennett, Jonathan. 'Analytic–Synthetic'. *Proceedings of the Aristotelian Society* 59 (1959). Reprinted in *Analyticity: Selected Readings*, pp. 152–78. Edited by J. F. Harris and R. H. Severens. Chicago: Quadrangle Books, 1970.

Bird, G. H. 'Analytic and Synthetic'. *The Philosophical Quarterly* 11 (1961), 227–37.

Black, Max. 'Necessary Statements and Rules'. *The Philosophical Review* 67 (1958), 313–41.

Blackburn, Simon. 'The Contingent A Priori and Negative Existentials'. In Blackburn, *Spreading The Word*, pp. 333–7. Oxford: Clarendon Press, 1984.

BonJour, Laurence. 'A Priori Justification'. Appendix A in BonJour, *The Structure of Empirical Knowledge*. Cambridge: Harvard University Press, 1985.

Bradley, Raymond, and Norman Swartz. *Possible Worlds*, pp. 149–77. Indianapolis, Ind.: Hackett, 1979.

Brody, Baruch. 'The Theory of Essentialism'. Chapter 5 in Brody, *Identity and Essence*. Princeton: Princeton University Press, 1980.

Butchvarov, Panayot. *The Concept of Knowledge*, Part 2. Evanston, Ill.: Northwestern University Press, 1970.

Canfield, John. 'Anthropological Science Fiction and Logical Necessity'. *Canadian Journal of Philosophy* 5 (1975), 467–79.

Carnap, Rudolf. 'Meaning and Synonymy in Natural Languages'. Appendix C in Carnap, *Meaning and Necessity*, 2nd edn. Chicago: University of Chicago Press, 1956.

——. 'Meaning Postulates'. Appendix B in Carnap, *Meaning and Necessity*, 2nd edn. Chicago: University of Chicago Press, 1956.

Casullo, Albert. 'The Definition of A Priori Knowledge'. *Philosophy and Phenomenological Research* 38 (1977), 220–4.

——. 'Kripke on the A Priori and the Necessary'. *Analysis* 37 (1977), 152–9. Also selection VIII, this volume.

Chisholm, Roderick M. 'Reason and the A Priori'. In Chisholm, *The Foundations of Knowing*, pp. 148–67. Minneapolis: University of Minnesota Press, 1982.

——. 'The Truths of Reason'. Chapter 3 in Chisholm, *Theory of Knowledge*, 2nd edn. Englewood Cliffs, NJ: Prentice-Hall, 1977. Also selection VI, this volume.

Chomsky, Noam, Hilary Putnam, and Nelson Goodman. 'Symposium on Innate Ideas'. *Boston Studies in the Philosophy of Science*, Vol. 3. Edited by R. S. Cohen and M. W. Wartofsky. Dordrecht: D. Reidel, 1967.

Cohen, L. J. *The Diversity of Meaning*, chaps. 6 and 10. London: Methuen, 1962.

Craig, E. J. 'The Problem of Necessary Truth'. In *Meaning, Reference, and Necessity*. Edited by Simon Blackburn. Cambridge: Cambridge University Press, 1975.

Dancy, Jonathan. 'A Priori Knowledge'. Chapter 14 in Dancy, *An Introduction to Contemporary Epistemology*. Oxford: Basil Blackwell, 1985.

Davies, Martin. *Meaning, Quantification, Necessity*, pp. 230–42. London: Routledge & Kegan Paul, 1981.

——, and Lloyd Humberstone. 'Two Notions of Necessity'. *Philosophical Studies* 38 (1980), 1–30.

Donnellan, Keith. 'The Contingent A Priori and Rigid Designators'. *Midwest Studies in Philosophy*, Vol. 2, pp. 12–27. Edited by P. French *et al*. Minneapolis: University of Minnesota Press, 1977.

——. 'Necessity and Criteria'. *Journal of Philosophy* 59 (1962), 647–58.

Dummett, Michael. 'Wittgenstein's Philosophy of Mathematics'. *The Philosophical Review* 68 (1959), 324–48. Reprinted in *Philosophy of Mathematics*, pp. 491–509. Edited by Paul Benacerraf and Hilary Putnam. Englewood Cliffs, NJ: Prentice-Hall, 1964.

Erwin, Edward. 'Are the Notions "A Priori Truth" and "Necessary Truth" Extensionally Equivalent?' *Canadian Journal of Philosophy* 3 (1974), 591–602.

Evans, Gareth. 'Reference and Contingency'. *The Monist* 62 (1979), 161–89. Reprinted in Evans, *Collected Papers*, pp. 178–213. Oxford: The Clarendon Press, 1985.

Ewing, A. C. 'The "A Priori" and the Empirical'. In Chapter 2 of Ewing, *The Fundamental Problems of Philosophy*. New York: Macmillan, 1951.

——. 'The Linguistic Theory of A Priori Propositions'. *Proceedings of the Aristotelian Society* 40 (1939–40), 207–44.

Frege, Gottlob. 'Are the Laws of Arithmetic Synthetic A Priori or Analytic?' In Frege, *The Foundations of Arithmetic*, 2nd edn., pp. 17–23. New York: Harper & Row, 1953.

Gasking, Douglas. 'The Analytic–Synthetic Controversy'. *Australasian Journal of Philosophy* 50 (1972), 107–23.

——. 'Mathematics and the World'. *Australasian Journal of Philosophy* 18 (1940), 97–116. Reprinted in *Logic and Language* (First and Second Series), pp. 427–45. Edited by Antony Flew. Garden City, NY: Doubleday, 1965.

Glymour, Clark. 'Equivalance, Underdetermination, and the Epistemology of Geometry'. Chapter 9 of Glymour, *Theory and Evidence*. Princeton: Princeton University Press, 1980.

Goldman, Alvin I. 'Innate Knowledge'. In *Innate Ideas*, pp. 111–20. Edited by S. P. Stich. Berkeley: University of California Press, 1975.

Grice, H. P., and P. F. Strawson. 'In Defense of a Dogma'. *The Philosophical Review* 65 (1956). Reprinted in *Analyticity: Selected Read-*

ings, pp. 54–74. Edited by J. F. Harris and R. H. Severens. Chicago: Quadrangle Books, 1970.

Haack, Susan. 'Some Metaphysical and Epistemological Questions about Logic'. Chapter 12 in Haack, *Philosophy of Logics*. Cambridge: Cambridge University Press, 1978.

Hahn, Hans. 'Logic, Mathematics, and Knowledge of Nature'. In *Logical Positivism*, pp. 147–61. Edited by A. J. Ayer. New York: The Free Press, 1959.

Hamlyn, D. W. 'A Priori and A Posteriori'. In *The Encyclopedia of Philosophy*, Vol. 1, pp. 140–4. Edited by Paul Edwards. New York: Macmillan, 1967.

——. 'A Priori Knowledge'. Chapter 9 of Hamlyn, *The Theory of Knowledge*. New York: Macmillan, 1970.

——. 'Analytic and Synthetic Statements'. In *The Encyclopedia of Philosophy*, Vol. 1, pp. 105–9. Edited by Paul Edwards. New York: Macmillan, 1967.

——. 'Contingent and Necessary Statements'. In *The Encyclopedia of Philosophy*, Vol. 2, pp. 198–205. Edited by Paul Edwards. New York: Macmillan, 1967.

——. 'On Necessary Truth'. *Mind* 70 (1961), 514–25.

Hanson, N. R. 'The Very Idea of a Synthetic A Priori'. *Mind* 21 (1962), 521–4.

Hempel, Carl G. 'On the Nature of Mathematical Truth'. *American Mathematical Monthly* 52 (1945), 543–56. Reprinted in *Philosophy of Mathematics*, pp. 366–81. Edited by Paul Benacerraf and Hilary Putnam. Englewood Cliffs, NJ: Prentice-Hall, 1964.

Hintikka, Jaakko. 'Are Logical Truths Analytic?' *The Philosophical Review* 74 (1965), 178–203.

——. 'Information, Deduction, and the A Priori'. *Noûs* 4 (1970), 135–52.

Jorgenson, Jorgen. 'On Empiric and A Priori Knowledge'. *Danish Yearbook of Philosophy* 6 (1969), 72–88.

Katz, Jerrold J. 'Analyticity and Contradiction in Natural Language'. In *The Structure of Language*, pp. 519–43. Edited by J. Fodor and J. J. Katz. Englewood Cliffs, NJ: Prentice-Hall, 1964.

——. 'Some Remarks on Quine on Analyticity'. *Journal of Philosophy* 64 (1967), 36–52.

Kim, Jaegwon. 'The Role of Perception in "A Priori" Knowledge: Some Remarks'. *Philosophical Studies* 40 (1981), 339–54.

Kitcher, Philip. 'A Priori Knowledge'. *The Philosophical Review* 76 (1980), 3–23.

——. 'Apriority and Necessity'. *Australasian Journal of Philosophy* 58 (1980), 89–101. Also selection X, this volume.

——. 'How Kant Almost Wrote "Two Dogmas of Empiricism"'. *Philosophical Topics* 12 (1981), 217–50.

——. 'Kant and the Foundations of Mathematics'. *The Philosophical Review* 84 (1975), 23–50.

——. 'The Nativist's Dilemma'. *The Philosophical Quarterly* 28 (1978), 1–16.

Kneale, William. 'Are Necessary Truths True by Convention?' *Proceedings of the Aristotelian Society*, Supplementary Volume 21 (1947), 118–33.

——, and Martha Kneale, *The Development of Logic*, chap. 10. Oxford: Clarendon Press, 1962.

Kripke, Saul A. 'Identity and Necessity'. In *Naming, Necessity, and Natural Kinds*, pp. 66–101. Edited by S. P. Schwartz. Ithaca: Cornell University Press, 1977.

Langford, C. H. 'A Proof that Synthetic A Priori Propositions Exist'. *Journal of Philosophy* 46 (1949), 20–4.

Levin, Michael E. 'A Definition of "A Priori" Knowledge'. *Journal of Critical Analysis* 6 (1975), 1–8.

Lewis, C. I. *An Analysis of Knowledge and Valuation*, chaps. 3–6. La Salle, Ill.: Open Court, 1946.

——. *Mind and the World Order*, chaps. 7–9. New York: Charles Scribner's Sons, 1929.

——. 'A Pragmatic Conception of the A Priori'. *The Journal of Philosophy* 20 (1923), 169–77. Reprinted in *Collected Papers of Clarence Irving Lewis*, pp. 231–9. Edited by J. D. Goheen and J. L. Mothershead. Stanford: Stanford University Press, 1970. Also selection I, this volume.

Linsky, Leonard. *Names and Descriptions*, chaps. 3 and 4. Chicago: University of Chicago Press, 1977.

Locke, Don. 'The Necessity of Analytic Truths'. *Philosophy* 44 (1969), 12–32.

Mackie, J. L. 'Empiricism and Innate Notions'. Chapter 7 in Mackie, *Problems From Locke*. Oxford: The Clarendon Press, 1976.

——. 'The Possibility of Innate Knowledge'. *Proceedings of the Aristotelian Society* 70 (1970), 245–57.

Maddy, Penelope. 'Perception and Mathematical Intuition'. *The Philosophical Review* 89 (1980), 163–96.

Malcolm, Norman. 'Are Necessary Propositions Really Verbal?' *Mind* 49 (1940), 189–203.

Martin, R. M. 'On "Analytic"'. *Philosophical Studies* 3 (1952), 42–7.

Reprinted in *Analyticity: Selected Readings*, pp. 179–87. Edited by J. F. Harris and R. H. Severens. Chicago: Quadrangle Books, 1970.

Mates, Benson. 'Analytic Sentences'. *The Philosophical Review* 60 (1951), 525–34.

Morawetz, Thomas. *Wittgenstein and Knowledge*, chaps. 2 and 5. Amherst, Mass.: University of Massachusetts Press, 1978.

——. 'Wittgenstein and Synthetic A Priori Propositions'. *Philosophy* 49 (1974), 429–34.

Moser, Paul K. 'Propositional Knowledge'. Forthcoming in *Philosophical Studies* 51 (1987).

O'Connor, D. J., and Brian Carr. 'A Priori Knowledge'. Chapter 6 in O'Connor and Carr, *Introduction to the Theory of Knowledge*. Minneapolis: University of Minnesota Press, 1982.

Pap, Arthur. 'The Different Kinds of A Priori'. *The Philosophical Review* 53 (1944), 465–84.

——. *Elements of Analytic Philosophy*, chap. 6. New York: Macmillan, 1949.

——. 'Logic and the Synthetic A Priori'. *Philosophy and Phenomenological Research* 10 (1950), 500–14.

——. 'Once More: Colors and the Synthetic A Priori'. *The Philosophical Review* 66 (1957), 94–9.

Parkinson, G. H. 'Necessary Propositions and "A Priori" Knowledge in Kant'. *Mind* 69 (1960), 391–7.

Parsons, Charles. 'Mathematical Intuition'. *Proceedings of the Aristotelian Society* (1979–80), 145–68.

Pears, D. F. 'Incompatibilities of Colours'. In *Logic and Language* (First and Second series), pp. 330–41. Edited by Antony Flew. Garden City, NY: Doubleday, 1965.

Plantinga, Alvin. *The Nature of Necessity*, chap. 1. Oxford: The Clarendon Press, 1974.

Pollock, John L. 'Truths of Reason'. Chapter 10 of Pollock, *Knowledge and Justification*. Princeton: Princeton University Press, 1974.

Putnam, Hilary. 'The Analytic and the Synthetic'. In Putnam, *Mind, Language, and Reality, Philosophical Papers*, Vol. 2, pp. 33–69. Cambridge: Cambridge University Press, 1975.

——. 'Analyticity and Apriority: Beyond Wittgenstein and Quine'. In *Midwest Studies in Philosophy*, Vol. 4, pp. 423–41. Edited by P. French *et al*. Minneapolis: University of Minnesota Press, 1979. Also selection V, this volume.

——. 'Identity Theory and the A Priori'. In Putnam, *Reason, Truth, and History*, pp. 82–5. Cambridge: Cambridge University Press, 1981.

——. 'It Ain't Necessarily So.' *The Journal of Philosophy* 59 (1962), 658–71.

——. 'Possibility and Necessity'. In Putnam, *Realism and Reason, Philosophical Papers*, Vol. 3, pp. 46–68. Cambridge: Cambridge University Press, 1983.

——. 'Red and Green All Over Again'. *The Philosophical Review* 66 (1957), 100–3.

——. 'Reds, Greens, and Logical Analysis'. *The Philosophical Review* 65 (1956), 206–17.

——. 'There Is At Least One A Priori Truth'. *Erkenntnis* 13 (1978), 153–70. Reprinted in Putnam, *Realism and Reason, Philosophical Papers*, Vol. 3, pp. 98–114. Cambridge: Cambridge University Press, 1983.

——. ' "Two Dogmas" Revisited'. In Putnam, *Realism and Reason, Philosophical Papers*, Vol. 3, pp. 87–97. Cambridge: Cambridge University Press, 1983.

Quine, W. V. 'Analyticity'. In Quine, *The Roots of Reference*, pp. 78–80. La Salle, Ill.: Open Court, 1974.

——. 'Carnap and Logical Truth'. In Quine, *The Ways of Paradox*, pp. 100–25. New York: Random House, 1966.

——. 'The Ground of Logical Truth'. Chapter 7 in Quine, *Philosophy of Logic*. Englewood Cliffs, NJ: Prentice-Hall, 1970.

——. 'Truth by Convention'. In Quine, *The Ways of Paradox*, pp. 70–99. New York: Random House, 1966.

——. 'Two Dogmas of Empiricism'. Chapter 2 in Quine, *From a Logical Point of View*, 2nd edn. New York: Harper & Row, 1963. Also selection III, this volume.

Quinton, Anthony. 'The A Priori and the Analytic'. *Proceedings of the Aristotelian Society* 64 (1963), 31–54. Reprinted in *Necessary Truth*, pp. 89–109. Edited by R. C. Sleigh. Englewood Cliffs, NJ: Prentice-Hall, 1972.

Reichenbach, Hans. 'The Philosophical Significance of the Theory of Relativity'. In *Albert Einstein: Philosopher-Scientist*, Vol. 1, pp. 287–312. Edited by P. A. Schilpp. New York: Tudor, 1949.

Rescher, Nicholas. 'The Instrumental Justification of Logic'. Chapter 14 in Rescher, *Methodological Pragmatism*. Oxford: Basil Blackwell, 1977.

——. 'A New Look at the Problem of Innate Ideas'. In Rescher, *Essays in Philosophical Analysis*, pp. 255–80. Pittsburgh: University of Pittsburgh Press, 1969.

Resnik, M. D. 'Mathematical Knowledge and Pattern Recognition'. *Canadian Journal of Philosophy* 5 (1975), 25–39.

Russell, Bertrand. 'How A Priori Knowledge is Possible'. Chapter 8 of

Russell, *The Problems of Philosophy*. Oxford: Oxford University Press, 1912.

———. 'What is an Empirical Science?' Chapter 17 of Russell, *The Analysis of Matter*. London: Routledge & Kegan Paul, 1927.

Salmon, Wesley. 'Synthetic A Priori Principles'. In Salmon, *The Foundations of Scientific Inference*, pp. 27–40. Pittsburgh: University of Pittsburgh Press, 1967.

Schiffer, Stephen. 'Naming and Knowing'. *Midwest Studies in Philosophy*, Vol. 2, pp. 28–41. Edited by P. French *et al*. Minneapolis: University of Minnesota Press, 1977.

Schlick, Moritz. 'Is There a Material A Priori?' In *Readings in Philosophical Analysis*. Edited by H. Feigl and W. Sellars. New York: Appleton-Century-Crofts, 1949.

Sellars, Wilfrid. 'Is There a Synthetic A Priori?' In *American Philosophers at Work*. Edited by Sidney Hook. New York: Criterion Books, 1956.

Sober, Elliott. 'Revisability, A Priori Truth, and Evolution'. *Australasian Journal of Philosophy* 59 (1981), 68–85.

Specht, E. K. 'Wittgenstein und das Problem des A Priori'. *Revue internationale de Philosophie* 23 (1969), 167–78.

Strawson, P. F. 'Necessary Propositions and Entailment Statements'. *Mind* 57 (1948), 184–200.

Stroud, Barry. 'Wittgenstein and Logical Necessity'. *The Philosophical Review* 74 (1965), 504–18. Also selection IV, this volume.

Swinburne, R. G. 'Analytic/Synthetic'. *American Philosophical Quarterly* 21 (1984), 31–42.

Swinburne, R. G. 'Analyticity, Necessity, and Apriority'. *Mind* 84 (1975), 225–43. Also selection IX, this volume.

Thompson, Manley. 'On A Priori Truth'. *The Journal of Philosophy* 78 (1981), 458–82.

Toulmin, Stephen. 'A Defense of "Synthetic Necessary Truth" '. *Mind* 58 (1949), 164–77.

———. 'The Escape From the A Priori'. In Toulmin, *Human Understanding*, pp. 495–503. Princeton: Princeton University Press, 1972.

———. 'The Origins of Epistemological Theory'. Chapter 5 in Toulmin, *The Uses of Argument*. Cambridge: Cambridge University Press, 1958.

Waismann, Friedrich. 'Analytic–Synthetic'. In Waismann, *How I See Philosophy*, pp. 122–207. London: Macmillan, 1968.

———. 'Is There A Priori Knowledge?' Chapter 3 in Waismann, *The Principles of Linguistic Philosophy*. London: Macmillan, 1965.

White, Morton. 'The Analytic and Synthetic: An Untenable Dualism'. In *John Dewey: Philosopher of Science and Freedom*. New York: The Dial

Press, 1950. Reprinted in *Analyticity: Selected Readings*, pp. 75–91. Edited by J. F. Harris and R. H. Severens. Chicago: Quadrangle Books, 1970.

——. *Toward Reunion in Philosophy*, chaps 7–9. Cambridge: Harvard University Press, 1956.

Yu, Paul. 'Analyticity and Apriority: The Quine–Putnam Dispute'. *Philosophia* 14 (1984), 41–64.

INDEX OF NAMES

Alexander the Great, 154
Ambrose, A., 119
Anscombe, G. E. M., 165
Aristotle, 36, 43, 44, 63, 100, 116, 117, 121, 154, 180
Austin, J. L., 171
Ayer, A. J., 8, 10, 11, 12, 13, 26, 86, 94, 173

Benfield, D., 123
Bennett, J., 184
Bochenski, I. M., 127
Bolzano, B., 127
Boole, G., 35
Brentano, F., 117, 126, 127, 142
Brody, B. A., 180
Butchvarov, P., 169

Canfield, J., 87
Carnap, R., 45, 46, 50, 54, 56, 60, 61, 66, 86, 94, 100, 102
Casullo, A., 5, 12, 161
Cavell, S., 74
Chisholm, R. M., 8, 12, 112
Church, A., 130
Cicero (Tully), 155, 181
Conway, P., 123

Darwin, C., 63, 100
Davidson, D., 161, 180, 190
Descartes, R., 94, 124
Devitt, M., 203
Dewey, J., 10
Donnellan, K., 14, 165, 199, 201
Duhem, P., 61
Dummett, M., 68, 69, 70, 74, 75, 79, 81, 84, 87, 88, 107
Duncan, G. M., 119

Einstein, A., 63, 100

Fair, D., 190
Fermat, P. de, 94, 96, 147
Field, H., 89
Fraassen, B. van, 197
Frankena, W. K., 143
Franklin, R. L., 182
Frege, G., 59, 62, 70, 72, 120, 121, 131, 151, 171

Gasking, D. A. T., 171
Gentzen, G., 97
George, R., 127
Goedel, K., 148
Goldbach, C., 147, 188
Grunbaum, A., 189

Haldane, E. S., 124
Harman, G., 161, 180, 190
Hempel, C. G., 58
Hick, J. H., 182
Hilbert, D., 148
Homer, 64
Hume, D., 26, 27, 42, 59
Humphrey, H., 150
Husserl, E., 119, 131

James, W., 10
Johnson, W. E., 117
Jourdain, E. B., 131

Kant, I., 5, 12, 13, 28, 29, 32, 33, 42, 43, 125, 126, 135, 136, 138, 145, 149, 161, 170, 173, 178, 184, 186, 187, 190, 193, 205
Kenny, A., 183
Kepler, J., 63, 100

Kitcher, P., 5, 9, 13, 190
Kornblith, H., 190
Kripke, S. A., 5, 12, 13, 97, 109, 110, 145, 161, 162, 164, 168, 169, 187, 190, 198, 199, 200, 201, 202, 203, 204, 206, 207
Kyburg, H. E., 2

Langford, C. H., 35, 36, 141
Lazerowitz, M., 119
Leibniz, G., 4, 12, 42, 45, 49, 112, 119, 120, 121, 126, 142, 161, 174
Leverrier, U. J., 199, 200
Lewis, C. I., 8, 9, 15, 35, 36, 50, 58, 66
Lewis, D. K., 89, 197
Linsky, L., 143
Lipps, T., 131
Locke, J., 59, 62, 124, 142
Lowinger, A., 61

Mach, E., 119
Malcolm, N., 124
Marcus, R., 155, 156
Menger, K., 35
Meyerson, E., 65
Mill, J. S., 18, 28, 29, 31
Montefiore, A., 183
Munitz, M. K., 161, 180

Nelson, L., 129, 130
Newton, I., 63, 93, 100
Nixon, R. M., 149, 150, 181

Peano, G., 88, 90, 91, 93, 97, 98, 111, 189
Peirce, C. S., 58, 107, 108
Plantinga, A., 180
Plato, 4, 11, 70, 75, 78, 82, 84, 99, 115, 116, 119, 154
Poincaré, H., 40
Ptolemy, 63, 100
Putnam, H., 3, 8, 11, 12, 85, 202

Quine, W. V., 1, 6, 11, 12, 13, 42, 65, 85, 86, 87, 98, 99, 100, 102, 104, 108, 109, 111, 134, 143, 154, 171, 173, 178
Quinton, A., 8, 171, 172, 184

Ross, G. R. T., 124, 127
Royce, J., 16
Russell, B., 17, 35, 36, 70, 103, 104, 151, 156

Schiffer, S., 201
Schrödinger, E., 155
Schwartz, S. P., 202
Scotus, D., 118
Sellars, W., 107
Sher, G., 190
Sleigh, R. C., 8
Smith, N. Kemp, 125, 161, 170
Socrates, 113, 114
Stalnaker, R., 197, 198, 206
Stroud, B., 11, 68, 87, 88
Swinburne, R. G., 8, 13, 170

Thomas Aquinas, 125
Thompson, M., 8
Tooke, J. H., 59
Turing, A., 92, 93, 94, 96, 109

Vesey, G. N., 187

Waismann, F., 170, 171
Whewell, W., 115, 116
White, M., 143
Whitehead, A. N., 35, 36
Williams, B., 183
Wittgenstein, L., 8, 11, 68, 69, 70, 71, 72, 74, 75, 77, 78, 79, 81, 82, 84, 85, 86, 87, 88, 89, 92, 98, 99, 109, 151, 164, 165
Wolter, A., 118

Xantippe, 113

Zeno, 189